Blues

The Complete Story

This is a **FLAME TREE** book
First published in 2007

Publisher and Creative Director: Nick Wells
Project Editor: Sara Robson
Picture Research: Melinda Révész
Designer: Lucy Robins

Special thanks to: Chelsea Edwards, Chris Herbert, Geoffrey Meadon, Claire Walker, Gemma Walters and Polly Willis

07 09 11 10 08

1 3 5 7 9 10 8 6 4 2

Created and produced by
FLAME TREE PUBLISHING
Crabtree Hall, Crabtree Lane
Fulham, London SW6 6TY
United Kingdom

www.flametreepublishing.com

Flame Tree Publishing is part of the Foundry Creative Media Co. Ltd.

ISBN 978-1-84451-812-8

A CIP record for this book is available from the British Library upon request.

Printed in China

Blues

The Complete Story

Bob Allen, Rebecca Berkley, Keith Briggs, Richard Buskin, Andrew Cleaton, Cliff Douse, Ted Drozdowski, Colin Irwin, Todd Jenkins, Howard Mandel, Bill Milkowski, Garry Mulholland, Robin Newton, Jim O'Neal, Bob Porter, Tony Skinner, David Whiteis

General Editor: Julia Rolf

Foreword by Paul Jones

Consulting Editor: Philip Van Vleck

FLAME TREE PUBLISHING

CONTENTS

LOUIS JORDAN
"T6"

HOW TO USE THIS BOOK

The reader is encouraged to use this book in a variety of ways, each of which caters for a range of interests, knowledge and uses.

- The book is organized into five main **categories: The Blues Story**; **Styles of the Blues**; **Influences of the Blues**; **Blues Instruments**; and **Playing Blues Guitar**.
- Each **category** is divided into the main **eras** of the blues or **styles** of music to enable the reader to quickly locate specific areas of interest. For **The Blues Story** this list includes The Thirties, The Eighties etc., and for **Styles of the Blues** this list includes Texas Blues and British Blues.
- Each **era** or **style** has a leading page that introduces the reader to the section. The remaining pages discuss the context within which it was created, the key artists and the development of the style.
- Each **entry** is introduced at the head of the page to enable ease of reference to specific areas of interest.
- Quotes from artists, producers and commentators are used throughout to enable the reader to get to grips with the feel and passion of the music.
- Lists of key artists and key tracks or albums relating to each era or style of music are used throughout to give a flavour of the artists and tracks that defined the music.
- Detailed picture credits give further information on the artists included.

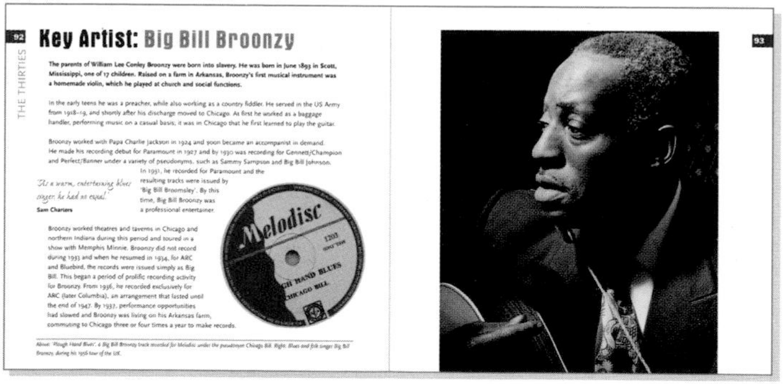
92 THE THIRTIES

Key Artist: Big Bill Broonzy

The parents of William Lee Conley Broonzy were born into slavery. He was born in June 1893 in Scott, Mississippi, one of 17 children. Raised on a farm in Arkansas, Broonzy's first musical instrument was a homemade violin, which he played at church and social functions.

In the early teens he was a preacher, while also working as a country fiddler. He served in the US Army from 1918–19, and shortly after his discharge moved to Chicago. At first he worked as a baggage handler, performing music on a casual basis; it was in Chicago that he first learned to play the guitar.

Broonzy worked with Papa Charlie Jackson in 1924 and soon became an accompanist in demand. He made his recording debut for Paramount in 1927 and by 1930 was recording for Gennett/Champion and Perfect/Banner under a variety of pseudonyms, such as Sammy Sampson and Big Bill Johnson. In 1931, he recorded for Paramount and the resulting tracks were issued by 'Big Bill Broomsley'. By this time, Big Bill Broonzy was a professional entertainer.

'As a warm, entertaining blues singer, he had no equal.'
Sam Charters

Broonzy worked theatres and taverns in Chicago and northern Indiana during this period and toured in a show with Memphis Minnie. Broonzy did not record during 1933 and when he resumed in 1934, for ARC and Bluebird, the records were issued simply as Big Bill. This began a period of prolific recording activity for Broonzy. From 1936, he recorded exclusively for ARC (later Columbia), an arrangement that lasted until the end of 1947. By 1937, performance opportunities had slowed and Broonzy was living on his Arkansas farm, commuting to Chicago three or four times a year to make records.

Above: 'Plough Hand Blues', a Big Bill Broonzy track recorded for Melodisc under the pseudonym Chicago Bill. Right: Blues and folk singer Big Bill Broonzy during his 1956 tour of the UK.

93

Entry title

Introduction to the entry

92

THE THIRTIES

Era or style of music

Key Artist: Big Bill Broonzy

The parents of William Lee Conley Broonzy were born into slavery. He was born in June 1893 in Scott, Mississippi, one of 17 children. Raised on a farm in Arkansas, Broonzy's first musical instrument was a homemade violin, which he played at church and social functions.

In the early teens he was a preacher, while also working as a country fiddler. He served in the US Army from 1918–19, and shortly after his discharge moved to Chicago. At first he worked as a baggage handler, performing music on a casual basis; it was in Chicago that he first learned to play the guitar.

Broonzy worked with Papa Charlie Jackson in 1924 and soon became an accompanist in demand. He made his recording debut for Paramount in 1927 and by 1930 was recording for Gennett/Champion and Perfect/Banner under a variety of pseudonyms, such as Sammy Sampson and Big Bill Johnson. In 1931, he recorded for Paramount and the resulting tracks were issued by 'Big Bill Broomsley'. By this time, Big Bill Broonzy was a professional entertainer.

Quotes from artists, producers and commentators

'As a warm, entertaining blues singer, he had no equal.'

Sam Charters

Information about the music

Broonzy worked theatres and taverns in Chicago and northern Indiana during this period and toured in a show with Memphis Minnie. Broonzy did not record during 1933 and when he resumed in 1934, for ARC and Bluebird, the records were issued simply as Big Bill. This began a period of prolific recording activity for Broonzy. From 1936, he recorded exclusively for ARC (later Columbia), an arrangement that lasted until the end of 1947. By 1937, performance opportunities had slowed and Broonzy was living on his Arkansas farm, commuting to Chicago three or four times a year to make records.

Above: 'Plough Hand Blues', a Big Bill Broonzy track recorded for Melodisc under the pseudonym Chicago Bill. Right: Blues and folk singer Big Bill Broonzy, during his 1956 tour of the UK.

Picture captions

FOREWORD

It's hard for me to recall with any clarity a time when I wasn't hearing the blues. Thanks to the influence of older boys at school (and sometimes my mother too) I was already spending my pocket-money on Lionel Hampton, Jimmy Rushing and Louis Armstrong records by the time Lonnie Donegan and Chris Barber hit us with 'Rock Island Line'. When Donegan mentioned Leadbelly and Big Bill Broonzy in a radio interview, they joined my collection; and inevitably I soon longed to have a go myself. The skiffle phenomenon meant that anyone could, and before long I was strumming away, like thousands of other teenage Worried Men, singing our Worried Songs.

I began to take music seriously, though, only when a T-Bone Walker album recommended by a friend introduced me to the blues harmonica of Junior Wells. Little Walter, Shaky Horton, both Sonny Boy Williamsons, Wells and James Cotton were my 'all-day study' for the next few years, and continued to be even after Manfred Mann, my 1960s 'boy band', began to have pop hits.

Even when my career moved me into acting in 1969 and throughout the 1970s, my blues record collection kept growing and much of my daytime was spent practising – until forming the Blues Band (pictured right) became my obvious next step. With the odd hiatus, we've been going for 28 years.

People ask 'What was it about this African-American music that made it so irresistible to middle-class white boys from the other side of the Atlantic?' (I, like my friend and colleague Dave Kelly's reply: 'It was only playing the blues that elevated me to the middle-class in the first place'.)

Many of us have tried to formulate accurate and convincing answers to the question, but when the subject itself is one that bypasses words, a verbal response inevitably misses something. I'm not saying that there's no such thing as the poetry of the blues, or that lyrics don't matter; they do – very much. But in a real sense, the language of the blues is independent from the meaning of any individual song, and communicates on other levels. This fact informs, for example, the notorious anecdote of the white ethno-musicologist quizzing the black bluesman about protest and discrimination in the blues – and getting absolutely nowhere. It also helps explain why so simple a musical form (though not quite so simple as some depict it) is able to convey so endless a variety of emotions and conditions – and to bypass the social, cultural, educational, and all other forms of standardization to which even middle-class white boys are subject.

I don't like the expression 'The Devil's Music'. For a start, the devil is not that clever or creative – and is all music except blues God's? Pops Staples sang gospel, but enjoyed the fact that 'down in Mississippi' he'd worked in the same place as Charley Patton; 'all music', he said, 'is [capable of being] good'.

I go with that.

Paul Jones 2007

THE BLUES STORY

The developments in popular music in the twentieth and twenty-first centuries have been vast and diverse, with a gradual shift from basic instruments and simple, melodic structures towards more complex works and an increasing use of advancing technology. However, the origins of most Western popular music can be traced back through its many artists and influences to the simplest of musical styles, the blues.

From its African-American roots in the chants of the cotton field slaves and the intricate finger-pickings of the Mississippi Delta blues guitarists, to the sophisticated jump bands of the 1940s, to the burgeoning British blues scene of the 1960s, to the current blues-rich musical community in Austin, Texas, blues music has transcended cultural divides, geographical boundaries and stylistic barriers to provide a wide-ranging influence that can be heard in music all over the world.

This first section of *Blues: The Complete Story* examines in detail the development of blues music, from the beginning of the twentieth century to the present day. Arranged chronologically by decade, there is discussion in each era of the social and historical context and an introduction examining the developments in blues music at the time. There then follows a focus on the key blues artists, together with many shorter synopses of other important blues figures of each period.

Bessie Smith is largely regarded as one of the most influential performers in the history of blues music.

Introduction

Few would deny that the blues has played a more important role in the history of popular culture than any other musical genre. As well as being a complete art form in itself, it is a direct ancestor to the different types of current popular music we know and love today. Without the blues there would have been no Beatles or Jimi Hendrix, no Led Zeppelin or Nirvana, Louis Armstrong or Miles Davis, James Brown or Stevie Wonder, Pink Floyd or Frank Zappa, Oasis or Blur ... the list is endless.

The blues emerged out of the hardships endured by generations of African-American slaves during the late nineteenth and early twentieth centuries. By 1900, the genre had developed to a three-line stanza, with a vocal style derived from southern work songs. 'Call and response' songs were a fundamental part of African slave labour, with the gang leader singing a line and the other workers following in response. This style was developed further by early blues guitar players, who would sing a line and then answer it on the guitar. They would sing when they were feeling depressed, or 'blue', and by 1910, the word 'blues' was commonly used in southern states to describe this musical tradition. Capitalizing on its popularity, the music industry published 'Memphis Blues' by W. C. Handy in 1912.

'The blues is a low-down, aching chill; if you ain't never had 'em, I hope you never will.'

Robert Johnson

By the 1920s, rural African-Americans had migrated to the big cities in search of work, bringing their music with them. Mamie Smith, a New York vaudeville singer, made the first known blues recording, 'Crazy Blues', with Okeh Records in 1920. Its success convinced singers such as Bessie Smith and Ma Rainey to follow suit. Louis Armstrong accompanied them on their recordings, absorbing some of their blues vibes into his jazz singing and trumpeting styles. Street musicians such as Blind Lemon Jefferson also started to make recordings, which inspired a whole generation of blues guitar players.

A memorial to the great W.C. Handy in Clarksdale, Mississippi.

W. C. HANDY
1873-1958
"Father of the Blues" composer
and family lived at this site
1903-05. In Clarksdale Handy
was influenced by Delta blues
which he collected and later
published as well as his own
famous and influential music.
MISSISSIPPI DEPARTMENT OF ARCHIVES AND HISTORY 1981

The 1930s were a crucial period in the development of the blues, for it was then that early Mississippi Delta blues performers Charley Patton, Son House and Robert Johnson travelled throughout the southern states, singing about their woes, freedom, love and sex to community after community. Johnson, who allegedly made a pact with the Devil in order to become a better guitar player, was the first true blues performance artist. On the east coast, musicians such as Blind Boy Fuller, Sonny Terry and the Rev. Gary Davis developed a more folky, 'Piedmont' blues style. In Kansas City, Count Basie was absorbing the blues and reinjecting it into the big band jazz style of the swing era. And in New York, Billie Holiday, one of the most famous blues/jazz singers of all time, began captivating audiences with her haunting, sensuous voice.

As urban blues grew and developed in cities all over the country, the 1940s witnessed the birth of a wide range of new musical styles. In Los Angeles, bandleaders Louis Jordan and Tiny Bradshaw pioneered jump blues, an energetic style based around singers and saxophone players. They still used the traditional call-and-response blues approach, but this time it was the singers ('shouters') and saxophonists ('honkers') who were exchanging phrases and passages. By the end of the decade, jump blues developed into rhythm and blues (R&B), in which more emphasis was placed on the singers than the instrumentalists. In Chicago, electric blues began to develop, as local bluesmen took Mississippi Delta ideas, amplified them and put them into a small-band context.

Popular Melody

Robert Johnson – 'Hellhound On My Trail' (1937)

By the 1950s, electric blues was in full swing, with B.B. King, Muddy Waters, John Lee Hooker, T-Bone Walker and Howlin' Wolf playing to packed houses in major cities. King pioneered across-the-string vibrato and note-bending techniques on his beloved guitar, 'Lucille'; these are now used today by all blues lead-guitar players. Hooker developed a different style, where he stomped continuously with his right foot while singing and playing. Wolf injected more power and frustration into the blues and Walker jazzed things up, but it was perhaps Muddy Waters, with his passionate singing and biting guitar tones, who popularized the style more than anyone else from this period. Some bluesmen, including Big Bill Broonzy, visited England, where their performances inspired local musicians to adopt the style. Chris Barber, a jazz bandleader, assembled his own blues outfit with guitarist Alexis Korner and harmonica player Cyril Davies; they went on to become Blues Incorporated.

The intricate guitar work and unusual tunings of Robert Johnson were a revelation.

The 1960s witnessed a musical and cultural revolution, as British guitar players such as Eric Clapton and Peter Green began to mimic American bluesmen, using solid body guitars and more powerful amps to get a harder, more driving sound than their American mentors. The Rolling Stones (named after a Muddy Waters song) developed a blues-influenced style, injecting rawness and attitude into mainstream chart music. These Brits had enormous worldwide success with their anglicized blues, much to the surprise of the American traditionals. But what went around came around, and the success of British bluesmen encouraged more listeners to check out some of the earlier, more authentic blues artists, whose audience numbers began to swell. 'They stole my music,' Muddy Waters said of the Rolling Stones, 'but they gave me my name.' Another musical phenomenon of the 1960s was Jimi Hendrix, an avant-garde bluester who expanded the boundaries of the electric lead-guitar style. His and Clapton's guitar tones prompted the birth of a number of other styles, including blues rock, hard rock and heavy metal.

From the 1970s onwards, fewer and fewer dedicated blues musicians have appeared, as more singers and players have adopted the spin-off styles that emerged out of it. However, Stevie Ray Vaughan and Gary Moore still managed to inject energy into it, Robben Ford expanded the blues-jazz chops repertoire and Robert Cray introduced the genre to a larger, more mainstream audience throughout the 1980s and 1990s. Other artists, including Bernard Allison, Walter Trout, Dave Hole and Susan Tedeschi, continue to play the blues to enthusiastic audiences around the world.

It might seem paradoxical that a music born out of loneliness, misery, poverty and depression should give so many listeners so much joy, but in reality the first blues songs were sung to raise the spirits of impoverished African-American slaves. The earliest blues singers empathized with their audiences because they had been through the same experiences. It seems fitting that such a sincere and worthy art form has endured to this day, spawning numerous musical children of its own.

Popular Melody

Stevie Ray Vaughan – 'Pride And Joy' (1983)

Jimmy Page, legendary guitarist for 1960s blues rock band the Yardbirds.

The Roots

Blues music is rooted in the enormous technological and social transformations that affected the USA and Western Europe at the turn of the twentieth century. The most striking changes were the advent of easier and cheaper travel; better communications; electric lighting; improvements in audio recording and moving pictures; increased urbanization; and the rise of the US, concurrent with the UK, as the world's leading military, economic and cultural power.

The budding empowerment of African-Americans, who no longer faced slavery, had more impact on the development of new forms of music than any other engine of change. The abolishment of slavery was the beginning of the end of white performers in blackface impersonating Negroes in minstrel shows. African-Americans in the US still may not have been treated equally, but they could gather more freely, and engage in group amusements without censure, loose threads of African retentions, Scotch-Irish ballads, Christian hymns, vaudeville themes, Spanish dance rhythms, marching-band fanfares and idiosyncratic expression began to be woven together by musicians who were either seeking their fortunes adrift from their childhood homes, or were immigrants exiled from age-old traditions.

Key Artists

Charley Patton
Ma Rainey

After the First World War, the US tried to regain its isolationist past. But newly efficient production methods and the rapid growth of cities lent the economy unbridled power. Money, speed, relocation and youth were ascendant – blues music sang their anthems. Blues was itself flexible enough to adapt to changes that continued at seemingly ever-faster rates, swallowing all prior conventions, throughout the twentieth century.

Many of the 'plantation songs' performed in the minstrel shows were published as sheet music.

MUSIC-LOVERS LIBRARY
PLANTATION SONGS
WITH PIANOFORTE ACCOMPANIMENT
1/6
NET.
CONTENTS.
Where de Golden Banjoes play
My old Kentucky Home
Dar's one more ribber for to cross
Old Folks at Home
Dat little black face
Massa's in de cold ground
Come where my love lies dreaming
Good news from home
Hard times come again no more
Ring de Banjo
The Yellow Rose of Texas
Come where the moonbeams linger
Belle Mahone
Let me kiss him for his mother
Rosalie, the prairie flower
I'm off to Charlestown
Uncle Ned
Camptown Races
Beautiful Isle of the Sea
Down the River
ASCHERBERG, HOPWOOD & CREW, Ltd.
16, Mortimer Street, London, W.1.
PRINTED IN ENGLAND.

Echoes of Distant Cultures

The blues was shaped by African culture, the experience of slavery and many other influences, but it emerged as a distinct form only around the turn of the twentieth century – some four decades after the abolition of slavery and several generations removed from the mother continent.

African retentions in timbres, tones and rhythms, and in the functional nature of music in daily life as practiced by people who were not necessarily professional musicians, interacted in America with European musical traditions, including Scotch-Irish fiddle tunes, English ballads, Christian songs and marching bands. Slaves with musical talent learned to entertain whites at plantation dances, balls and parties, performing reels, jigs, waltzes and popular songs of the day. The work songs and hollers of those labouring in the fields often harked back to the chants of their African ancestors, while in the churches Protestant hymns took on an African-American character to emerge as 'Negro spirituals'.

'In the beginning, Adam had the blues, 'cause he was lonesome. So God helped him and created a woman. Now everybody's got the blues.'

Willie Dixon

Africanisms survived in the work and game songs, call-and-response patterns, vocal and instrumental phrasings, syncopations, oral traditions, folk customs and beliefs, pentatonic scales and flattened 'blue notes', as well as in instrumentation. The banjo can be traced back to Africa, along with other bowed or plucked stringed instruments, including the one-string 'diddley bow' – the beginning instrument of many blues guitarists. The fife and drum music of rural southeast America – a mixture of blues, spirituals and folk pieces played on homemade bamboo-cane fifes and marching drums – can be traced back to black musicians who played in the militia units during and before the Civil War; this genre also has its counterparts in African music.

The beginnings of Delta blues can be traced back to the Mississippi cotton plantations.

Minstrels, Spirituals & Ragtime

After America's Civil War, itinerant songsters, musical roustabouts on the riverboats and travelling minstrel show troupes spread their music far and wide. Early forms of music that would become the blues began to develop not only on the plantations, where former slaves and their descendants now toiled as sharecroppers, but also in towns and cities along the Mississippi and Ohio Rivers.

The music makers' repertoires variously included 'jump-ups' (unrelated lines sung over simple chorded accompaniments), ditties, old plantation melodies, breakdowns (uptempo dance pieces), church songs, bad man or folk hero ballads and derogatory 'coon songs' (sung in minstrel shows by blackface performers), as well as popular white music, show tunes and – in some areas, as black musicians acquired formal training – classical works. The jubilee singing of black spiritual ensembles drew national and international attention, and the ragtime craze that swept the country from the 1890s to the First World War established America's fascination with the secular music of African-Americans. The syncopated rhythms of ragtime fuelled the sales of pianos, sheet music and piano rolls. Ragtime embodied the spirit of a country liberating itself from Victorian mores (while at the same time, blacks were still subjected to discrimination, oppression and lynch-mob violence).

Popular Melody

Traditional – 'Arwhoolie (Cornfield Holler)' (1800s/1900s)

The blues drew from many sources to give voice to an African-American identity and response in the troubled era of Jim Crow laws, enacted to restrict the rights and opportunities of America's free but unequal black citizens. The lyrics often expressed a desire to move on to a better place or a better mate; songs of lost love and mistreatment sometimes had a double meaning – as codified protests or commentary secretly directed towards the white boss man and his social order. Risqué sexual double-entendres also abounded, as blues inherited the vulgar side of ragtime's early notoriety as low-class and disreputable, denounced by churchgoers as the 'devil's music' played in dens of temptation, violence and evil. It may have been born of sorrow and hardship, consigned to the margins of society, yet blues sought not to wallow in pain and misery but to raise the spirits in cathartic release, often with humour or irony – to get rid of the blues by singing them.

Minstrel troupes such as the Ethiopian Serenaders were popular touring entertainers.

AUTHORIZED EDITION
ETHIOPIAN SERENADERS
Pell
Harrington
White
Germon
NEW YORK
WILLIAM HALL & SON
FIRTH POND & C°.

The Blues Begins to Spread

Blues took hold in Mississippi, Texas, Georgia, Louisiana, Missouri, the Carolinas and several other southern states. Waves of northward migration would eventually establish Chicago as the blues capital, but in earlier years St Louis and Memphis were more significant urban blues centres. The cotton plantation system of the Mississippi Delta spawned a concentrated and prolific blues subculture, as workers sought weekend release from their toils.

A primary function of the blues was as dance music, played by banjoists, mandolinists and guitarists; string bands with fiddles; harmonica blowers and washboard, fife and drum, and jug bands. In the top rung of entertainers were pianists; the piano remained the dominant instrument in blues for several decades. Most blues performers also worked as fieldhands or labourers, but some made a living from their music, roaming the countryside, playing for workers on plantations and farms or in levee and lumber camps. In towns and cities black musicians were also able to join brass bands, mandolin clubs, singing quartets and dance orchestras, such as the one led by W.C. Handy (1873–1958). Handy drew from his encounters with the blues in the Delta (c. 1903) to write orchestrated versions such as 'Yellow Dog Rag' (later re-christened 'Yellow Dog Blues') and 'Memphis Blues'.

In his autobiography *The Father Of The Blues*, published in 1941, Handy described songs that were apparently blues, which he had heard in St Louis and Evansville, Indiana (*c.* 1892), and just after that in Henderson, Kentucky, as well as some form of proto-blues in his native Florence, Alabama. Contemporary documentation of turn-of-the-century blues is virtually non-existent; New Orleans was a blues piano centre, by the recollections decades later of Jelly Roll Morton (1890–1941) and Pops Foster (1892–1969). Among the pianists remembered as playing blues at the sporting houses were Alfred Wilson, Kid Game and a Creole woman, Mamie Desdunes (Desdoumes), who was playing in New Orleans in 1902, the same year in which Ma Rainey (1886–1939) recalled hearing blues in Missouri. John Jacob Niles later wrote of a blues singer from Louisville, Kentucky named Black Alfalfa (a.k.a. Ophelia Simpson), who in 1898 was performing a song called 'Black Alfalfa's Jail-House Shouting Blues'.

Popular Melody

Traditional – 'Joe Turner Blues' (1893–97, published by W.C. Handy in 1915)

Napoleon Strickland, described as the 'fife-blowingest man in the state of Mississippi', with his fife and drum band.

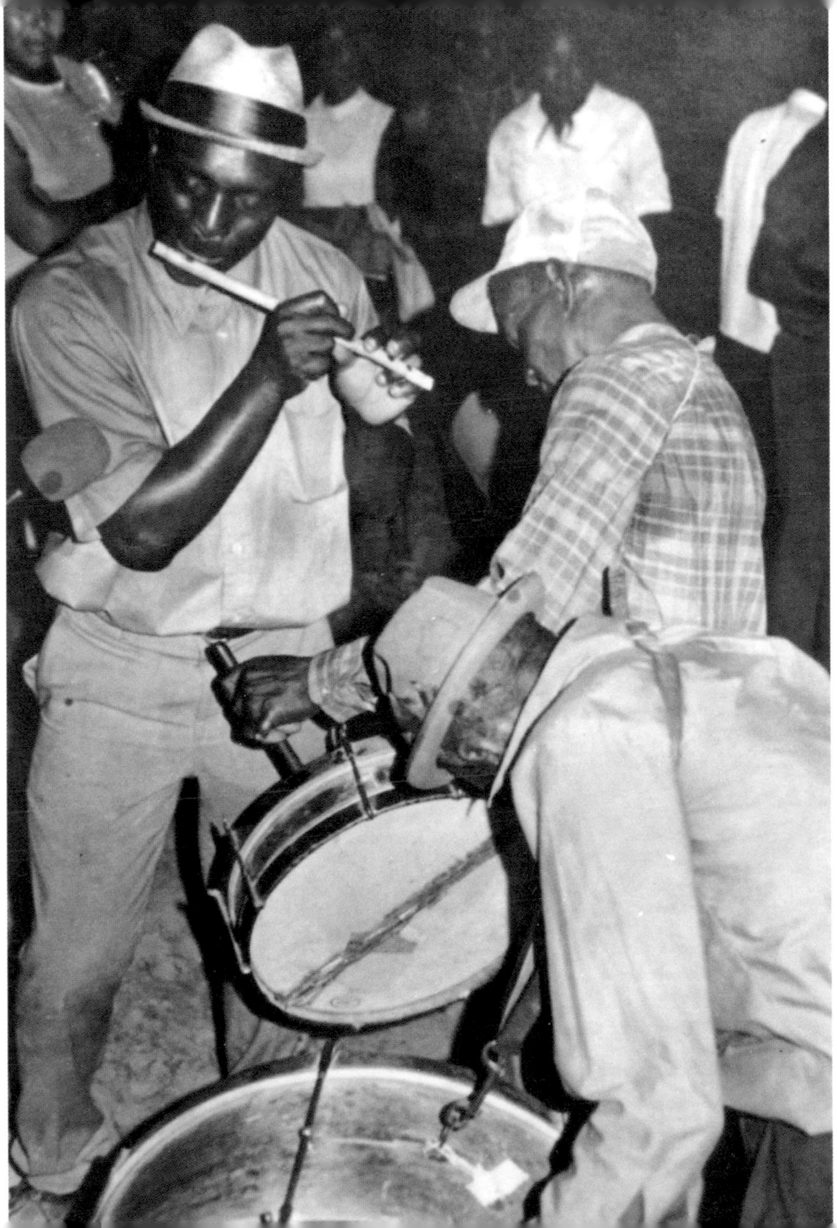

Evidence of Early Blues Songs

While most recollections of early blues songs – including those of bluesmen such as Big Bill Broonzy (1893–1958) from Mississippi and Leadbelly (1888–1949) from northwest Louisiana – were published decades after the fact, a few researchers did file more timely reports of early blues or blues-like songs.

Charles Peabody, a Harvard archeologist working on an excavation at the Stovall Plantation in the Mississippi Delta in 1901, wrote of the 'autochthonous music' he heard the black workers singing; folklorist Howard Odum collected a number of blues songs in Georgia and Mississippi, from both local musicians and travelling performers between 1905 and 1908, as well as some from North Carolina. Besides this, songs dating back to 1890 were collected by Gates Thomas in Texas. Various compositions published in the 1890s and early 1900s contained some structural or lyrical resemblance to blues, although the blues form had yet to congeal; 'I Got The Blues' by New Orleans violinist Antonio Maggio – the 1908 instrumental that was perhaps the earliest such number to use blues in the title – was advertised as an 'up-to-date rag'.

Popular Melody

Robert Cole, James W. and J. Rosamond Johnson – 'Under The Bamboo Tree' (1902)

Few recordings of black performers were made in the earliest eras of cylinders, piano rolls and 78-rpm discs; of those that were made, most were spirituals, coon songs or comedy routines. The primary dissemination of black music was still done via sheet music (including 'ballits' sold on the streets by itinerant songwriters) and public performances. Blues had yet to make a name for itself and was in fact only just beginning to be called 'blues' – some early bluesmen remembered the songs being called 'reels' or 'reals'. But a folk blues repertoire was forming (although not yet being recorded) from songs such as 'Make Me A Pallet On The Floor', 'Joe Turner Blues', 'East St. Louis', 'Stack O' Lee' and 'John Henry', along with other southern airs noted by Handy.

The earliest secular recordings listed in Blues And Gospel Records 1890–1943 are cylinders by a banjo duo, the Bohee Brothers (1890–92); another banjo team, Cousins and DeMoss, recorded a one-sided disc in 1897. In London the American singer Belle Davis, one of the first black women to record, provided a taste of the blues to come in her 1902 recording 'The Honeysuckle And The Bee'.

The 'father of the blues', composer and music collector W.C. Handy.

Handy
at 19!

The Teens

Blues made a leap forward into the public consciousness of America in 1912, when Baby Seals, Hart Wand and W.C. Handy (1873–1958) became the first composers to publish blues sheet music, or at least to register blues with the copyright office.

Many more 'blues' were to follow, often from the pens of New York songwriters. Not all compositions named 'blues' were actually blues in structure or feel – many such songs of the era were rags, vaudeville tunes or Tin Pan Alley pop pieces, with 'blues' fashionably attached to the end of the title. The real breakthrough for blues came with Handy's 'St. Louis Blues', which innovatively incorporated traditional folk and blues elements, along with a touch of habañera that Handy had heard in Cuba. In the years following its first publication in 1914, it became one of the most widely recorded compositions of all time and topped the sales lists for sheet music and piano rolls.

'I wrote "St. Louis Blues" in the key of G because colored people can moan better in that key. It has a mournful plaintiveness.'

W.C. Handy

The Blues Influence in Vaudeville

Prior to the record industry's discovery that there was a niche market for blues and jazz among black buyers – sparked by the success of Mamie Smith's (1883–1946) recording of 'Crazy Blues' in 1920 – what little black music was recorded was done so with white audiences in mind. The first singers to record any of Handy's blues in 1914 were white, in fact, and so were many other vaudeville singers who began to incorporate the blues (something of a novelty at the time) into their repertoires, including the young star billed as 'Queen of the Blues', Marion Harris, and even Sophie Tucker. In New York, the most famous of the early black vaudevillians, Bert Williams, was in the nineteenth year of his recording career when he finally waxed 'I'm Sorry I Ain't Got It, You Could Have Had It If I Had It Blues' in 1919, followed by two blues in 1920, both of which preceded 'Crazy Blues'.

African-American blues songs and spirituals such as 'Deep River' began to be performed in vaudeville shows.

AMERICAN NEGRO MELODY

DEEP RIVER

TRANSCRIBED BY

S. COLERIDGE-TAYLOR

Piano Solo, Op. 59, No. 10		.50

ALEXANDER KELBERINE

Piano, Four hands		.50
Two Pianos, Four hands	Complete	.60

JAMES H. ROGERS

Organ Solo		.50

MAUD POWELL

Violin and Piano		.50

KARL RISSLAND

'Cello and Piano		.50
Trio for Violin, 'Cello and Piano		.60
String Quartet, for Two Violins, Viola and 'Cello		.75

WILLIAM ARMS FISHER

Song, with Piano accompaniment. Op. 19, No. 1 (High, in G; Medium, in F; Medium Low, in E; Low, in D)		.50
Part Song for Mixed Voices, with Piano accompaniment.	Octavo No. 13,136	.15
Part Song for Men's Voices, unaccompanied.	Octavo No. 13,252	.15

VICTOR HARRIS

Trio for Women's Voices, with Piano accompaniment.	Octavo No. 13,196	.12

OLIVER DITSON COMPANY
THEODORE PRESSER CO., DISTRIBUTORS
1712 CHESTNUT STREET
• PHILADELPHIA •

Blues on Wax

Another black act, Dan Kildare's string band, featuring two banjos, had recorded 'St. Louis Blues' in 1917 in London, where they were entertaining white Britons at clubs and dancehalls; they were billed as Ciro's Club Coon Orchestra.

Banjoists also played in the bands accompanying some of the early female blues singers. The guitar would supplant the banjo as blues came to fruition, but even so the record labels were late in bringing Sylvester Weaver, the first recorded blues guitarist, to the studio in 1923, and later still in rounding up the great blues singer-guitarists such as Blind Lemon Jefferson (*c.* 1897–1929), Lonnie Johnson (*c.* 1894–1970) and Charley Patton (*c.* 1891–1934). Seminal figures such as Henry 'Ragtime Texas' Thomas (1874–1930), Frank Stokes and banjoists Gus Cannon (1885–1979) and Papa Charlie Jackson (*c.* 1890–1938) only began to record in the 1920s, but their music echoed sounds from the dawn of the blues and before. The most extensive recording of early black ballads and pre-blues was done by Leadbelly (1888–1949) at the behest of folklorists John (1867–1948) and Alan (1915–2002) Lomax, but not until the 1930s and 1940s.

Popular Melody

W.C. Handy – 'Memphis Blues' (1912)

The Early Blues Diva

Even from its emergence, blues was a multi-faceted phenomenon, developing both as a grassroots folk music and as a professional entertainment medium on a more commercial level. It also continued to influence and be affected by musicians from other genres – from jazz and gospel to old-time country and pop. The blues' first proven stars atop the black showbusiness ladder were the divas who travelled the vaudeville circuit. Well before their recording careers began, Ma Rainey (1886–1939), Sara Martin (1884–1955), Ida Cox (1896–1967) and a young Bessie Smith (1894–1937), among others, had years of experience in tent shows and vaudeville revues; women such as Alberta Hunter (1895–1984) also worked their way in to cabarets, supperclubs and white society venues. That they were advertised not just as singers but as 'comediennes' underscored the nature of their art; they could turn tears into laughter and survive in the face of adversity. When the doors to the recording industry opened to them in the 1920s, they were already on centre stage.

Ida Cox, who remained a largely independent performer and wrote many of her own songs.

Key Artist: Charley Patton

Although not really the 'Founder of the Delta Blues', as one reissue album title touted, Charley Patton more than anyone defined not only the genre but also the image of the hard-living, rambling Delta bluesman, leaving trouble in his wake as he rolled from plantation to plantation and woman to woman.

His rough vocal timbre – combined with the poor sound quality of the few surviving Paramount 78s he recorded – may have caused some listeners to regard him as primitive, yet even guitarists such as John Fahey, his biographer, have been awed by both the power and the complexity of his music.

'If I were going to record for just my pleasure I would only record Charley Patton songs.'

Bob Dylan

Under the influence of an older guitarist named Henry Sloan on the Dockery Plantation, Patton, probably born in 1891 in Bolton, Mississippi, developed into the most famous and formidable Delta bluesman of the early twentieth century. By his biographers' accounts, he was leading the way long before his belated recording debut in 1929. Patton, of mixed black, white and Native American ancestry, was an animated performer who clowned with the guitar and beat on the instrument for percussive effects. He taught or influenced guitarists such as Tommy Johnson, Willie Brown, Roebuck 'Pops' Staples and Howlin' Wolf during his stays in the Dockery area, and later, further north in the Delta, added Son House, Robert Johnson and others to the list.

Patton's Lasting Influence

Patton's first Paramount disc, 'Pony Blues'/'Banty Rooster Blues', was his biggest hit. His recorded repertoire drew from traditional black folk songs, white pop tunes, religious songs, dance pieces and frolics, as well as his own creative wellspring as a composer and storyteller. His records are noteworthy for his descriptions of topical events, such as the great Mississippi River flood of 1927, and for the local lore and real-life characters that he worked into songs such as 'Tom Rushen Blues' and 'High Sheriff Blues'. He died in 1934, but his influence persists into the twenty-first century; Bob Dylan included a tribute song – 'High Water Everywhere (For Charley Patton)' – on his 2001 album *Love And Theft*.

Charley Patton, the first great Delta bluesman and a key influence on all who followed.

Key Artist: Ma Rainey

Gertrude 'Ma' Rainey, the 'Mother of the Blues', had been singing the blues for some two decades before she commenced her influential series of recordings for the Paramount label in 1923. She even laid claim to naming the music 'the blues' after hearing the singing of a young girl in Missouri in 1902, where Rainey was performing with a tent show.

Born Gertrude Pridgett on 26 April 1886, Rainey began performing in her native Columbus, Georgia as a schoolgirl, before joining a number of travelling revues and minstrel shows, working southern theatres, circuses, carnivals and other venues. She teamed with William 'Pa' Rainey, whom she married in 1904, to perform as 'Rainey and Rainey, Assassinators of the Blues'. Known for her flamboyant stage shows, jewelled attire and colourful lifestyle, she was already one of the best-known blues singers in the South when recruited by Paramount.

Key Tracks

'Booze And Blues Blues'
'See See Rider Blues'
'Mountain Jack Blues'
'Daddy Goodbye Blues'
'Black Cat Hoot Owl Blues'

A Versatile Performer

Rainey helped to shape the character, style and presentation of blues in its formative years, and her role and stature in the blues genre escalated during her brief but prolific career (1923–28). Her records were noted not only for the powerful majesty of her singing, but also for the variety of outstanding accompaniment by acclaimed jazz, blues and jug band musicians. Ma Rainey possessed an earthier, more downhome southern style than most of the early blues queens, and was effective working with bluesmen such as Tampa Red, Georgia Tom Dorsey and Blind Blake, as well as with jazz musicians. She retired in 1935 and died four years later, but her influence is evident in the work of her protégé Bessie Smith and many others. Among Rainey's classics were the original version of 'See See Rider', 'Bo-Weavil Blues', 'Moonshine Blues' and 'Ma Rainey's Black Bottom' (also the title of an award-winning play written in the 1990s by August Wilson, with a Rainey studio recording session as its setting).

Ma Rainey, a flamboyant blues singer with a powerful voice who mentored others, including Bessie Smith.

A-Z of Artists

Gus Cannon (Vocals, banjo, jug, kazoo, guitar, fiddle, piano, 1885–1979)

A pioneering bluesman who became a central figure in the Memphis jug band scene, Gus Cannon may have been the first blues recording artist, if tales of music he recorded as early as 1898 are true. Cannon performed as Banjo Joe on medicine shows in the teens and 1920s and recorded his first sides under that name. Inspired by the success of the Memphis Jug Band, Cannon reconfigured his act into Cannon's Jug Stompers and signed with Victor in 1928. Among the Cannon songs reworked by latter-day folk revivalists is 'Walk Right In', which became a number-one pop hit in the US for the Rooftop Singers in 1963. The notoriety enabled Cannon to record an album for Stax Records in 1963, although his participation in the blues revival of the 1960s was limited.

Georgia Tom Dorsey (Vocals, piano, 1899–1993)

Thomas A. Dorsey earned his greatest fame as the 'Father of Gospel Music' after leaving his blues career behind in 1932, but in his early days he was an important blues performer, songwriter, arranger and studio musician. In his youth in ragtime-era Atlanta and in Chicago from 1916, Dorsey developed his piano-playing skills at barrelhouses and rent parties. He also worked with jazz orchestras and Ma Rainey's band before teaming up with Tampa Red in 1928. Dorsey composed songs for the duo as well as material for Ma Rainey and others, and had a special knack for the risqué double-entendre – ironic for a man best known for religious classics such as 'Precious Lord (Take My Hand)'.

Key Tracks

'Walk Right In' Gus Cannon
'Viola Lee Blues' Gus Cannon
'White House Station' Gus Cannon
'It's Tight Like That' Georgia Tom Dorsey
'Precious Lord (Take My Hand)' Georgia Tom Dorsey

Dorsey achieved his greatest success as a music publisher and was founder of the National Convention of Gospel Choirs and Choruses, Inc. Despite his stature in religious circles, Dorsey continued to give credit to the blues, both as a valid expression of the human condition and as a contributing element in the development and acceptance of gospel music.

The multi-talented Georgia Tom Dorsey (third from left) with Ma Rainey's band.

A-Z of Artists

Mississippi John Hurt (Vocals, guitar, 1892–1966)

A songster and fingerpicking guitarist from Avalon, Mississippi, John Hurt excelled in the pre-blues black folk ballad tradition as well as in blues, gospel and dance instrumentals. He spent most of his life working on farms and entertaining at local parties. His first opportunity to record came in 1928, when the fiddle/guitar duo of Narmour and Smith informed OKeh Records of a talented black guitar picker that they knew. Hurt not only contributed songs such as 'Candy Man' and 'Avalon Blues' to the blues canon, but also reinvigorated the folk legends of Casey Jones, Frankie & Albert and Stack O' Lee.

Tommy Johnson (Vocals, guitar, *c.* 1896–1956)

Johnson was a highly influential early blues artist due to the impact of his three 1928 records for Victor, which earned him a niche as Mississippi's first black recording star. Johnson recorded only three more 78s after that, for Paramount, but the songs he recorded for Victor (including 'Cool Drink Of Water' and 'Canned Heat Blues') became entrenched in the repertoires of many bluesmen to follow. His notoriety as a drinker no doubt contributed to his quick decline. He ceased recording after 1929 and spent his remaining years playing streets and house parties in Mississippi.

'I saw him at Newport '63 and he just killed me. His voice, his face, his attitude, his gentle innocence, his real profound thoughts; I was just lost, lost into the world of John Hurt.'

Dick Waterman

Daddy Stovepipe (Vocals, harmonica, guitar, 1867–1963)

Daddy Stovepipe – a.k.a. Mobile, Alabama native Johnny Watson – is an obscure figure, with only a scattering of recording sessions to his credit, but he represents an important era of blues and pre-blues music. He was one of the first downhome blues performers to record (in 1924), and his recorded work has much in common with the jug-band melodies of Memphis, a similarity enhanced by the addition of his wife, Mississippi Sarah, on vocals and jug during the 1930s. Watson performed as a one-man band on streets and in medicine shows in Mississippi, Texas and elsewhere, before going to Chicago, where he played for tips on Maxwell Street.

Formidable guitar picker and gentle folk blues narrator Mississippi John Hurt.

The Twenties

The US in the 1920s was a place of constant change and development. Workers and the newly burgeoning middle class turned into consumers due to relatively higher wages. The international political advantages that came from having just won a major war buttressed a 'lost generation' of artistic types, who took up residence in Europe. New moral codes, sophistication and cynicism abounded.

Some African-Americans benefited from the prosperity, but far from all of them. It was the age of the Harlem Renaissance, of black sports heroes, black revues on Broadway and exotic 'jungle' music in New York and abroad. Yet the Great Migration brought tens of thousands of former farm workers from the southern US to northern industrial areas, seeking jobs and fairer treatment. Although in many ways conditions were better than they had been back home, racist oppression did not end. Corrupt urban governments and landlords exploited the new immigrant population, while employers and labour unions prevented black workers from earning wages equivalent to those of their white counterparts. Meanwhile, back in the South, with the Ku Klux Klan trumpeting white supremacy, it sometimes seemed as if conditions were scarcely better than they had been under slavery.

Key Artists

Leroy Carr
Blind Lemon Jefferson
Lonnie Johnson
Bessie Smith

Against the backdrop of new wealth juxtaposed with poverty and desperation, blues music grew and took root as never before among African-Americans, white Americans and audiences overseas. Advances in the recording industry and radio broadcasts made it a fully fledged popular music style. From acoustic guitar pickers on the streets of Texas towns to the 'classic blues' women who sang in well-appointed theatres backed by jazz musicians, listeners and dancers responded to a newly charged atmosphere of interchange, creativity and inspiration.

Ethel Waters surrounded by dancers at the Cotton Club show in Harlem, New York.

Breaking with Tradition

Although one still often hears the term 'folk music' – a label that implies rustic simplicity, ingenuous lack of artifice and a hand-to-hand passing down of ideas from mentor to student – to describe much of the blues played and recorded during the 1920s, the reality and the music itself were far more complex than that.

No doubt there were strong regional and local traditions that might be described as 'folk', some centred around southern plantations like Dockery's, where Charley Patton (*c.* 1891–1934) had learned from older guitarists such as Henry Sloan; others more broadly based, such as along the Eastern Seaboard between Georgia and the Carolinas, where Blind Blake (*c.* early 1890s–c. 1933), Blind Willie McTell (1901–59), Blind Boy Fuller (1908–41), Rev. Gary Davis (1896–1972) and others interacted and shared ideas. Certainly, many blues songs' lyrical content, as well as their harmonic and melodic structures, rhythms and even, arguably, the 12-bar form itself, could be traced to traditions that extended back for generations.

'The blues wasn't recognized much until the blues singers got a break, 'til they got a chance, see. And then the blues began to spread.'

Georgia Tom Dorsey

But at the same time, even in remote, rural areas in the 1920s, people were listening to radios and purchasing (or at least hearing) records. One need only listen to the ragtime-influenced guitar patterns played by a 'folk' blues artist such as Blind Blake, or the melange of blues, pop tunes, vaudeville-like comedy routines and novelty songs purveyed by the Mississippi Sheiks to know that these were artists who had a keen ear for 'mainstream' popular entertainment, and who worked diligently and consciously to create music that would please listeners and dancers who shared those tastes. When Gus Cannon (1885–1979) was discovered working as a yard man in Memphis in the early 1960s, his awestruck young admirers asked him where he'd learned his material. 'From the radio,' he answered, instantly shattering virtually all the preconceptions they'd had about him.

Dockery's plantation in Mississippi, where Charley Patton honed his craft.

DOCKERY FARMS
EST. 1895 BY
WILL DOCKERY 1865-1936
JOE RICE DOCKERY
OWNER.

Evolution and Growth

At the very least, the most important event in terms of recorded blues in the 1920s occurred in a decidedly urban, and urbane, context. On 10 August 1920, a vaudeville singer and Harlem nightclub chanteuse named Mamie Smith (1883–1946) entered a New York recording studio and cut a song called 'Crazy Blues', the first recording by an African-American singer to be billed specifically as a 'blues'. Her band was a classy one, anchored by stride piano genius Willie 'The Lion' Smith (1897–1973) and possibly featuring cornettist Johnny Dunn.

Clearly, songwriter Perry Bradford, who had urged OKeh to do the session, had a pop hit on his mind when he planned the date. But it was Bradford's genius to figure out that a song like 'Crazy Blues', might tap into a market of potential listeners that, until then, virtually no one in the recording industry had sought to infiltrate.

'Crazy Blues' sold upwards of a million copies in its first six months, and in its wake a new genre was born. These days that genre is usually referred to as 'classic blues', a name that neither does it justice nor describes it very well. At its best, it combined the sophisticated improvisational musicianship of 1920s-era jazz with the earthy vocal declamations of women singers whose material did, indeed, often invoke 'folk' traditions or portray the day-to-day lives and struggles of urban and rural African-Americans. But the musical context (often a single pianist, but not infrequently an ensemble graced with skilled soloists) was strictly first-class, or was at least staged to look that way.

The 'classic blues' sound was no doubt also similar to what these singers had been doing in live performance, especially in the South, for some time. Many if not most of them either got their start or spent significant amounts of time performing in tent shows, minstrel revues and along the rugged Theater Owners' Booking Association (TOBA) African-American vaudeville circuit. The shows that they took out on the road after recording their hits reflected both the sound and style of the records, and the stage acts that they had been honing throughout their professional lives.

Popular Melody

Bessie Smith – 'Young Woman's Blues' (1926)

Gus Cannon, banjo player who it is claimed may have been the first blues recording artist ever.

Two-Way Streets

Ragtime, jazz and/or vaudeville influences can be heard not only in the sophisticated musical backings and well-tempered diction that characterize most of the 'classic blues' singers' recorded output (and, one assumes, their performances), but also in the work of some of the most putatively 'pure' folk bluesmen of the era.

For that matter, some of those 'folk' artists were, in fact, city-born or came of musical age in an urban environment. Even that prototypical 'country' bluesman Blind Lemon Jefferson (*c.* 1897–1929) cut his teeth among the barrelhousers, ragtimers, pimps and hustlers of Dallas's notorious Deep Ellum district. Conversely, even at their most musically refined, 'classic blues' women such as Ida Cox (1896–1967), Victoria Spivey (1906–76) and the various unrelated Smiths often dealt in material with lyrics as nasty and uncompromisingly funk-drenched as anything that might have emanated from a plantation juke (or a backstreet urban gin mill) on a Saturday night.

Blues from the Heart

None of this is to suggest that there is anything inauthentic or faked about the blues recorded and performed in the 1920s, be it 'classic blues' backed by a single pianist or a full jazz orchestra, or the downhome stylings of a lone Mississippi guitar picker. That records may be recorded and sold as commodities, or that music may be played and sung for profit, does not detract from either's artistic worth or legitimacy – the 'folk'/'commercial' dichotomy is, in this context, arbitrary and false. Whether performed in a backwoods shack or a big-city theatre, blues did (and does) express the deepest emotional and aesthetic truths of its purveyors, both as a people and as individuals.

Popular Melody

Blind Lemon Jefferson – 'That Black Snake Moan' (1926)

It is the abiding genius of this music that it is also at once culturally specific and grandly universal, voicing desires, dreams, joys and frustrations common across the human condition. In the 1920s, it evolved to new levels of sophistication as well as artistic and emotional honesty, setting the context and the standards for the developments that would transpire in the decades that lay ahead.

As the blues grew in popularity, the genre began to dominate 1920s record catalogues.

Victor Records
VOCAL BLUES
RELIGIOUS
SPIRITUALS
RED HOT DANCE TUNES
SERMONS
NOVELTIES

Key Artist: Leroy Carr

Vocalist/pianist Leroy Carr's life and career belie the myth that pre-war acoustic blues artists were necessarily 'rural' or 'primitive'. Carr was born not on a plantation but in Nashville, Tennessee on 27 March 1905. His father worked as a porter at Vanderbilt University. After his parents separated, his mother brought him and his sister to Indianapolis (known in the vernacular as 'Naptown'), which at the time was a major nexus of the US automotive industry.

Young Leroy taught himself piano and left school at an early age to go out into the world and seek his fortune; he travelled with a circus, he spent time in the military, he worked as a meat packer and as a bootlegger. But by the mid-1920s he was a professional entertainer, performing at private parties and in clubs around Indiana Avenue, Indianapolis's primary black nightlife strip. Some time during these years he met guitarist Francis 'Scrapper' Blackwell (1903–62), who shared his urbane, somewhat wistful musical sensibilities. The two developed an uncanny musical telepathy; they could interweave melodies of pristine delicacy one moment, then charge into a drive-'em-down barrelhouse stomp the next, goading folks back on to the dance floor.

'I am in love with Leroy Carr; I can play his stuff all night and not give a damn if people like it!'

Barrelhouse Chuck

A Successful Formula

In 1928 the duo had their first recording session for Vocalion. 'How Long, How Long Blues', their debut release, turned out to be their most successful. A melancholy pastiche of images of loss and resignation – lonesome train whistles, departed lovers, desolate mountain vistas – set to a pop-tinged melody line of eight bars, it was sophisticated in feel, yet 'country' enough in its lyric content to strike a familiar chord in listeners down home. In Mississippi, Robert Johnson became a devotee; plenty of others shared his tastes, and the team of Carr and Blackwell quickly became one of the most popular acts in blues. They followed

Far Right: Vocalist and pianist Leroy Carr, who died from alcoholism at the age of 30.

up their first hit with a series of sides, almost all of them featuring Carr's understated yet emotionally rich vocals – 'Naptown Blues', 'Rocks In My Bed', 'We're Gonna Rock', 'Mean Mistreater Mama', 'Blues Before Sunrise' – which may not have sold quite as well as 'How Long ...', but were more than sufficient to maintain their careers for the next seven years or so.

The Liquor Takes its Toll

The blues life has never been an easy one, and both Carr and Blackwell (who had also been a bootlegger before he became a bluesman) were heavy drinkers. Their last session together was in February 1935; less than two months later, Carr died from the effects of acute alcoholism. His partner soldiered on for a while, but he was devastated by the loss and eventually dropped out of music. He was 'rediscovered' in 1959, and enjoyed a brief comeback until his death a few years later.

Despite his undeniable influence on Robert Johnson and others (Johnson's 'Love In Vain' carries distinct echoes of both 'How Long ...' and another Carr/Blackwell song, 'When The Sun Goes Down'), and despite the popularity the Carr/Blackwell duo enjoyed in their heyday (among male blues singers, only Blind Lemon Jefferson could claim as many admirers), Leroy Carr is under-recognized today. Perhaps his location in a northern city outside of Chicago or Detroit is a hindrance; maybe his style remains too subtle for those who still insist on associating blues only with sledge-hammer emotions or gutbucket 'primitivism'. But in his own quiet way, Leroy Carr earned himself an honoured place in the pantheon next to Jefferson, Lonnie Johnson, Bessie Smith and the others who helped to codify modern blues in the 1920s.

Carr's friend and musical soul-mate, guitarist Scrapper Blackwell.

Key Artist: Blind Lemon Jefferson

Although he is often cited as the first 'folk' bluesman to record, Blind Lemon Jefferson was actually much more than that: he was America's first male blues pop star. On the strength of his recordings for the Paramount label – some of which are said to have sold upwards of 100,000 copies – Jefferson became a celebrity throughout the southern blues circuit and beyond.

Jefferson was born in Couchman, Texas, most likely in 1897. 'Lemmon' was probably his given name. He may have been partially sighted, at least as a youth. He taught himself guitar early on, and by his mid-teens he had travelled as far as Dallas to perform. There he sang on street corners and in the jukes and whorehouses that lined Deep Ellum, the wide-open entertainment district that ran along Elm Street in the city's African-American quarter. He teamed up with Huddie 'Leadbelly' Ledbetter for a while, before Leadbelly went to prison in 1918.

'Lemon was fat, dirty, dissolute, but his singing was perhaps the most exciting country blues singing of the 1920s.'

Samuel Charters

In 1925, someone – possibly pianist Sammy Price – recommended him to a Paramount Records talent scout. For Paramount, Jefferson recorded approximately 100 sides (counting alternate versions), of which 42 were issued. In 1927 he also paid a brief visit to the OKeh label, for whom he cut a version of his already popular '(That) Black Snake Moan', as well as the first incarnation of 'Match Box Blues', which he soon re-cut for Paramount. He became such a celebrity that Paramount adorned some of his discs with a designer label featuring that now-famous photo of him, surrounded by bright lemon-yellow trim.

'Don't Play Me Cheap!'

By all accounts, he carried himself like the star he was. He usually travelled alone – or at least without a personal guide – and he comported himself like a dandy, decked out in suits, demanding respect and appropriate remuneration everywhere he went (one of his favourite catchphrases was 'Don't play me cheap!'). Although many of his best-known songs – 'Tin Cup Blues', ''Lectric Chair Blues', 'Match Box Blues' – portrayed a man suffering under oppressive conditions, his musical persona was that of a

Right: Blind Lemon Jefferson, an inventive guitarist and one of the biggest blues stars of his day.

BLIND LEMON
JEFFERSON
King of the Country Blues
First in-depth documentary of
Blind Lemon Jefferson and his music

resolute survivor. His voice was high-pitched and supple, his diction and enunciation crisp and sure. His lyrics expressed the desires, passions and day-to-day struggles of working-class black people with an unadorned yet poetic directness that had never before been captured on disc.

As a guitarist he was superbly inventive within the confines of the 12-bar form, to which he generally adhered – at least on record. Creating separate voices with his basslines and his trademark high-treble arpeggios, and sometimes interrupting the rhythmic flow for a bar or two of unaccompanied single-string solo work, his playing reflected the two-handed contrapuntal attack of the pianists he'd no doubt heard as a young man in the gin mills of Deep Ellum.

'See That My Grave is Kept Clean'

In December of 1929, Jefferson was found dead on a sidewalk in Chicago, apparently having lost his way in a snowstorm and suffered a heart attack. Pianist Will Ezell took him back to Texas, where he was buried in Wortham Cemetery, not far from where he was born.

Not long afterwards, Rev. Emmet Dickinson recorded what was probably the first 'tribute' record in the history of blues muisc – a sermon entitled 'The Death Of Blind Lemon Jefferson'. That an artist whose recording career spanned less than half a decade would receive such an encomium is remarkable; that a Christian minister would record it is even more so – in those days, church-going Christians were advised to shun the blues. But Dickinson's words eloquently captured the feelings of the many who had listened to Jefferson's records and danced at his shows over the years: 'Blind Lemon Jefferson is dead, and the world today is mourning over this loss ... there is a vacancy in our hearts that will never be replaced.'

Next Page: Deep Ellum – Elm Street in Dallas, Texas – as it would have looked in the days when Blind Lemon Jefferson played there.

AD OFFICES
M FRESHMAN LIQUOR CO.
OFFICES
ST.
LIQUO

E.
E.M.
KAHN
& CO.

Key Artist: Lonnie Johnson

Alonzo 'Lonnie' Johnson will probably be forever classified as a 'blues' guitarist, and – at least in his later years – he seemed to accept the label, albeit somewhat gruffly. But in fact he was a consummate musician, deft enough to move between jazz, pop and blues stylings with ease, and inventive enough to imbue everything he touched with new angles of vision and fresh improvisational ideas.

Johnson was born into a musical New Orleans family on 8 February, probably in 1894. At a young age he began performing around town (on violin and piano) with his parents and siblings. In 1917, the year he purchased his first guitar, he landed an overseas tour with Will Marion Cook's Syncopated Orchestra. When he returned home, he discovered that his entire family, except his brother James, had died in the flu epidemic of 1918. He and James left for St. Louis, where they played in the riverboat bands of Fate Marable and Charlie Creath, with whom Johnson recorded in 1925.

'Lonnie Johnson is one of my favorite guitar players … he kind of bridged the gap between blues and jazz.'

Catfish Keith

A Prolific Recording Career

Also in 1925, Johnson won a blues contest sponsored by OKeh Records, the first prize for which was a recording contract. He ended up cutting, by his own recollection, 572 sides for the label, many (but not all) of which were 12-bar blues. He also worked, and sometimes recorded, with such jazz stalwarts as Eddie Lang, Louis Armstrong and Duke Ellington.

As a bluesman, Johnson sang in a fluttery, somewhat thin voice, which was nonetheless effective in delivering his sometimes violently misogynistic lyrics. His apparent lack of emotion heightened the threat as he drawled out ultimatums like 'Woman, get out of my face/or I'll take my fist and knock you down' (from 'Cat You Been Messin' Around') with dead-eyed, murderous serenity. Even on ballads such as 'Careless Love' ('I'm goin' to shoot you and shoot you four, five times/And stand over you until you finish dyin''), he sounded like a man hurt beyond all caring. Meanwhile, his lithe guitar lines and horn-like phrasing amplified (and sometimes mercifully tempered) such lyric themes with improvisational *élan* and an ever-present sense of swing.

Right: Lonnie Johnson, a highly influential guitarist.

Echoes of Johnson's Influence

In 1948 Johnson hit the R&B charts with 'Tomorrow Night', a sentimental ballad that he followed up with several other pop-styled hits. He was nonetheless billed as a 'blues singer' when he toured overseas in 1952. The vicissitudes of the music industry forced him to take a day job shortly thereafter. In the early 1960s, upon his 'rediscovery', he often found himself playing coffeehouses and being booked on 'folk blues' packages with the likes of Muddy Waters and Big Joe Williams. He is said to have been rather imperious in such settings, but audiences enjoyed his slicked-up versions of traditional blues and pop themes. He made his last recordings for Folkways in 1967.

Following a 1969 automobile accident, Lonnie Johnson suffered a stroke; he died on 6 June 1970. Although he was inducted into the Blues Hall Of Fame in 1997, he is still not often mentioned in the same breath as Blind Lemon Jefferson, Charley Patton or Robert Johnson, yet his influence was at least as important as theirs. Robert Johnson, in fact, was so enamoured of him that it is said he sometimes tried to pass himself off as a relative. Echoes of Lonnie's fusion of blues themes with a jazz-like harmonic and rhythmic sensibility resonate through the work of fretmen such as Charlie Christian, T-Bone Walker and many others, including Walker devotees such as B.B. King. Johnson was undeniably a blues trailblazer and an important figure in the evolution of mainstream American popular music.

Next Page: New Orleans c. 1900, where Johnson grew up.

Key Artist: Bessie Smith

Born into crushing poverty in Chattanooga, Tennessee on 15 April 1894, Bessie Smith sang on street corners for tips as a girl, and in her teens she danced in a minstrel show. While honing her craft and expanding her territory, she relocated to several different cities; by the early 1920s she was starring in her own revue, touring the TOBA circuit along the Eastern Seaboard and through the South.

In 1923 she signed with Columbia Records. Her second session with Columbia resulted in 'Ain't Nobody's Business If I Do', a street-savvy declaration of defiance that became one of her theme songs, and which remains a classic of the genre. On the strength of that record and her subsequent releases, Smith garnered national fame and toured widely, not just in the South but in northern cities where African-American migrants were pouring in, seeking jobs and better living conditions than they had been able to find back home. It was for these audiences that Bessie Smith crafted her music and her persona as a tough-talking, urbane woman of power who nonetheless retained memories of her southern roots.

'We had a lot of great singers back then … Ethel Waters, Ida Cox, Sippie Wallace, Clara Smith, Trixie Smith – they were great singers but they couldn't reach Bessie.'

Little Brother Montgomery

The lyrics of the songs Smith recorded dealt with the harsh realities of African-American life, although their overall themes – love, loss, betrayal, defiance and perseverance in the face of hard times – were universal. Even at her most mournful she undergirded her sorrow with steely resolve, as if determined to shout down suffering with the pure force of will.

The Empress of the Blues

Although her vocal range was limited, Smith employed a broad variety of vocal effects – growls, sobs, burnished hollers, church-like ascents and moans – that heightened her appeal for sophisticated jazz aficionados as well as the working-class blues audience that remained her core listenership. In 1925 she recorded some sessions with Louis Armstrong, who responded to her vocal lines on fare such as 'You've Been A Good Old Wagon' and 'St. Louis Blues' with unerring zest – he obviously treated her as a musical equal, and he riffed off her leads as if she were a fellow horn player.

Right: The 'Empress of the Blues', Bessie Smith.

Eventually she became known as the 'Empress of the Blues', but even that title doesn't come close to truly reflecting her importance. Like her erstwhile contemporary Ma Rainey, and like other 'race heroes', such as Jack Johnson, Joe Louis, Jesse Owens and Paul Robeson, as well as such latter-day figures as Muhammad Ali, Aretha Franklin and James Brown, she came to symbolize more than mere excellence in her chosen field. With her air of brazen self-confidence, her apparently fearless strutting of her appetites (sexual and otherwise), her defiant refusal to compromise her selfhood or her integrity (at least in public), even her flair for ostentation and conspicuous consumption, she became a role model and heroine for African-American admirers who saw in her success a vision of what 'the race' might some day be able to achieve.

A Tragic End on 'Blues Alley'

In the early morning of 26 September 1937, Smith was travelling along Highway 61, just outside of Clarksdale, Mississippi. The car in which she was riding sideswiped a truck. She was severely injured, with one of her arms torn nearly loose at the elbow. A white physician stopped to help her; after he loaded her into his car, that car was also hit. The ambulance that finally arrived took her to Clarksdale's 'colored' hospital, where she died, primarily from loss of blood.

So ended the life of one of the blues' most monumental talents. Bessie Smith represented not just the crowning glory of the 'classic blues' style, or of 1920s-era African-American popular music, or even of the blues as a whole. She was, and is, an artist against whom all others, male and female, black and white, in all areas of entertainment and popular art, continue to be judged.

Next Page: The room where Smith died at the Riverside Blues Hotel, a former hospital near Clarksdale, Mississippi.

A-Z of Artists

Texas Alexander (Vocals, 1900–54)

Alger 'Texas' Alexander's broad-toned, pugnacious vocal delivery recalled older work songs and field hollers, while his themes evoked the hard-travelling lives of migrant workers and hoboes. His recordings on OKeh in the 1920s paired him with sophisticated instrumentalists such as Clarence Williams, Lonnie Johnson and King Oliver. In his later years, he often worked alongside his cousin, vocalist-guitarist Lightnin' Hopkins; the pair recorded for Aladdin in 1947.

Deford Bailey (Vocals, harmonica, guitar, 1899–1982)

Deford Bailey was a member of the original Grand Ole Opry and was its first big star, until he was dismissed from the troupe in 1941. His 'Pan American Blues', a harmonica train imitation, was one of the early Opry's most readily identifiable themes. Bailey recorded for both Brunswick and Victor, and while a member of the Opry he also toured with the show. A drive is currently underway to induct him into the Country Music Hall Of Fame, an institution that seldom, if ever, embraces black artists.

Key Tracks

'Penitentiary Moan' Texas Alexander
'Corn-Bread Blues' Texas Alexander
'Pan American Blues' DeFord Bailey
'Barbecue Blues' Barbecue Bob
'Kokomo Blues' Scrapper Blackwell

Barbecue Bob (Vocals, guitar, 1902–31)

Barbecue Bob Hicks was a mainstay of the 1920s Atlanta scene. His 12-string guitar technique featured percussive, banjo-like flailing and sometimes a bottleneck slide, instead of the rag-style fingerpicking often associated with the Southeast. Hicks recorded over 60 sides for Columbia, including his trademark 'Barbecue Blues'. He remained a popular entertainer in Atlanta jukes until his death.

Scrapper Blackwell (Vocals, guitar, 1903–62)

Francis 'Scrapper' Blackwell is best known as Leroy Carr's musical partner, but he was also a gifted artist in his own right. In 1928 he recorded 'Kokomo Blues', which Kokomo Arnold covered as 'Original Old Kokomo Blues', before Robert Johnson retooled it as 'Sweet Home Chicago'. After Carr died in 1935, Blackwell retired from music until 1959, when he was 'rediscovered'. In the midst of a somewhat tentative comeback, he was shot to death in an Indianapolis alley.

Harmonica player Deford Bailey was one of the original stars of the Grand Ole Opry.

A-Z of Artists

Blind Blake (Vocals, guitar, *c.* early 1890s–*c.* 1933)

Among the most influential instrumentalists in the blues, Blind Blake remains a mystery man in terms of his personal life. Born either Arthur Blake or Arthur Phelps, probably in Florida (Jacksonville or Tampa), he purveyed a ragtime-influenced, polyrhythmic picking technique that combined jaw-dropping technical virtuosity with an impeccably crafted symmetry. He approached his fretboard like a piano or even an entire orchestra, balancing themes, tonal attack, inflections and cadences, yet never losing either his improvisational flair or his seemingly limitless capacity for speed.

'I ain't never heard anybody on a record yet beat Blind Blake on the guitar.'

Rev. Gary Davis

He recorded about 80 sides for Paramount (some with jazz clarinettist Johnny Dodds); after the label folded in 1932 he disappeared from sight. He is generally thought to have died about a year later. Generations of guitarists, from Rev. Gary Davis on down, owe much of their inspiration and their art to his genius.

Ida Cox (Vocals, 1896–1967)

An important figure in the so-called 'classic blues' genre, Ida Cox (née Prather) performed in minstrel and tent shows as a teenager. She had already become a vaudeville star when she began to record for the Paramount label in 1923. Apart from her gifts as a vocalist, she was an independent spirit who wrote much of her own material and managed several touring companies (e.g. Darktown Scandals and Raisin' Cain).

She was one of the relatively few 'classic blues' singers who continued to prosper during the Depression. In 1939 she appeared at John Hammond's landmark Spirituals To Swing concert in Carnegie Hall, but the market for her style of music dwindled in subsequent years and she suffered a stroke in the mid-1940s. Nevertheless, she continued to record and perform, on and off, until her death. Her final recording, from 1961, featured Coleman Hawkins on tenor sax.

Blind Blake, a virtuoso guitarist whose personal life remains a mystery.

A-Z of Artists

Cow Cow Davenport (Vocals, piano, *c.* 1894–1955)

Charles Davenport's best-known recording is 1928's 'Cow Cow Blues', a barrelhouse workout that kicks off with a chiming stop-time intro before plunging into a proto-boogie-woogie theme. Davenport recorded over 30 sides for various labels, and he worked in venues ranging from vaudeville theatres to house rent parties. Although slowed by a stroke in 1938, he continued to perform sporadically (sometimes as just a vocalist) until his death almost 20 years later.

Peg Leg Howell (Vocals, guitar, 1888–1966)

James Barnes 'Peg Leg' Howell, who lost his right leg after being shot when he was about 21 years old, led a three-man band – Peg Leg Howell & his Gang – in Atlanta during the mid- to late 1920s. He recorded for Columbia between 1926 and 1929 and continued to perform locally until the mid-1930s. He was 'rediscovered' in the blues revival of the early 1960s and in 1963 cut an album on Testament.

Alberta Hunter (Vocals, 1895–1984)

Memphis-born Alberta Hunter ran away to Chicago as a young girl to seek her fortune as an entertainer. She survived the cutthroat world of early-twentieth-century jazz long enough to establish herself as a front-line vocalist, albeit in a somewhat less declamatory style than that favoured by some of her contemporaries. She recorded (sometimes using pseudonyms) for Black Swan, Paramount and other labels; she also appeared in several musical stage revues. She toured overseas with the play Showboat (starring Paul Robeson) in the late 1920s, and in the 1930s she expanded her touring territory to include both Russia and the Middle East. Hunter retired in the mid-1950s and became a registered nurse in New York, but in the early 1960s she began to record again. In 1977, at the age of 82, she returned to performing and continued as a beloved and still-potent purveyor of dusky jazz and blues torch songs and ballads, mostly in upscale nightclub and concert settings, until her death.

Key Tracks

'Cow Cow Blues' Cow Cow Davenport
'New Prison Blues' Peg Leg Howell
'Broke And Hungry Blues' Peg Leg Howell
'My Man Is Such A Handy Man' Alberta Hunter
'Down Hearted Blues' Alberta Hunter

Alberta Hunter, one of the classic blueswomen of the era.

A-Z of Artists

Papa Charlie Jackson (Vocals, banjo, *c.* 1890–1938)

New Orleans-born Charlie Jackson brought a jazzman's sophistication to an instrument still too often overlooked by blues historians. He alternated single-string solos with percussive chording and dexterous fingerpicking, allowing him to bridge styles and genres with rare facility. He released more than 60 sides of his own, and he also recorded with Freddie Keppard, Tiny Parham and Kid Ory, as well as both Ma Rainey and Ida Cox.

Blind Willie Johnson (Vocals, guitar, *c.* 1902–47)

Texas-born Willie Johnson, a purveyor of sacred material who would probably have been appalled at being categorized as a 'blues' artist, was blinded at the age of seven when his stepmother threw lye in his face after being beaten by his father. He sang in a hoarse, declamatory voice and his fretwork combined tonal purity and pinpoint accuracy (even when using a pocket-knife slide) with an emotional intensity unsurpassed by any acoustic guitarist, regardless of genre.

His masterpiece, the instrumental 'Dark Was The Night (Cold Was The Ground)', invokes soul-chilling existential dread. Other works – 'Jesus Make Up My Dying Bed', 'Keep Your Lamp Trimmed And Burning' – are testament to his faith and the resolute certainty with which he held it. Johnson, who recorded 30 sides for Columbia in 1927–30, died after contracting pneumonia, having spent a night sleeping in wet clothes after his house burned down.

Key Tracks

'Airy Man Blues' Papa Charlie Jackson
'Shake That Thing' Papa Charlie Jackson
'Jesus Make Up My Dying Bed' Blind Willie Johnson
'John Henry' Furry Lewis

Furry Lewis (Vocals, guitar, 1893–1981)

Born in Greenwood, Mississippi, Walter 'Furry' Lewis played medicine shows as a young man. After moving to Memphis, he recorded 23 sides for Vocalion and Victor between 1927 and 1929. Despite a somewhat chaotic guitar technique, he was an indefatigable entertainer and he became a beloved figure among younger-generation aficionados throughout his post-1959 'rediscovery' period. In 1975 he had a cameo alongside Burt Reynolds in the film *W.W. And The Dixie Dance Kings*.

Following a background in medicine shows, Furry Lewis became a popular entertainer.

A-Z of Artists

Blind Willie McTell (Vocals, guitar, 1901–59)

A skilled purveyor of the ragtime-influenced Piedmont fingerpicking style, Atlanta-based Blind Willie McTell incorporated pop songs and novelty numbers, as well as blues, into his repertoire . His voice was unusually tender and expressive for a musician who made his living as a street singer, adding depth and poignancy to deftly crafted meditations on infatuation and loss. His recording career extended from 1927–56 and his style remained the same throughout. His gift of conveying intense emotion through low-key, intimate vocals rather than flamboyant shouting have made him one of the most revered of the south-eastern acoustic blues artists.

Memphis Jug Band (Vocal/instrumental group, 1927–34)

They did not invent the style, but guitarist/harpist Will Shade (a.k.a. Son Brimmer) and his rollicking aggregation were among the most popular and influential of the jug and string bands that proliferated around Memphis and Louisville, during the 1920s and 1930s. Their members over the years included such luminaries as Furry Lewis, harpist Big Walter Horton and guitarist Casey Bill Weldon, as well as occasional female guest vocalists. Their repertoire included some blues, but their speciality was tightly arranged pop and novelty numbers, some of which have become standards, and all of which they performed with a theatrical, vaudevillian flair.

Key Tracks

'Statesboro Blues' Blind Willie McTell
'Broke Down Engine Blues' Blind Willie McTell
'Stealin' Stealin'' Memphis Jug Band
'Sitting On Top Of The World' Mississippi Sheiks
'Stop And Listen Blues' Mississippi Sheiks

Mississippi Sheiks (Vocal/instrumental group, 1926–35)

The Mississippi Sheiks were Lonnie Chatmon (guitar, violin) and Walter Vinson (guitar), sometimes joined by Chatmon's brothers Sam (guitar, violin) and Armenter (a.k.a. Bo Carter, guitar), as well as Charlie McCoy (banjo, mandolin); the vocals were shared between the group members. Their repertoire blended blues themes with contemporary pop/novelty tunes, similar to a jug band's but somewhat less hokey in its delivery. They recorded for OKeh and Bluebird; their 'Sitting On Top Of The World' has become a standard, subsequently interpreted by Howlin' Wolf and Cream, among many others.

Blind Willie McTell was among the blues musicians based along the Eastern Seaboard.

A-Z of Artists

'Hambone' Willie Newbern (Vocals, guitar, 1899–1947)

A resident of Brownsville, Tennessee, Willie Newbern had only one recording session, for OKeh in Atlanta in 1929. Although he was not widely known outside his area, he influenced quite a few musicians: he recorded the first known version of 'Roll And Tumble Blues' and is said to have taught it to Charley Patton, among others. Allegedly he was killed while serving time in prison.

Mamie Smith (Vocals, 1883–1946)

Mamie Smith's first recording session, for OKeh in 1920, resulted in a pair of nondescript pop songs, but her manager Perry Bradford then talked the label into recording her as a blues singer. On 10 August 1920, fronting a band dubbed the Jazz Hounds – featuring stride pianist Willie 'The Lion' Smith (no relation) and possibly also cornettist Johnny Dunn – Smith cut the first record ever billed as a 'blues': 'Crazy Blues'. It sold upwards of a million copies, and in support she toured with a show that featured trapeze artists, comedians, dancers and other embellishments from her vaudeville past.

Despite her horn-like vocal timbre and emotional delivery, Smith was not really a blues singer. But 'Crazy Blues' virtually defined the genre – at least as a recorded popular music – for a generation of women vocalists who followed, each one of whom came in through the door that Mamie Smith had opened.

Key Tracks

'Roll And Tumble Blues' 'Hambone' Willie Newbern
'She Could Toodle-Oo' 'Hambone' Willie Newbern
'Crazy Blues' Mamie Smith
'Don't Care Blues' Mamie Smith
'Trixie's Blues' Trixie Smith

Trixie Smith (Vocals, 1895–1943)

Atlanta-born Trixie Smith was a vaudeville trouper when, in 1922, she cut her first records on Black Swan. Although she did not have the vocal prowess of front-line blues stars like Bessie Smith (no relation), she recorded steadily until 1926 – often with top-flight jazz orchestras such as Fletcher Henderson's – and sporadically thereafter. In the 1930s, after her recording career slackened off, she continued in show business, appearing in musical revues and films.

Mamie Smith with her Jazz Hounds in 1922. Note Bubber Miley on trumpet and a youthful Coleman Hawkins on saxophone.

A-Z of Artists

Victoria Spivey (Vocals, piano, 1906–76)

Houston native Victoria Spivey cut her first sides for OKeh in 1926 and she was soon one of the most popular artists of the 'classic blues' era. An eloquent lyricist alongside her vocal gifts, Spivey worked steadily into the 1940s; in 1962 she emerged from retirement as the head of blues label Spivey Records, on which she recorded herself and other 'rediscovered' blues artists. She continued to record and perform, based in New York City, until her death.

Henry Thomas (Vocals, quills, guitar, 1874–1930)

A son of former slaves, Henry 'Ragtime' Thomas specialized in the quills, a pan-pipe-like instrument made from hollow reeds. He was itinerant for most of his life, a fact reflected in songs such as 'Railroadin', in which Thomas names train stops from Fort Worth to Chicago. His 'Bull Doze Blues', renamed 'Goin' Up The Country', became a 1960s hit for Canned Heat, who recreated his quills intro note for note.

Key Tracks

'Black Snake Blues' Victoria Spivey
'Dirty Woman Blues' Victoria Spivey
'Railroadin' Henry Thomas
'His Eye is on the Sparrow' Ethel Waters
'That's No Way To Get Along' Rev Robert Wilkins

Ethel Waters (Vocals, 1896–1977)

Ethel Waters' most significant blues releases, on Cardinal and Black Swan, were recorded in the early 1920s. Versatile and ambitious, she soon moved into a more pop-oriented direction, and she also began to work in films and theatrical productions. It was in theatre that she eventually made her greatest mark, but after a mid-1950s religious conversion she joined evangelist Billy Graham's crusade, with which she remained until her death.

Rev. Robert Wilkins (Vocals, guitar, 1896–1987)

Mississippi-born Robert Wilkins' blues style, as evidenced on records he made for Victor, Brunswick and Vocalion from 1928–35, featured vivid lyric imagery couched in asymmetrical verses, laid over rudimentary but serviceable strumming. After being ordained in the 1930s, Wilkins quit the blues for religious music. 'Prodigal Son' on the Rolling Stones' *Beggars Banquet* (1968) was a cover of Wilkins' 'That's No Way To Get Along' – ironically, a blues that the Stones recast in a more biblical light.

Victoria Spivey in a 1920s photograph signed by the blues star to bandleader Luis Russell.

ELSHA
N.Y.
For my dear friend
Louis Russell
Ever
Victoria Spive
9/25/29.

The Thirties

As if at the convenience of history, the stock market crash of 1929 severed the 1920s from the 1930s. The breach was economic but its consequences were pervasive, sweeping away economic values and social illusions, and affecting all aspects of life for Americans and Europeans alike.

America's compliant 1920s middle class became the 1930s 'new poor'. Rural African-Americans were pitched back into conditions akin to servitude; those in the urban North and West after the Great Migration struggled anew to adapt. Poverty's ubiquity lent it unusual moral standing, reflected in movies and songs. Businessmen lost status; the wealthy were subjected to cultural ridicule and liberal reform unleashed by one of their own, President Franklin D. Roosevelt. Clashes over small-town and big-city values were replaced by battles over wages and hours between capital and labour.

Key Artists

Albert Ammons
Big Bill Broonzy
Robert Johnson
Leadbelly

Popular culture found easy ways forth. Network radio, paid for by advertisers, took hold; outlets competed for local and niche audiences, hiring bluesmen to host shows aimed at African-American listeners, for example. The record industry almost expired, but live music, especially for dancers, thrived. Movies, combining social realism and romantic fantasy, offered the decade's most iconic imagery. Within 10 years, movies and touring bands displaced theatre and vaudeville as transmitters of a popular culture, available for the first time to millions simultaneously, sea to sea – and beyond. That culture was centred on jazz, steeped in the blues, immersed in transition. In April 1939 the New York World's Fair opened a vision to a future dominated by technology, which 1930s music and art had essentially come to represent. Five months later the decade ended with the beginning of the Second World War. Music and art faced another wild ride.

The shadow of the Great Depression hung over 1930s America.

Political Change

The early part of the 1930s was dominated by one major event: the collapse of American financial institutions that led to what is known as the 'Great Depression'. The disaster was underway as the decade began, and hit its lowest point in 1932.

Significantly, in the final quarter of that year, there was not a single blues recording session anywhere in America. The Depression hung over America like a dark cloud and economic conditions improved very slowly. While the government instituted many reforms and programmes to help the unemployed, it could only do so much. It would take a wartime economy in the next decade to pull the country out of the doldrums.

The 1930s also saw a rise in radical political activity. Critics of capitalism found eager followers, workers banded together in labour unions, and artists and intellectuals were drawn to Marxism as a solution to the problems of America. The infamous trials of the Scottsboro Boys in Alabama, involving rape charges by two white women against eight black men, dominated the news pages during 1931–32 and the Communist Party (CP) was in the middle of that battle. The National Association for the Advancement of Colored People (NAACP), founded in 1909, had been working to expose the racial injustice of the country through traditional methods and was moving cautiously; however, it was upstaged by the CP, which organized marches, demonstrations and letter-writing campaigns. Lawyers from the CP-controlled International Labor Defense represented the defendants and won an appeal of the initial guilty verdict. The second, third and fourth trials were rife with CP attempts to bribe witnesses and manipulate the situation. It was the NAACP that prevailed in its work through the legal system to gain limited victories for some of the defendants. Throughout the remainder of the decade, the CP would be at the forefront of the racial struggle.

'Piano dominated blues music in the twenties and thirties and 'til the late forties. See, acoustic blues that original Sonny Boy Williamson was playing, Big Bill Broonzy, and Memphis Minnie, they all used piano.'

Billy Boy Arnold

Labourers gamble their cotton money in a juke joint, a place where blues musicians could often find work.

The New Record Labels

The repeal of the Volstead Act in 1933 meant that Americans could once more legally consume alcoholic beverages, while the rise of the new jukebox industry helped to fuel the revival of the record business. Such race record stalwarts of the 1920s as Paramount and Gennett had found it impossible to survive the change in economic conditions. But the void was quickly filled by Victor's new Bluebird imprint; the revived American Record Corporation (ARC) and the brand new Decca label. The vast majority of great blues records would appear on those labels for the remainder of the decade.

Geographically, Chicago became a primary location for blues recording by all three labels. In terms of public performance, much of the country blues was played on street corners or at private functions such as parties. The pianists tended to work indoors, playing in brothels, barrelhouses, taverns and clubs. By the end of the decade, brothels and barrel-houses were a less frequent destination and for all blues players of reputation, the tavern and nightclub became more a source of work.

The Rise of Boogie-Woogie

There were new trends in the music of the 1930s. Boogie-woogie, which was heard in the 1920s, developed into a national phenomenon in the 1930s. Its great exponents, such as Albert Ammons (1907–49), Pete Johnson (1904–67) and Meade 'Lux' Lewis (1905–64), would become stars of radio and movies. Most blues artists were recorded with a fairly minimal accompaniment. There were many solo performances and rarely would a recording session involve more than guitar, harmonica, piano and bass. But with the migration to Chicago by so many artists, changes began to occur. Tampa Red (1904–81) was a catalyst for new ideas among Chicago musicians and among those in his circle were Big Bill Broonzy (1893–58), Memphis Minnie (1897–1973), John Lee 'Sonny Boy' Williamson (1914–48) and 'Big Maceo' Merriweather (1905–53). Washboard Sam (1910–66) was the pioneer of blues percussion, but when artists such as Minnie and Broonzy used drums for some of their 1937 recordings, new vistas began to open. Some would be slow to adopt this new sound, but those who did explore it were able to move towards new audiences.

Popular Melody

Kokomo Arnold – 'Milk Cow Blues' (1934)

Meade 'Lux' Lewis was among the main exponents of the burgeoning boogie-woogie piano style.

The Blues Arrives at Carnegie Hall

In December 1938, record producer John Hammond organized a concert at Carnegie Hall in New York entitled 'From Spirituals To Swing, An Evening Of American Negro Music'. It was dedicated to the memory of Bessie Smith (1894–1937) and was sponsored by a CP magazine, *New Masses*. The concert was a huge success, with almost 3000 people in attendance.

While there were jazz and gospel performers featured the blues was well represented by Sonny Terry (1911–86), Broonzy, Joe Turner (1911–85) and boogie-woogie piano stars Ammons, Lewis and Johnson. The event generated universal praise in the press and made stars out of most of its participants. In the aftermath of the concert, a new nightclub called Café Society opened in New York's Greenwich Village, catering to integrated audiences and performances of black jazz, blues and gospel music. Most of the concert's performers appeared there at one time or another. Another Spirituals To Swing concert was held a year later and featured Broonzy, Terry and Ida Cox (1896–1967) as the blues performers.

Popular Melody

Sonny Boy Williamson – 'Good Morning Little School Girl' (1937)

The Blues Becomes More Citified

By 1939, the big swing bands were at the forefront of American show business. Well-established stars such as Basie and Duke Ellington (1899–1974) had used the blues as a basis for much of what they performed; they were now joined by orchestras led by Erskine Hawkins and Buddy Johnson, who continued that tradition. In the early years of the next decade, Lionel Hampton (1908–2002) and Cootie Williams also led large orchestras following the same trail.

Despite the fact that great country blues would continue to be performed and recorded, it was clear that the momentum in blues music was moving in the direction of a more urban sound. The changes begun in blues in the late 1930s would come to fruition in the next decade; in time, some blues influence would play a part in most styles of American music, including gospel and country.

New York's Carnegie Hall – the venue for John Hammond's seminal Spirituals To Swing concert, featuring blues, gospel and jazz music.

Key Artist: Albert Ammons

Albert Clifton Ammons was born in Chicago, Illinois in March 1907. As a young man he learned from Jimmy Yancey, who cast a long shadow over Chicago blues pianists through his work at rent parties, social functions and after-hours jobs. Ammons came to know other pianists and the blues specialists gathered together in Chicago, echoing what was happening with the stride pianists in Harlem.

Among the Chicago group, in addition to Yancey, were Clarence 'Pine Top' Smith, Jimmy Blythe, Cripple Clarence Lofton, Hersal Thomas and Ammons' close friend Meade 'Lux' Lewis. Ammons was the youngest of these men and he learned from all of them. He also drew inspiration from stride-piano great Fats Waller, a major star in black entertainment circles. Lewis and Smith had recorded boogie in the 1920s, and among blues pianists boogie-woogie, with its eight-beats-to-the-bar pattern in the left hand, became an adjunct to the basic style.

Ammons' Big Break

Ammons worked at jobs outside music, led his own swing combos and played with other bandleaders until his big break: a residency at the Club DeLisa, the most important nightspot on Chicago's south side. This engagement, which began in 1935, led to his discovery by John Hammond and his first recordings, for Decca, in February 1936.

'...I listened to Albert Ammons this morning and it was everything. It was sex, it was life, it was truth. It was marvellous.'

Jools Holland

In 1938, Ammons was invited to appear in New York for Hammond's Spirituals To Swing concert at Carnegie Hall. He served as accompanist to Sister Rosetta Tharpe and Big Bill Broonzy, and had his own feature number, 'Boogie Woogie'. He was also teamed with Lewis and Kansas City pianist Pete Johnson for two selections, 'Jumpin' Blues' and 'Cavalcade Of Boogie'. The audience response was a clear indicator that boogie-woogie had arrived. The occasion also served as a launch-pad for this trio of pianists. Ammons, Johnson and Lewis were linked for several years; they appeared in duo or trio settings, occasionally with the addition of vocalist Joe Turner, and recorded for Vocalion, Blue Note and Victor.

Right: Albert Ammons (right) with Pete Johnson – two of the great boogie-woogie masters.

They toured the US, using Café Society in New York as a base, and also appeared in movies and on radio broadcasts.

The Rhythm Kings

In 1944, during his final extended New York engagement, Albert Ammons recorded two sessions for the Commodore label. One was a solo date, while the other involved an all-star aggregation billed as Albert Ammons & his Rhythm Kings – the same name that Ammons had used on his first recording session. When he returned to Chicago the following year, he signed with the brand-new Mercury label and began a new series of Rhythm Kings recordings. Until this time, the thematic material used in boogie-woogie was usually the blues or simple, riff-based melodies; Ammons, however, began to adapt his thundering left-hand patterns to pop songs. It is here that we get fresh treatments of standards such as 'Deep In The Heart Of Texas', 'Roses Of Picardy' and 'Swanee River'. Ammons made it clear that, in his hands, a boogie-woogie approach could be applied to any musical source.

Ammons made his final Mercury session just before the start of the second American Federation of Musicians recording ban in January 1948. No doubt the future would have held much for this giant of piano blues but, shortly after appearing at the Inaugural Ball for President Truman, he contracted a mysterious disease – later diagnosed as congestive heart failure – which eventually led to his death in December 1949.

Next Page: Albert Ammons with his band in the Club DeLisa, Chicago in 1936.

Key Artist: Big Bill Broonzy

The parents of William Lee Conley Broonzy were born into slavery. He was born in June 1893 in Scott, Mississippi, one of 17 children. Raised on a farm in Arkansas, Broonzy's first musical instrument was a homemade violin, which he played at church and social functions.

In the early teens he was a preacher, while also working as a country fiddler. He served in the US Army from 1918–19, and shortly after his discharge moved to Chicago. At first he worked as a baggage handler, performing music on a casual basis; it was in Chicago that he first learned to play the guitar.

Broonzy worked with Papa Charlie Jackson in 1924 and soon became an accompanist in demand. He made his recording debut for Paramount in 1927 and by 1930 was recording for Gennett/Champion and Perfect/Banner under a variety of pseudonyms, such as Sammy Sampson and Big Bill Johnson. In 1931, he recorded for Paramount and the resulting tracks were issued by 'Big Bill Broomsley'. By this time, Big Bill Broonzy was a professional entertainer.

'As a warm, entertaining blues singer, he had no equal.'
Sam Charters

Broonzy worked theatres and taverns in Chicago and northern Indiana during this period and toured in a show with Memphis Minnie. Broonzy did not record during 1933 and when he resumed in 1934, for ARC and Bluebird, the records were issued simply as Big Bill. This began a period of prolific recording activity for Broonzy. From 1936, he recorded exclusively for ARC (later Columbia), an arrangement that lasted until the end of 1947. By 1937, performance opportunities had slowed and Broonzy was living on his Arkansas farm, commuting to Chicago three or four times a year to make records.

Above: 'Plough Hand Blues', a Big Bill Broonzy track recorded for Melodisc under the pseudonym Chicago Bill. Right: Blues and folk singer Big Bill Broonzy, during his 1956 tour of the UK.

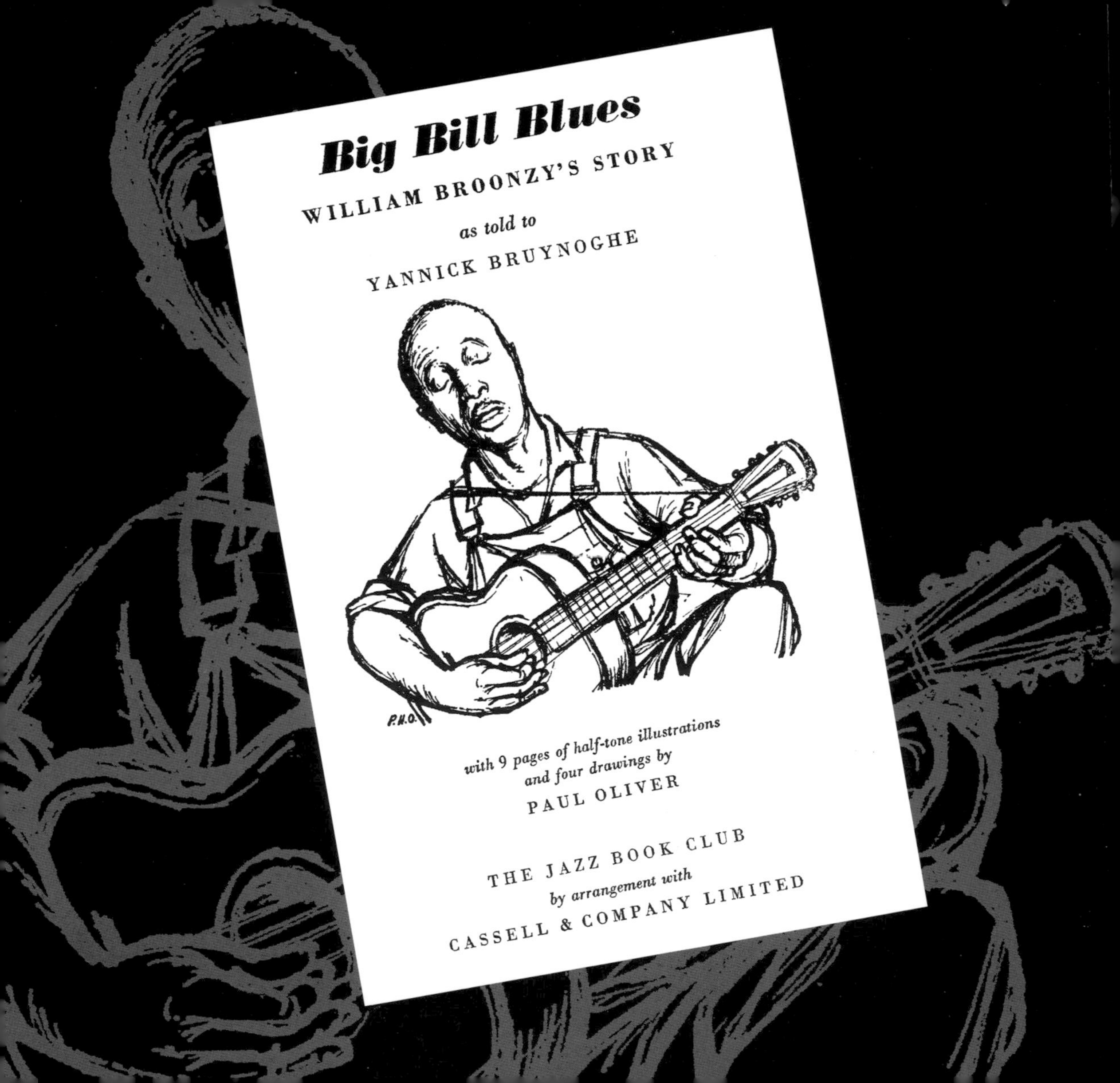

Big Bill Blues

WILLIAM BROONZY'S STORY

as told to

YANNICK BRUYNOGHE

with 9 pages of half-tone illustrations and four drawings by

PAUL OLIVER

THE JAZZ BOOK CLUB

by arrangement with

CASSELL & COMPANY LIMITED

Spirituals to Swing

In 1938 Broonzy was part of the cast for the John Hammond production 'Spirituals To Swing', a concert held at Carnegie Hall in New York City. He made the most of the opportunity and renewed his career as an entertainer, shortly afterwards appearing at major clubs in New York as well as Chicago. He appeared in the movie *Swingin' The Dream* in 1939, toured with Lil Green during 1941–42 and had theatre dates in New York and Los Angeles in the early 1940s. He released records on a regular basis and by the end of his career he had written and recorded hundreds of songs.

European Tours

For some time, Broonzy's record dates had alternated between the spare accompaniment of piano and bass, and larger ensembles often featuring two horns. As time wore on, the country aspects of his recording sessions were given scant attention. When he signed with Mercury in 1949, his recording began to take on the flavour of the emerging R&B sound. While he continued to record he was, for a time, employed as a janitor at Iowa State University, but things changed markedly when he made his first overseas tour. He toured England, France and Germany as a solo artist during September and October 1951; he made recordings in each country and proved to be extremely popular.

Another tour in early 1952 came immediately after his final sessions for Mercury. From this point forward, Broonzy would revert to his country blues origins and record prolifically for a variety of European labels. In 1955 his autobiography, *Big Bill Blues*, was published. Further European appearances came during 1955–57 but after the shows Big Bill Broonzy was diagnosed with cancer, from which he died in August 1958 in Chicago.

Big Bill Blues – *Broonzy's autobiography, published in 1955.*

Key Artist: Robert Johnson

While blues music has produced dozens of great, innovative musicians, vocalists and songwriters, the continuing influence of Robert Johnson over the years has shown that no other performer has succeeded in combining all the elements in quite the exceptional way that he did.

He was born Robert Leroy Johnson in May 1911 in Hazelhurst, Mississippi to Julia Dodds and Noah Johnson. Julia Dodds was the wife of Charles Dodds Jr., a farmer forced to leave Mississippi a few years prior to Robert's birth. Julia had taken up with Johnson in the absence of Charles, who settled in Memphis and adopted the name C.D. Spencer. Julia remarried in 1916, to Willie Willis. Robert lived with them in Robinsonville, Mississippi and was raised as Robert Spencer. It wasn't until his early teens that he was informed about his real father and began to call himself Robert Johnson. Already a keen harmonica player, Johnson began to take an interest in the guitar at this time; he built a rack for his harmonica and was soon picking out accompaniments on the guitar to his harp and voice. He came under the tutelage of Willie Brown, then living in Robinsonville, and Charley Patton, a frequent performer at the area juke joints.

'Amongst all of his peers I felt he was the one that was talking from his soul without really compromising for anybody.'

Eric Clapton

Johnson married Virginia Travis in Penton, Mississippi in February 1929. The couple moved in with Robert's half-sister on a plantation in the Robinsonville area. Robert worked as sharecropper, while continuing his interest in music, and Virginia became pregnant. Who knows which way his life may have turned at this time had his wife not died in childbirth in April 1930.

Music as a Full-Time Occupation

Within weeks of this tragedy, Son House moved to Robinsonville to work with Willie Brown prior to his recording debut for Paramount in late May 1930. During this brief time, Robert became intensely interested in Son House and his music, although the older man regarded Robert as little more than a beginner. Before the end of 1930, Robert Johnson decided to devote himself completely to music, and headed back to Hazelhurst.

Right: Blues guitar legend Robert Johnson.

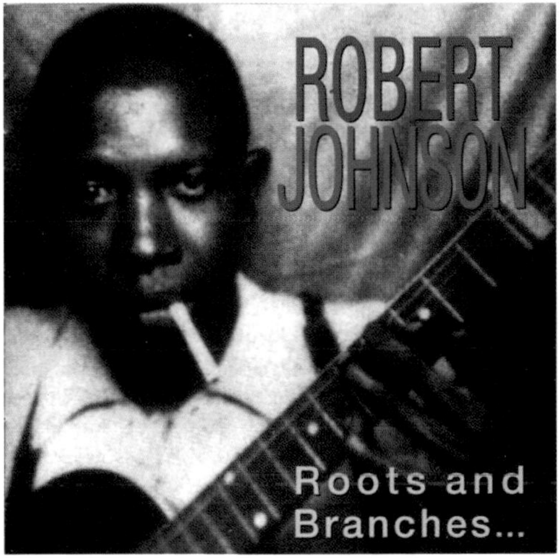

Robert met Ike Zinnerman, a bluesman who became his next mentor. The two men worked the area around Hazelhurst, occasionally encountering artists such as Johnny Temple or Tommy Johnson, and Robert began to blossom. He was working street corners, juke houses, lumber camps – wherever he could make money. In time he returned to the Mississippi Delta area. On a trip back to Robinsonville he encountered Willie Brown and Son House, who were astonished at how well he could play – and so was born the delicious blues legend of how Johnson sold his soul to the devil in return for his guitar-playing abilities. Johnson soon settled in Helena, Arkansas, which remained his main base of operations for the rest of his life.

Rambling Man

By 1934 he had become a constant traveller. His reputation spread and he had a large following throughout Mississippi and Tennessee. He relied on women to care for him in his constant travels, but he longed to make records. His quest led him to H.C. Speir in Jackson, Mississippi. Speir was a talent scout for ARC records and he passed his recommendation up the line. A recording session was arranged in San Antonio, Texas in November 1936 and Johnson recorded 16 titles in the space of a week. The following June in Dallas, Texas he recorded 13 more.

These 29 songs are the Johnson legacy. 'Terraplane Blues'/'Kindhearted Woman Blues', the first record to be released, was the bestselling track but was still only a modest success. The first LP of this material, *King Of The Delta Blues Singers*, was issued by Columbia in 1961 and inspired a whole new generation of blues musicians. When the CD box-set version, *The Complete Recordings*, was released in 1990, the worldwide public was finally ready for Johnson's genius and it became an enormous hit. Robert Johnson died of pneumonia in August 1938, following an incident in which he was poisoned at a juke joint near Greenwood, Mississippi.

Next Page: Robinsonville, where Johnson grew up.

Key Artist: Leadbelly

Huddie Ledbetter was born in January 1888 in Mooringsport, Louisiana. He was exposed to music from an early age and began playing guitar before he was in his teens. The music he performed was composed of shouts, hollers and Native American songs, as well as ballads, religious songs and dance tunes from a variety of traditions.

He became a popular entertainer at functions in his community, which was almost entirely black. By 1901 he had left home and he spent time in the red-light district of Shreveport. It was here that he first encountered early blues songs such as 'The Dirty Dozens'. By the time he was 15, he had his own guitar and his own pistol. In 1910 he was playing in the Deep Ellum area of Dallas and it was probably in 1912 that he met Blind Lemon Jefferson, the Dallas street singer. This is also about the time Huddie acquired his 12-string guitar. Ledbetter and Jefferson worked together over the next three years and Ledbetter absorbed much from the younger man, including his slide guitar technique.

In December 1917, Ledbetter killed his cousin's husband, for which he was convicted and received a sentence of seven to 30 years in jail. He served his time at the Central State Prison Farm, near Houston, Texas. During his time in prison, Huddie picked up the nickname 'Leadbelly'. He was frequently called upon to entertain Governor Pat Neff during his visits to Sugarland. On one occasion in 1924, Leadbelly created an impromptu blues, which – legend has it – so impressed Neff that he promised to pardon him. He was set free in January 1925, but after his release he continued to exhibit violent behaviour. In January 1930, in Mooringsport, he knifed a white man and was sentenced to six to 10 years' hard labour at Angola State Penitentiary.

'Leadbelly was a man who decided he was going to be a champion in life. Everything he did, he did it with his whole personality: sing, dance, fight, work.'

Alan Lomax

Leadbelly with session pianist Paul Mason Howard playing the dolceola, a type of fretless zither.

LEAD
BELLY
MY
LAST
GO
ROUND

Lomaxes to the Rescue

As luck would have it, folklorists John and Alan Lomax visited Angola in July of 1933 as part of John's quest to document American folk songs and ballads using portable disc-recording equipment. Leadbelly recorded for them at Angola; among the songs were 'Ella Speed', 'Frankie And Albert' and a gentle waltz called 'Goodnight Irene'. When it became known that John Lomax was returning to Angola in July 1934, Leadbelly saw an opportunity. As his petition for release was being ignored, he recorded his song 'Governor O.K. Allen'. Lomax brought it to the governor's office and Leadbelly was released in August 1934.

At the end of the year, Lomax arranged for Leadbelly to perform at a dinner given by the Modern Language Association in Philadelphia. Within days, the two visited New York and were written up in the *New York Herald Tribune*. This led to Leadbelly's first commercial recording sessions (for ARC) in early 1935. He also continued to record for John – and later John's son Alan – Lomax for the Library of Congress.

An Acrimonious Split

Financial disagreements caused Leadbelly to split from John Lomax and instead reach an arrangement with Mary Elizabeth Barnicle, a professor who introduced Leadbelly to the liberal and radical community that provided much of his growing audience. He made no commercial recordings from 1936–38 and his last association with John Lomax came when *Negro Folk Songs As Sung By Leadbelly* was published in November 1936. The book received favourable reviews and Leadbelly was profiled in Life magazine, after which he appeared on a radio series and began to write new songs.

He was arrested again for felonious assault in 1939. Alan Lomax, trying to raise money for his defence, contacted Musicraft Records to arrange a recording session. The songs Leadbelly recorded were issued on an album titled *Negro Sinful Songs*. He was convicted and served eight months. In 1940 Leadbelly recorded for RCA Victor and by the summer of 1941 he had begun a lengthy association with Moses Asch. With the exception of some 1944 recordings for Capitol, the remainder of his recordings were released on Asch/Stinson/Folkways. He continued to be a popular attraction on the folk circuit until his death in 1949.

Huddie 'Leadbelly' Ledbetter – murderer, convict and undisputed blues hero.

A-Z of Artists

Kokomo Arnold (Guitar, vocals, 1901–68)

Born and raised in Georgia, James Arnold was taught to play guitar by his cousin. He moved to Buffalo, New York in his late teens and to Chicago in 1929. He worked outside music, making bootleg whiskey, but also played occasional jobs. He first recorded for Victor in 1930 as Gitfiddle Jim and was signed to Decca in September 1934, scoring an instant hit with 'Milk Cow Blues'/'Old Original Kokomo Blues'. The former was a song covered by artists as diverse as Bob Wills, Elvis Presley and George Strait, while the flip side – written about a brand of coffee – provided Arnold with a lifelong nickname.

A left-handed, bottleneck stylist who had 76 sides issued on Decca, Arnold recorded for the last time in 1938. He mainly worked outside music after 1940, although he did play some Chicago dates during the folk music revival of the early 1960s.

Big Maceo (Piano, vocals, 1905–53)

Major Merriweather was born in Georgia and taught himself to play piano. He moved to Detroit in 1924 and worked at the Ford Motor Company, also playing jobs, mostly as a soloist, before moving to Chicago. There he developed a friendship with Tampa Red and they recorded for Bluebird in 1941. His 'Worried Life Blues' is a blues standard, while 'Chicago Breakdown' is an instrumental blues masterpiece. He suffered a stroke in 1946, following which his career was sharply curtailed.

Key Tracks

'Milk Cow Blues/Old Original Kokomo Blues' Kokomo Arnold
'Rainy Night Blues' Kokomo Arnold
'Worried Life Blues' Big Maceo
'Chicago Breakdown' Big Maceo
'Future Blues' Willie Brown

Willie Brown (Guitar, vocals, 1900–52)

An associate of Charley Patton, Brown was a part of the Mississippi blues scene in the early 1920s. While he started out playing with Patton and Tommy Johnson, he teamed up with Son House in 1926 and accompanied his Paramount session in May 1930, also cutting four songs of his own. Brown played with Robert Johnson frequently in the years prior to Johnson's death. He recorded for the Library of Congress in 1941 but then left the music business.

Pianist Big Maceo, whose 'Worried Life Blues' became a blues standard.

A-Z of Artists

Sleepy John Estes (Guitar, vocals, 1899–1977)

John Adams Estes was born in Ripley, Tennessee. He teamed up with mandolinist Yank Rachell to work the area from 1919 until the late 1920s. His first recordings were made for Victor in 1929 and included his celebrated 'Divin' Duck Blues'. He left Brownsville for Chicago in 1931.

With harmonica player Hammie Nixon, Estes worked medicine shows, fish fries and hobo camps, touring much of the country in the late 1930s. He recorded six sides for Champion in 1935, including 'Drop Down Mama', and he later recorded for Decca from 1937–40. After two sessions for Bluebird in 1941 he returned to Brownsville and left the music scene, with the exception of two recording sessions for Sun in 1952. He had completely lost his sight by 1950. 'Rediscovered' in 1962, he recorded for several labels and began an extensive comeback, which included at least one album of electric blues with younger musicians. He toured the US, Europe and Japan steadily until his death.

Key Tracks

'Divin' Duck Blues' Sleepy John Estes
'Drop Down Mama' Sleepy John Estes
'Someday Baby' Sleepy John Estes
'Rag Mama Rag' Blind Boy Fuller
'Trucking My Blues Away' Blind Boy Fuller

Blind Boy Fuller (Guitar, vocals, 1908–41)

Fuller was born Fulton Allen in Wadesboro, North Carolina and was one of 10 children. He learned to play guitar as a teenager and by the mid-1920s was working for tips around Rockingham, North Carolina. He had lost his sight by 1928. He teamed up with artists such as Gary Davis, Bull City Red and Sonny Terry and worked the area around Durham, North Carolina in the mid-1930s.

He first recorded for ARC in 1935 and, with the exception of two sessions for Decca in 1937, recorded for ARC/Vocalion/OKeh until June 1940. He cut well over 100 sides during that time. Fuller was known for the wide variety of music he played, including pop songs, religious material, ragtime and blues, and because of that range he is considered a unique figure in the pantheon of Carolina blues stylists. He underwent kidney surgery in 1940 and suffered blood poisoning, which ultimately killed him.

Sleepy John Estes backstage at London's Royal Albert Hall, 1966.

Stella

A-Z of Artists

Son House (Guitar, vocals, 1902–88)

The son of a musician, Eddie James House Jr. was born in Riverton, Mississippi. House was preaching sermons by his mid-teens and travelled widely in the 1920s. He did not learn guitar until the age of 25, but soon thereafter was torn between his faith and his love of the blues. After killing a man in a Lyon juke joint and serving two years in jail, House encountered Charley Patton, whose connections at Paramount Records landed him a recording session in 1930.

The intensity and passion of House on songs such as the two-part 'Preachin' The Blues' have rarely been approached in the blues field. However, the records sold poorly and House worked functions in the Delta, often in the company of Willie Brown, for much of the 1930s. He recorded for the Library of Congress in 1941–42, before leaving music in 1943 and moving to Rochester, New York. Rediscovered in 1964, he recorded for a number of labels and toured widely for the rest of the decade.

Skip James (Vocals, guitar, 1902–69)

Born in Bentonia, Mississippi and raised on a nearby plantation, Nehemiah 'Skip' James played the guitar professionally from a young age and also taught himself to play the piano. His distinctive E-minor guitar tuning, three-finger picking technique and melancholy, high-pitched vocals gave him a unique sound, and his recording session for Paramount in 1931 resulted in some of the most affecting and haunting country blues ever recorded. Songs such as 'Devil Got My Woman', 'I'm So Glad' and '22-20 Blues' still stand out as masterpieces of their genre.

'Someone who once heard Caruso sing said that he was so moved that his heart shook. That's the way I felt the first time I heard Son House.'

Martin Scorsese

In the 1930s James drifted away from the music scene to concentrate on a career in the church, before being 'rediscovered' in the 1960s. He performed at the 1964 Newport Folk Festival and recorded a handful of albums for Takoma, Melodeon and Vanguard, while his 'I'm So Glad' was covered by the British blues-rock band Cream. His revived career was sadly cut short by his death from cancer in 1969.

Son House, whose role in the development of blues in the genre's early days was significant.

A-Z of Artists

Pete Johnson (Piano, 1904–67)

Born in Kansas City, Missouri, Kermit Holden Johnson teamed up with Joe Turner at the Sunset Café in the early 1930s and went to New York for the Spirituals To Swing concert in 1938. He recorded with Turner for Vocalion (the famous 'Roll 'Em Pete'), as well as alone and with Albert Ammons and Meade 'Lux' Lewis. Beginning in 1944, he recorded for Brunswick, National, Apollo and Swingtime, and was often featured with Turner. He suffered a heart attack in 1958 and was only sporadically active after that.

Meade 'Lux' Lewis (Piano, 1905–64)

Born in Chicago and inspired by Jimmy Yancey, Meade Anderson 'Lux' Lewis recorded an early boogie-woogie masterpiece, 'Honky Tonk Train Blues', for Paramount in 1927 (the song was also recorded for Parlophone, 1935 and Victor, 1937). He recorded for Decca in 1936 ('Yancey Special') and Vocalion, Blue Note and Solo Art throughout 1941, almost always as a soloist or with Albert Ammons and Pete Johnson. He recorded for many other labels between 1944–61.

John & Alan Lomax (Folklorists, John Avery Lomax 1867–1948; Alan Lomax 1915–2002)

John Lomax was born in Goodman, Mississippi and raised near Fort Worth, Texas. Although his initial interest lay in cowboy songs, a friendship with a servant named Nat Blythe sparked an interest in black music. With the 1910 publication of *Cowboy Songs And Other Frontier Ballads*, his reputation was established. His work on black music took root with a consultancy to the Library of Congress in 1933.

Key Tracks

'Dive Bomber' Pete Johnson
'Death Ray Boogie' Pete Johnson
'Honky Tonk Train Blues' Meade 'Lux' Lewis
'Yancey Special' Meade 'Lux' Lewis

Alan Lomax was 18 when he joined his father to record musicians and singers in their natural habitat. In July 1933, the Lomaxes arrived at Angola Penitentiary, where they discovered Leadbelly. Alan continued his father's essential fieldwork, most notably by finding Son House and discovering Muddy Waters in 1941. Much of Alan's best field recordings were released commercially on Atlantic Records (*The Songs Of The South*, which contained Fred McDowell's first recordings). His 1993 memoir, *The Land Where The Blues Began*, recounts all of these adventures.

Alan Lomax, second-generation American musicologist.

A–Z of Artists

Mississippi Fred McDowell (Guitar, vocals, 1904–72)

Self-taught as a guitarist, music was only a sideline for McDowell for the first 60 years of his life. He worked in the Memphis area before settling in Como, Mississippi to work as a farmer in 1929; he didn't own a guitar until 1940. Discovered and recorded by Alan Lomax in 1959, McDowell's first recordings were issued on Atlantic and Prestige/International.

A bottleneck specialist, McDowell was recorded in 1964 by Chris Strachwitz for Arhoolie Records. This provided a springboard to prominence for McDowell, who soon moved into regular appearances at festivals and on the folk-music circuit. From that point until 1971, he recorded regularly and appeared in three films, including the documentary *Fred McDowell* (1969). He was championed by younger performers such as the Rolling Stones, who covered McDowell's tune 'You Got To Move' on their 1971 album *Sticky Fingers*.

Memphis Minnie (Guitar, vocals, 1897–1973)

Lizzie Douglas was born in Algiers, Louisiana but was raised in Walls, Mississippi. She learned banjo and guitar at a young age and ran away to Memphis in 1910 to work the music circuit under the name Kid Douglas. She toured with the Ringling Brothers circus for several seasons prior to 1920 and also worked in jug bands, where she met and married 'Kansas' Joe McCoy.

They made their recording debut as Kansas Joe and Memphis Minnie for Columbia in 1929, and recorded for Victor in 1930 and Vocalion during 1930–34. Minnie moved to Chicago in the early 1930s and divorced McCoy in 1935. She recorded for Decca and Bluebird before returning to Vocalion/OKeh/Columbia from 1935–49. She teamed with her third husband, Ernest 'Little Son Joe' Lawlers, in 1939. Minnie then ran a vaudeville company before leaving the music business in the mid-1950s.

Key Tracks

'You Got To Move' Mississippi Fred McDowell
'Baby Please Don't Go' Mississippi Fred McDowell
'Bumble Bee' Memphis Minnie
'Nothing In Rambling' Memphis Minnie
'I'm So Glad' Memphis Minnie

Mississippi Fred McDowell, who was an unknown amateur until the blues revival of the 1960s.

A-Z of Artists

Little Brother Montgomery (Piano, vocals, 1906–85)

Eurreal Wilford Montgomery was born in Louisiana and taught himself piano, dropping out of school to work functions and juke joints. He first recorded for Paramount in 1930 ('Vicksburg Blues'/'No Special Rider') and then for Bluebird and ARC in 1935–36. Often featured with traditional jazz bands in addition to his primary work as a soloist, Montgomery settled in Chicago in 1942 and worked as a sideman for other recording artists. He continued to tour and record throughout the 1960s and 1970s.

Jimmy Rushing (Vocals, 1899–1972)

James Andrew Rushing was born in Oklahoma City, Oklahoma into a musical family. He worked in California in the mid-1920s as a pianist and vocalist, joined Walter Page's Blue Devils in Oklahoma City in 1927 and made his recording debut with the band in 1929. He played with the Bennie Moten band in Kansas City from 1929, before joining the first Count Basie band in 1935. He remained with Basie until 1950 and recorded more than 50 songs, including his signature song 'Mister Five By Five'.

Key Tracks

'Vicksburg Blues'/'No Special Rider' Little Brother Montgomery
'Mister Five By Five' Jimmy Rushing
'Going To Chicago' Jimmy Rushing
'Driving Wheel Blues' Roosevelt Skyes
'Night Time Is The Right Time' Roosevelt Skyes

Roosevelt Sykes (Piano, vocals, 1906–83)

Born in Elmar, Arkansas and raised in St. Louis, Sykes taught himself piano. He made his recording debut for OKeh in 1928 but also recorded for Paramount (as Dobby Bragg) and Victor (as Willie Kelly) from 1929–33. He settled in Chicago in 1931 and created the blues standards '44 Blues', 'Driving Wheel Blues' and 'Night Time Is The Right Time'. Sykes' powerful, lusty style adapted well to modern trends and he remained a prolific recording artist well into his 70s.

Accomplished pianist and revolutionary bandleader Count Basie from whom Jimmy Rushing plied his trade.

Murray Korman N.Y.

Tampa Red (Guitar, piano, kazoo, vocals, 1904–81)

Hudson Woodbridge was born in Smithville, Georgia and rasied in Tampa, Florida by his maternal grandmother. A self-taught musician, he worked juke joints throughout Florida in the early 1920s, before moving to Chicago in 1925. He made his recording debut as Tampa Red for Paramount in 1928. He then teamed with Georgia Tom Dorsey, later a major gospel songwriter, and recorded extensively for Vocalion until 1932, creating blues standards such as 'It's Tight Like That'.

Red also recorded as a soloist, in a successful duo with pianist Big Maceo Merriweather and in jug-band settings. He recorded for Bluebird in 1934 and remained with Bluebird/RCA Victor until 1953, cutting more than 220 titles including the blues standard 'It Hurts Me Too'. Tampa Red lost interest in music in the mide-1950s, but did make two solo LPs for Prestige/Bluesville in 1960.

Key Tracks

'It Hurts Me Too' Tampa Red
'It's Tight Like That' Tampa Red
'Strange Things Are Happening Every Day' Sister Rosetta Tharpe
'Up The Country Blues' Sippie Wallace
'I'm A Mighty Tight Woman' Sippie Wallace

Sister Rosetta Tharpe (Guitar, vocals, 1915–73)

Born in Arkansas, Rosetta Nubin was the daughter of a missionary. She had learned to play guitar by the age of six and accompanied her mother at church functions. The family moved to Chicago and Tharpe signed with Decca in 1938. Sister Rosetta was essentially a gospel performer, but with Lucky Millinder's Orchestra (1941–43) she recorded blues as well as spirituals. In 1944 she teamed up with blues pianist Sammy Price and made hit records including 'Strange Things Are Happening Every Day'.

Sippie Wallace (Vocals, 1898–1986)

Beaulah Thomas was raised in Houston, Texas. From an early age she sang in church and worked with her pianist brother Hersal Thomas. She moved to Chicago in 1923 and recorded for OKeh, creating blues standards such as 'Up The Country Blues' and 'I'm A Mighty Tight Woman'. 'Rediscovered' in 1966, she recorded two albums prior to a 1970 stroke. Her final album, *Sippie* (1983), received a W.C. Handy award and a Grammy nomination.

Tampa Red and Big Maceo enjoyed a relaxed musical dialogue similar to that of Leroy Carr and Scrapper Blackwell in the 1920s.

TAMPA RED & BIG MACEO

THE GREAT PIANO/GUITAR DUO 1941-1946

HISTORIC * SONG * RECORDING

BLUES COLLECTION

A-Z of Artists

Washboard Sam (Washboard, vocals, 1910–66)

Robert Brown was born in Walnut Ridge, Arkansas and was the half-brother of Big Bill Broonzy. He left home to play with street singers in the Memphis area in the mid-1920s. In 1932 he moved to Chicago and teamed up with Sleepy John Estes and Hammie Nixon. He made his recording debut for Bluebird in 1935 and stayed with Bluebird/RCA until 1949; he recorded more than 150 titles, many of which featured Broonzy on guitar.

Peetie Wheatstraw (Piano, vocals, 1902–41)

William Bunch was born in Tennessee but raised in Arkansas. He played guitar and piano in his youth, left home in the mid-1920s and settled in East St. Louis, Illinois. He made his recording debut in 1930 for Vocalion as Peetie Wheatstraw. A popular and prolific recording artist for Decca and Vocalion until his death, Wheatstraw was billed as 'The Devil's Son-In-Law'. His recordings often also featured a prominent guitarist such as Kokomo Arnold or Lonnie Johnson. He died in an automobile accident less than a month after his final recording session.

Bukka White (Guitar, piano, vocals, 1906–77)

Booker T. Washington White was raised on a farm outside Houston, Texas; his father taught him guitar in 1915. Two years later he learned piano and by 1921 he was working barrelhouses and honky tonks in St. Louis. Inspired by a meeting with Charley Patton, he hoboed through the South for much of the 1920s. He made his recording debut for Victor in 1930 as Washington White.

He recorded 'Shake 'Em On Down' for Vocalion in 1937 and the record was a considerable hit. White recorded 12 titles for Vocalion in March 1940, which are among the finest examples of pre-war country blues. He served in the US Navy during the Second World War and retired from music, until being 'rediscovered' in 1963.

Key Tracks

'Red River Dam Blues' Washboard Sam
'Suicide Blues' Peetie Wheatstraw
'Doin' the Best I Can' Peetie Wheatstraw
'Parchman Farm' Bukka White
'Shake 'Em On Down' Bukka White

Pianist Peetie Wheatstraw recorded with guitarists such as Kokomo Arnold and Lonnie Johnson.

A-Z of Artists

Josh White (Guitar, vocals, 1908–69)

Joshua Daniel White was born in Greenville, South Carolina to a preacher father and a mother who sang in church. He worked in tandem with street singers such as Blind Blake and Blind Joe Taggart for much of the 1920s. His recording debut was made for Paramount in 1928 but his work for Banner/ARC beginning in 1932 is considered to be his most important. He recorded sacred music (as 'Joshua White, The Singing Christian') in addition to blues under his own name or as 'Pinewood Tom'. After 1940, he was increasingly involved with folk music, where he was promoted to white audiences.

Big Joe Williams (Guitar, vocals, 1903–82)

Joe Lee Williams was born in Crawford, Mississippi to tenant farmer parents and by the age of five he was playing a homemade guitar. He left home in 1915 to hobo through the South. Williams worked tent shows and medicine shows with a jug band and as a soloist from 1918–24. Often accompanied by Little Brother Montgomery, he played brothels, labour camps and barrelhouses throughout Mississippi and Louisiana during the 1920s.

'Big Joe (Williams) was great to work with and learn from because he was such a character. He was one of the last of the old-time itinerant blues singers.'

Charlie Musselwhite

He made his recording debut for Bluebird in 1935 and one of his early recordings, 'Baby Please Don't Go', became a blues standard. He frequently recorded with Robert Nighthawk and Sonny Boy Williamson on Bluebird sessions in the late 1930s. Although Williams played both six- and 12-string guitars, he is most famous for playing a nine-string instrument of his own construction. He toured constantly and recorded into his late 70s.

Josh White recorded a variety of blues, gospel and folk music under various pseudonyms.

A-Z of Artists

Sonny Boy Williamson (Harmonica, vocals, 1914–48)

John Lee Williamson was born in Jackson, Tennessee. He taught himself harmonica at an early age and left home in his mid-teens to hobo with Yank Rachell and Sleepy John Estes through Tennessee and Arkansas. He settled in Chicago in 1934 and made his recording debut for Bluebird in 1937. His first song, 'Good Morning Little School Girl', became a blues standard.

Williamson was friendly with Big Bill Broonzy and frequently worked Chicago clubs with him. During the years 1939–45 he worked Chicago's Maxwell Street for tips, but in 1947 his record 'Shake The Boogie' became a number-four hit on the Race charts. Williamson was the most gifted and influential harmonica stylist of the pre-war era and was very much in demand to play on recordings by other artists. He was murdered coming home from a job in 1948, after which his name and reputation were taken on by harmonica player Rice Miller – or 'Sonny Boy Williamson II', as he became known.

Key Tracks

'Good Morning Little Schoolgirl' Sonny Boy Williamson
'Shake The Boogie' Sonny Boy Williamson
'I Love To Hear My Baby Call My Name' Jimmy Yancey
'Yancey Special' Jimmy Yancey
'35th And Dearborn' Jimmy Yancey

Jimmy Yancey (Piano, 1898–1951)

James Edward Yancey was born in Chicago and toured the vaudeville circuit as a dancer in his childhood. He learned piano from his brother Alonzo in 1915 and was soon working rent parties and small clubs around Chicago. He made his recording debut in 1939 for Solo Art and continued to record intermittently, often in the company of his wife, singer Estella Yancey. Yancey was especially adept at slow blues and had a unique ability to develop his own left-hand basslines.

John Lee 'Sonny Boy' Williamson – the first of the great blues harmonica players.

The Forties

The 1940s encompassed a wide range of musical art, reflecting extremes of economic hardship and recovery, global war and rebuilding. Empowered by necessarily full-tilt production, US industry recovered from the Depression, though the cream of its youth was siphoned off to fight on distant fronts, and returned to a strange new world.

Great Britain suffered air strikes, privations and threat of occupancy – traumas which took years to heal. Continental Europe, including Russia and on to the Far East, was gripped by government-sanctioned genocide, military invasion and destruction. At the decade's end, the world was divided by victory and defeat.

Blues music, along with jazz and all other popular musical styles and performance arts, was pressed into service during the Second World War as uplifting propaganda and social balm. Trends of the 1930s did not come to a jolting halt, but nothing was immune from change. The youngest of the Mississippi Delta blues artists headed for Memphis and Chicago, with newly cheap electric guitars and other gear; adding soulful balladry and urgent rhythms to their folky older country repertoire, they upped the tempo and prepared a path for a whole new brand of pop music called rock'n'roll. Rock and R&B were not even dreamt of when the 1940s began, but as the decade drew to a close blues music had moved into a new era.

Key Artists

John Lee Hooker
Big Joe Turner
T-Bone Walker

Chicago, a Mecca for young blues artists of the 1940s.

America Emerges from the Great Depression

The 1940s was a decade of wrenching, often violent change in America. War clouds were on the horizon as 1939 turned into 1940. In the autumn of 1940, Franklin Delano Roosevelt was elected to his third term as President of the United States; he created the Fair Employment Practices Committee the following year.

The idea was to investigate and report on discrimination in employment. The executive order was largely ignored in the South and where changes were attempted, such as in Mobile, Alabama or Beaumont, Texas, racial violence ensued. The Roosevelt administration offered tepid support and in 1942 the committee was folded into the War Manpower Commission.

'The Chicago blues is based on the country blues that John Lee Williamson and Big Joe Williams and Robert Nighthawk and all those guys was producing in the late thirties and early forties.'

Billy Boy Arnold

American industry quickly geared up for the war effort. There were no new American automobiles produced between 1942–46 but defence plants were built, modified, adapted and retrofitted with astonishing quickness. Defence plants meant jobs and the nation was finally ridding itself of the yoke of the Great Depression. Defence jobs in California meant the migration of thousands of black people from Texas and Louisiana, while jobs in the Midwest resulted in new arrivals from Mississippi and Arkansas; much of the nation's manpower was in uniform.

The music industry was also undergoing great changes. The American Society of Composers, Authors and Publishers (ASCAP), the performing rights society, had been challenged by a group of radio-station owners protesting the high fees for on-air musical performances. Broadcast Music Incorporated (BMI) was formed in 1940 as an alternative and presented an opportunity for black songwriters who had been largely ignored by ASCAP.

Music fans dance to R&B at a juke joint near Clarksdale, Missouri.

The Record Industry Recovers

James C. Petrillo, the head of the American Federation of Musicians (AFM), called a strike of union musicians against the record labels, effective 1 August 1942. The ban held until the autumn of 1943, when Decca Records settled with the union. RCA and Columbia held out for another 14 months, but Decca's agreement meant that other companies could begin recording under the same terms.

All of a sudden, new labels began to appear at an astonishing pace in New York, Chicago and Los Angeles. BMI, anxious to stockpile compositions for its catalogue, would advance money to labels with BMI-affiliated publishing companies. The combination of BMI involvement and RCA and Columbia sitting on the sidelines opened the door for jump bands and blues singers. Many of the new labels, such as Savoy, Aladdin and Modern, specialized in black jazz, blues and gospel.

The jump band led by saxophonist Louis Jordan (1908–75) was the number one combo in the country. Similar groups led by Roy Milton (1907–83) and Eddie Vinson (1917–88) were finding an audience. Boogie-woogie, once embraced by jazz bands, was now being abandoned but picked up on by those little combos, which utilized the rhythm in very different ways.

Popular Melody

Amos Milburn – 'Chicken Shack Boogie' (1947)

Billboard, the record industry trade paper, traced the sales progress of records and its dilemma as to what to call 'black music' was apparent. In 1942 *Billboard* tracked it as the Harlem Hit Parade, changed this name to Race Records in 1945 and in 1949 called it Rhythm & Blues. Finally, they had come up with a term that applied to all secular black music that wasn't bebop or traditional jazz: R&B.

The Golden Age of the Saxophone

The saxophone really came to prominence during the 1940s. While its use in jazz big bands and combos was not new, the style was quickly adopted by the jump bands. Recording artists such as Hal Singer (b. 1919) and Big Jay McNeely (b. 1927) found an instrumental road directly to the audience, and saxophone-dominated R&B instrumentals became a growth industry.

'Landing Blues' by Birmingham Sam (a.k.a. John Lee Hooker) on Savoy; 'You're Not Going To Worry My Life Any More' by Lightnin' Hopkins on Aladdin; John Lee Hooker's 'John L's House Rent Boogie' on Modern. Hooker's 'Stutterin' Blues', which was released on the Rockin' label.

SAVOY
RECORDS
LANDING BLUES
(H. A. Oliver)
BIRMINGHAM SAM
and his Magic Guitar
5558-A
NOT LICENSED FOR RADIO BROADCAST · FOR HOME USE ON PHONOGRAPHS

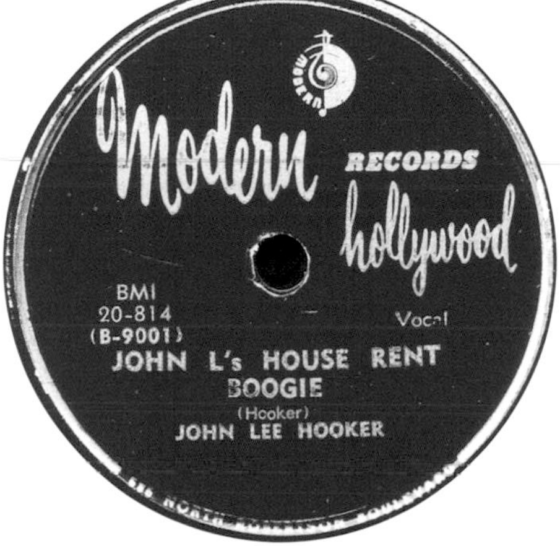
Modern
RECORDS
hollywood
BMI
20-814
(B-9001)
Vocal
JOHN L's HOUSE RENT
BOOGIE
(Hooker)
JOHN LEE HOOKER

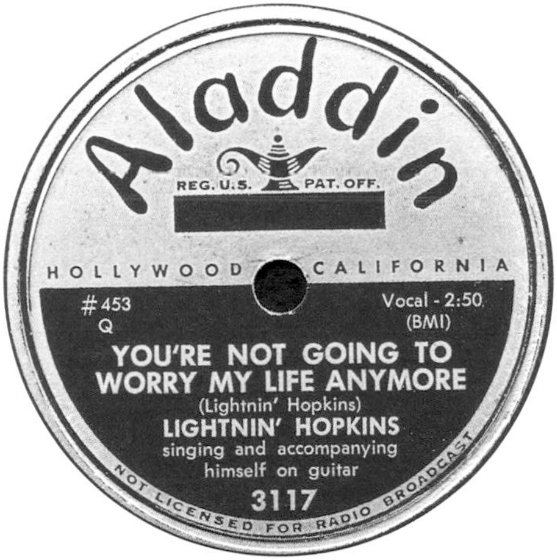
Aladdin
REG. U.S. PAT. OFF.
HOLLYWOOD CALIFORNIA
#453
Q
Vocal - 2:50
(BMI)
YOU'RE NOT GOING TO
WORRY MY LIFE ANYMORE
(Lightnin' Hopkins)
LIGHTNIN' HOPKINS
singing and accompanying
himself on guitar
3117
NOT LICENSED FOR RADIO BROADCAST

ROCKIN'
GR 15127
(Lois-BMI)
2:14
Vocal by
John Lee Booker
STUTTERING BLUES
(John Lee Booker)
JOHN LEE BOOKER
525

Shouters and Crooners

Country blues was still being recorded but more and more artists were moving towards a more urban sound. Shouters such as Big Joe Turner (1911–85), Wynonie Harris (1913–69), Jimmy Witherspoon (1922–97) and Roy Brown (1925–81) were an important part of the scene, and smooth blues balladeers such as Charles Brown (1922–99) and Amos Milburn (1927–80) added their abilities to the mix.

Vocal groups such as the Ravens and Orioles were very much a part of R&B, as were the big bands of Lionel Hampton, Erskine Hawkins, Buddy Johnson and Lucky Millinder – bandleaders who had been able to keep up with the new trend. Artists such as Sonny Terry (1911–86), Brownie McGhee (1915–96), Memphis Slim (1915–88) and Champion Jack Dupree (1910–92) were being recorded in an R&B context. In time, things would shake out and these artists would return to their original styles. Others that couldn't keep up would be shunted aside by the industry.

Popular Melody

Jimmy Witherspoon – 'Ain't Nobody's Business If I Do Pt. 2' (1949)

R&B Hits the Airwaves

In 1948 President Truman ordered the desegregation of the US military. Between the battle over civil rights and the growing concern with Communism, Truman was challenged when he stood for re-election in the autumn of 1948; he prevailed nonetheless. James C. Petrillo called another strike of the AFM to take effect on 1 January 1948. This one was not as successful, since many of the smaller labels found ways to circumvent the action. Still, there were many small labels, started after the settlement of the 1942 strike, which did not survive 1948. Radio station WDIA in Memphis instituted a black music policy in 1949. It was a huge success and other stations began to play more R&B on the airways. More radio play increased the sales of black records and exposed the music to more people.

In December 1948, Detroit bandleader and saxophonist Paul Williams recorded a song called 'The Hucklebuck'. It was an R&B instrumental that became the biggest black record of 1949. It also started a dance craze: the first to come out of the black community during the 1940s. The next decade would have a lot of new dances, a lot more R&B and, right around the corner, rock'n'roll.

Amos Milburn, a supremely talented blues pianist and adaptable singer.

Baldwin

Key Artist: John Lee Hooker

John Lee Hooker was born on 22 August 1917 near Clarksdale, Mississippi. He got his first instrument from singer Tony Hollins, but he was taught how to play by his stepfather, Will Moore. Moore would play weekends at jukes and functions in various Delta locations, often in the company of Charley Patton or Son House. Moore's trademark was a rhythmic pattern that his stepson picked up and made his own. He called it the boogie.

By 1933, John Lee Hooker had left Mississippi and his family for good. He played some music in Memphis but soon left for Cincinatti, where he stayed for several years. He had a steady job outside music and played parties and functions on weekends. During his time in Cincinnati, he also sang with several different gospel quartets. In 1943, Hooker moved to Detroit. He found work at clubs on the east side of the city, around Hastings Street, but still had his basic employment outside music until he was discovered by Bernie Bessman. Hooker's first recording for Bessman's Sensation label was in September 1948.

'With one chord, John Lee Hooker could tell you a story as deep as the ocean....'

Carlos Santana

'Boogie Chillen' Hits the Chart

The first Hooker record, 'Boogie Chillen', was a huge success. Sensation was a subsidiary of Pan American Record Distributors, a local record wholesaler, and Bessman, recognizing his inability to promote a record nationally, licensed 'Boogie Chillen' to Modern Records in Los Angeles. The record reached number one on *Billboard* magazine's Race Records chart and John Lee Hooker's career as an entertainer was launched. Within weeks of the Modern release of 'Boogie Chillen', Hooker was recording for a variety of labels under an enormous number of pseudonyms. He was Texas Slim on King, Delta John on Regent, Birmingham Sam on Savoy, Johnny Williams on Prize, Staff and Gotham, the Boogie Man on Acorn and John Lee Booker on Chance and Chess. It didn't seem to affect his sales on Modern, where he had solid sellers such as 'Hobo Blues', 'Crawlin' King Snake Blues' and another number-one hit on the Billboard R&B charts, 'I'm In The Mood'. For most of his career, Hooker paid little attention to the exclusivity aspect of recording contracts.

Right: John Lee Hooker (left) with his first cousin and fellow blues guitarist, Earl Hooker.

Throughout 1948–51, Hooker worked mostly in Detroit. Playing solo or duo, he was very irregular in his patterns, rarely adhering to the 12-bar structure. In the city, Hooker sometimes worked with a small group he called the Boogie Ramblers, where his work followed the more traditional form. His first major roadwork was done in 1952, with Eddie Kirkland on second guitar; they picked up accompanists as needed. It wasn't until 1955 when Hooker signed with Vee Jay that he began recording regularly with a band. Hooker had several hits on Vee Jay, the biggest being 'Boom Boom'.

Reaching New Audiences

As the 1950s turned into the 1960s, Hooker's music began to appear on LP. He performed at both the Newport Folk Festival and Newport Jazz Festival in 1960, gaining exposure to large numbers of white college students for the first time. Beginning in 1962, he became a regular on the European club and concert circuit. At home, he spent much of the early 1960s working coffeehouses and folk-music clubs. He signed a three-year deal with Bluesway in 1966, where he made excellent albums with blues bands until the label folded and was taken over by the parent label, ABC Records, in 1970. He frequently recorded for European labels while overseas. In 1970 Hooker teamed up with a California rock band, Canned Heat, and the resultant album, *Hooker 'N Heat* (1971), introduced Hooker to rock'n'roll fans.

The final glorious chapter in John Lee Hooker's career began with an association with the Rosebud Agency, which handled Hooker's bookings from the mid-1980s. Around the same time, Hooker developed a friendship with rock star Carlos Santana and the fruit of that relationship was *The Healer* (1989), an album that was a huge hit and vaulted Hooker back to stardom. In 1990, he recorded the soundtrack for the film *The Hot Spot*, overdubbing tracks with Taj Mahal and Miles Davis. Over time Hooker toured less frequently but continued to record and rack up awards. He died in 2001.

Next Page: Boogie guitarist John Lee Hooker relaxes in the studio.

Key Artist: Big Joe Turner

Joseph Vernon Turner was born on 18 May 1911 in Kansas City, Missouri. He dropped out of school after sixth grade and worked with blind singers on the streets. The blues was in the air in Kansas City and when Turner joined in with the street singers he would make up blues lyrics. Turner was functionally illiterate and never learned to read or write properly.

He studied records in his late teens and cited Leroy Carr, Lonnie Johnson, Bessie Smith and Ethel Waters as favourites. By 17, he had teamed up with Pete Johnson at the Backbiter's Club. There were no microphones at the time and Turner's voice became the stuff of legend as locals told stories of hearing him 10 blocks away. He became the first of a new breed of performer: the blues shouter.

'I was sitting up there thinking, "now when is he gonna run out of words?" And then I was thinking "when is he gonna run out of something to play?" But they never ran out of nothing.'

Jay McShann on Big Joe Turner & Pete Johnson

A Fruitful Partnership

In the early 1930s, Turner and Johnson moved to the Black and Tan club, where Turner learned to tend bar. After Prohibition ended in 1933 the pair moved to the Cherry Blossom, a larger spot which had a floor show, including the orchestra of George E. Lee. It was during this time that Johnson and Turner travelled to out-of-town locations such as Omaha and St. Louis. In 1935 the pair moved to the Sunset Café, where they were heard by John Hammond and invited to appear at the Spirituals To Swing concert in New York. A big hit at the concert, Johnson and Turner soon joined forces with Albert Ammons and Meade 'Lux' Lewis, and began a four-year run at a New York nightclub, Café Society, which featured black entertainment. Johnson and Turner made their recording debut for Vocalion but Joe moved over to Decca in 1940. He was a guest vocalist on jazz dates featuring the Varsity Seven, Benny Carter, Joe Sullivan and Art Tatum, and was paired with artists such as pianists Sammy Price and Willie 'The Lion' Smith on his own recordings.

In the summer of 1941, Turner went to Los Angeles to appear in Duke Ellington's musical *Jump For Joy*. Turner was added to the cast after the show had opened but Ellington had written a blues for Turner to

Right: Powerful blues shouter Big Joe Turner, who provided an essential link between the blues and rock'n'roll music.

perform in the show, 'Rocks In My Bed'. It became Turner's signature song following the show's close in late September, and his return to New York's Café Society.

In 1945, he signed with National Records who recorded him in New York, Chicago and Los Angeles, backed by small groups that often included horns. In 1947–48 he recorded sessions in California for Aladdin, Swingtime and MGM. He lived in New Orleans for a time in the late 1940s and early 1950s, but in 1951 he signed with Atlantic Records; here began the period of his greatest popularity.

Atlantic Years

The Atlantic partners, Ahmet Ertegun and Herb Abrahmson, felt that Turner could thrive in the R&B style that was so popular with black audiences. Turner responded with big hits such as 'Chains Of Love', 'Honey Hush' and 'Shake, Rattle & Roll', forming an important link between the blues and the forthcoming rock'n'roll style. He recorded in Chicago (with electric guitarist Elmore James) and New Orleans, but more often in New York with the arrangements of Jesse Stone. Atlantic also recorded a jazz album, *The Boss Of The Blues* (1956), which reunited Turner with Pete Johnson. The Atlantic association lasted until 1961 and for the next decade Turner freelanced with various different labels.

He settled in southern California in the mid-1950s; by the early 1960s he was a regular at European clubs and festivals. In the US, apart from when touring the festivals, he mainly worked in California. His career was revived by an association with Norman Granz and Pablo records, which produced LPs with top jazz stars such as Count Basie on a regular basis, from 1973 until Turner's death. He was prominently featured in the film *Last of the Blue Devils* (1979), a reunion of Kansas City musicians from the 1930s and 1940s. He earned a Grammy nomination for his Muse album *Blues Train* (1982), recorded with the young New England-based band, Roomful of Blues.

Next Page: Turner appearing in the 1956 film Shake, Rattle & Rock, *which included footage of Turner and Fats Domino in concert.*

BC
No.3

Key Artist: T-Bone Walker

Aaron Thibeaux Walker was born in Linden, Texas on 28 May 1910, the only child of Rance and Movelia Walker. The family moved to Dallas in 1912 and as a pre-teen Walker would lead Blind Lemon Jefferson around the Dallas streets. He taught himself guitar and worked streets and functions until he toured with various travelling shows in the mid- to late 1920s. He made his recording debut for Columbia in 1929 ('Trinity River Blues'/'Wichita Falls Blues') as Oak Cliff T-Bone. The name T-Bone is a phonetic corruption of his middle name.

'I believe that it all comes originally from T-Bone Walker. B.B. King and I were talking about that not long ago and he thinks so, too.'

Freddie King

Walker worked locally with artists as diverse as Cab Calloway and Ma Rainey before moving to the Los Angeles area in 1934, where he worked his own combo at the Little Harlem Club and gradually built a following. He recorded one title ('T-Bone Blues') with the Les Hite orchestra and worked with that band on tours through Chicago and New York for much of 1939–40. He returned to the Little Harlem Club, where he reformed his own group. He played guitar on a record date with Freddie Slack's orchestra in July 1942 and, at the end of the date, recorded two songs ('Mean Old World'/'I Got A Break Baby') for Capitol Records. On the strength of that record he began to tour and to work whites-only clubs in Hollywood. He made frequent stops at the Rhumboogie club in Chicago from 1942–45 and in 1945 he made recordings for the Rhumboogie and Mercury labels.

Black & White

In September 1946, Walker signed an exclusive contract with Black & White Records and worked with producer Ralph Bass. He recorded 49 titles in the next 15 months, among

Far Right: A versatile musician, Walker (left) is pictured here with jazz greats Dizzy Gillespie (seated) and James Moody.

which were all his bestsellers. He had hit records with such well-remembered titles as 'Call It Stormy Monday' and 'T-Bone Shuffle'. He became a national touring attraction and his acrobatic stunts, such as playing the guitar behind his head and doing the splits on stage, helped him to become a major star. Because of the second AFM recording ban, Walker could not make any new recordings during 1948, but the large stockpile of sides he had recorded provided new releases into 1950. Black & White had gone out of business in 1948 and the masters had been acquired by Capitol.

In the spring of 1950, he signed with Imperial Records. Of the 52 titles he recorded over the next four years there were no national hits, but the music is of a high quality. He signed with Atlantic in 1955 and, once again, there were no big sellers but a considerable amount of memorable music. He continued to tour nationally while headquartered in Los Angeles.

An International Star

In 1962, Walker went to Europe with the American Folk Blues Festival and developed a circuit for himself that led to frequent visits overseas; he was now a part of the American festival scene as well. He freelanced his recording deals and recorded for a variety of labels in a numbeer of countries. His Polydor album *Good Feelin'* (1969) won a Grammy award in 1970. He continued to tour and record until shortly before his death.

Walker was a smooth blues singer with some of the qualities of a crooner, but it was his guitar work that made him such an important artist. He was an influence, to some degree, on almost all of the key guitarists of the post-Second World War generation. His sound, his unhurried phrasing and his self-editing ability are hallmarks of his style. T-Bone Walker certainly never overstayed his welcome.

T-Bone Walker, electric guitar pioneer and great showman.

A-Z of Artists

Charles Brown (Piano, vocals, 1922–99)

Charles Mose Brown was born in Texas City, Texas and had extensive classical piano training as a youth. He moved to Los Angeles in 1943 and by September 1944 had become the vocalist-pianist in Johnny Moore's Three Blazers. The Blazers had several hits before Brown went solo in 1948 and scored success with songs such as 'Trouble Blues' (1949) and 'Black Night' (1951). He regained international renown later in his life and continued to record up until his death.

Roy Brown (Vocals, 1925–81)

Roy James Brown was born in New Orleans and raised in Texas and Louisiana. A strong blues shouter, Brown was one of the first stars of New Orleans R&B. He led his own group, Roy Brown & his Mighty, Mighty Men, and wrote most of the material he recorded. He began recording for DeLuxe in 1947 in New Orleans, and had hit records with 'Long About Midnight' (1948), 'Rockin' At Midnight' (1949) and 'Hard Luck Blues' (1950).

Key Tracks

'Trouble Blues' Charles Brown
'Black Night' Charles Brown
'That's All Right' Arthur 'Big Boy' Crudup
'My Baby Left Me' Arthur 'Big Boy' Crudup
'Twelve Gates To The City' Rev. Gary Davis

Arthur 'Big Boy' Crudup (Guitar, vocals, 1905–74)

Arthur William Crudup was born in Forest, Mississippi and did not learn to play the guitar until his 30s. He worked functions in the Clarksdale area before moving to Chicago in 1940, signing with Bluebird in 1941 and finding considerable popularity on record. Crudup is perhaps best remembered as an outstanding blues songwriter; several of his tunes, such as 'That's All Right' and 'My Baby Left Me', were covered by pop and rock stars, notably Elvis Presley.

Rev. Gary Davis (Guitar, harmonica, banjo, vocals, 1896–1972)

Gary D. Davis was born in Laurens, South Carolina and was completely blind by the age of 30. He taught himself harmonica, banjo and guitar and played in string bands throughout the teens, going on to work the Carolinas as a street singer in the 1920s. Davis began recording regularly in the mid-1950s. His unique guitar playing shows traces of ragtime, blues and other early music. He stands with Blind Blake as the finest of Piedmont-area guitar stylists.

Arthur 'Big Boy' Crudup, whose compositions were covered to great effect by Elvis Presley.

A-Z of Artists

Champion Jack Dupree (Piano, vocals, 1910–92)

William Thomas Dupree was born in New Orleans. He learned piano at an early age and in the 1920s worked barrelhouses as a soloist, as well as playing with traditional jazz bands. From the early 1930s, he worked as a prizefighter and took occasional music jobs. Dupree was discovered in Chicago and signed to OKeh records in 1940. Among those early sides were the first recordings of 'Junker's Blues' and 'Cabbage Greens'.

After US Navy service, Dupree settled in New York and recorded for several small labels often in the company of Brownie McGhee. He became known for his strong, two-fisted piano and for his humorous songs and vocals. Dupree settled in Switzerland in 1960 and became one of the most visible blues artists in Europe over the next 30 years.

Key Tracks

'Junker's Blues' Champion Jack Dupree
'Cabbage Greens' Champion Jack Dupree
'Old Time Shuffle Blues' Lloyd Glenn
'Who Threw The Whiskey In The Well' Wynonie Harris
'All She Wants To Do Is Rock' Wynonie Harris

Lloyd Glenn (Piano, arranger, 1909–85)

Lloyd Colquitt Glenn Sr. was born and raised in San Antonio, Texas. He worked with several southwestern territory bands before joining Don Albert in 1934 in the role of pianist and chief arranger. He moved to California in the early 1940s. Glenn became the prototype of the studio pianist-arranger for blues and R&B record dates while working on sessions for T-Bone Walker, Lowell Fulson and others. A fine blues and boogie-woogie pianist, Glenn recorded hit instrumentals for Swingtime ('Old Time Shuffle Blues' and 'Chica Boo') in 1950–51.

Wynonie Harris (Vocals, 1913–69)

Raised in Omaha, Nebraska, Wynonie Harris first came to prominence in the Lucky Millinder Orchestra of 1944, where he had a number-one Race chart hit, 'Who Threw The Whiskey In The Well'. A leather-lunged shouter in the Big Joe Turner tradition, Harris had a long successful run on King records, which produced huge hits such as 'Good Rockin' Tonight' as well as a wealth of other material. He specialized in raunchy, risqué songs, but was rarely active in the last few years of his life.

Wynonie Harris, one of the great blues shouters of the era.

A-Z of Artists

Helen Humes (Vocals, 1909–81)

Helen Elizabeth Humes was born in Louisville, Kentucky and made her recording debut for OKeh in 1927. She spent 1938–41 in the Count Basie Orchestra, singing mostly ballads. She moved to California in 1945 and recorded for many different labels while working as a solo artist. She had solid hits with 'Be Baba Leba' in 1945 and 'Million Dollar Secret' in 1950. A versatile singer, Humes had a sweet voice and could adapt to almost any material. She returned to her music in the 1970s after a 10-year absence, and remained active until her death.

Bull Moose Jackson (Tenor saxophone, vocals, 1919–89)

Benjamin Joseph Jackson was born in Cleveland, Ohio and replaced Wynonie Harris as male vocalist with the Lucky Millinder Orchestra in 1945. From 1947 until the late 1950s he toured with his own group, the Buffalo Bearcats. He recorded for Queen/King from 1945; among his biggest hits were 'I Love You, Yes I Do', 'I Can't Go On Without You', 'Little Girl, Don't Cry' and 'Why Don't You Haul Off And Love Me'. Jackson alternated ballads, jump tunes and risqué novelties, as well as occasionally recording instrumentals featuring his saxophone.

Key Tracks

'Million Dollar Secret' Helen Humes
'I Love You, Yes I Do' Bull Moose Jackson
'I Can't Go On Without You' Bull Moose Jackson
'Double Crossing Blues' Little Esther
'Release Me' Little Esther

Little Esther (Vocals, 1935–84)

Esther Mae Washington was born in Galveston, Texas. She moved to the Los Angeles area at the age of five and in 1949 was discovered by Johnny Otis. Her first recording with Otis, 'Double Crossing Blues', was a number-one R&B hit in 1950. In that year the pair had two more number ones on the R&B chart, 'Mistrustin' Blues' and 'Cupid's Boogie'. On her own after 1951, Esther continued to record but her career suffered ups and downs due to her narcotics addiction. As Esther Phillips, she returned in 1962 with yet another R&B number-one, 'Release Me', and other hits.

Esther Phillips, a.k.a. Little Esther, who had several big R&B hits.

A-Z of Artists

Brownie McGhee (Guitar, vocals, 1915–96)

Walter Brown McGhee was born in Knoxville, Tennessee. He learned to play guitar before his tenth birthday and dropped out of school to play throughout the state in the late 1920s. He met Sonny Terry in 1939 and they joined forces almost immediately. McGhee began recording for OKeh in 1940 and moved to New York.

McGhee recorded solo for several labels, notably Savoy. He was recorded in an R&B context throughout 1948–58, in addition to his own Piedmont-style acoustic blues and duets with Terry. The duo toured England in 1958, going on to become regular visitors to Europe. McGhee continued to make his own recordings during the folk-blues revival and the duo continued into the mid-1970s.

Big Jay McNeely (Tenor saxophone, b. 1927)

Cecil James McNeely was born and raised in Los Angeles. Inspired by Illinois Jacquet, McNeely played in high school with future jazz stars Sonny Criss and Hampton Hawes. He was discovered by Johnny Otis and made his recording debut in 1948 with a number-one hit, 'Deacon's Hop'. He had another hit in 1959 with 'There Is Something On Your Mind'. A stomping, screaming wildman, McNeely was the quintessential showboating saxophonist of the 1950s.

Key Tracks

'Barbecue Any Old Time' Brownie McGhee
'Deacon's Hop' Big Jay McNeely
'There Is Something On Your Mind' Big Jay McNeely
'Confessin' The Blues' Jay McShann
'Hands Off' Jay McShann

Jay McShann (Piano, vocals, 1916–2006)

James Columbus McShann was born in Muskogee, Oklahoma and moved to Kansas City in 1936. He formed a big band in 1940 and recorded for Decca in 1941–43. The band featured vocalist Walter Brown and alto saxophonist Charlie Parker, and had a big hit with 'Confessin' The Blues'. McShann had a hit record on Vee Jay in 1955 with 'Hands Off' and continued to work in the Kansas City area. Prominently featured in the film *Last of the Blue Devils* (1980), McShann was a masterful pianist with equal parts jazz and blues in his style.

Saxophone honker Big Jay McNeely drives the crowd wild with his stage antics.

A-Z of Artists

Memphis Slim (Piano, vocals, 1915–88)

John Len Chatman was born in Memphis, Tennessee. Influenced by barrelhouse pianists such as Roosevelt Sykes, Slim forged an early career in Memphis playing in cafes, juke joints and other music venues around the Beale Street area. He moved to Chicago in 1937, where he worked with Big Bill Broonzy. He began recording in 1940 and formed his band, the House Rockers, after the Second World War. Slim recorded with several different record labels throughout the 1940s and 1950s and formed successful working partnerships with musicians such as Matt Murphy and Willie Dixon. He had several hits on the Miracle label in 1948–49, including 'Messin' Around' and 'Blue And Lonesome'.

A prolific recording artist and first-rate blues pianist, Slim was also a songwriter who wrote most of his own material, including the oft-covered blues standard 'Every Day I Have The Blues'. He went to Europe in 1962 with the American Folk Blues Festival and settled in Paris, where he continued to tour and record until his death.

Amos Milburn (Piano, vocals, 1927–80)

Joseph Amos Milburn Jr. was born in Houston, Texas, and he began recording in 1946 for Aladdin records. Milburn was an exceptionally popular performer between the late 1940s and mid-1950s, with number-one R&B hits such as 'Chicken Shack Boogie', 'Bewildered' and 'Roomin' House Boogie' (all 1948–49). Beginning in 1949, he toured and recorded with his own band, the Aladdin Chickenshackers, and continued his string of hits with 'Bad, Bad Whiskey' and 'One Scotch, One Bourbon, One Beer'. The success of the latter inspired a series of songs with liquor-related themes.

Key Tracks

'Messin' Around' Memphis Slim
'Blue And Lonesome' Memphis Slim
'Having Fun' Memphis Slim
'Bewildered' Amos Milburn
'Bad, Bad Whiskey' Amos Milburn

Milburn was a superb pianist, equally at home with slow blues, rolling boogie-woogie, ballad material, novelties and jump blues. He worked frequently with Charles Brown in the late 1950s but became inactive in music after a stroke in 1970.

Rocking blues pianist Memphis Slim, in a publicity poster for Fontana Records.

MEMPHIS
SLIM
EXCLUSIVITÉ DISQUES
fontana

A-Z of Artists

Roy Milton (Drums, vocals, 1907–83)

Roy Bunny Milton was born in Wynnewood, Oklahoma. He had his own bands before moving to Los Angeles in 1935, where he formed the Solid Senders combo in 1938 and worked small clubs throughout the city. He began recording in 1945 and had a lengthy relationship with Specialty records throughout 1946–54, which produced such hits as 'R.M. Blues', 'Information Blues' and 'Best Wishes'. The Solid Senders featured pianist Camille Howard and three horns along with the leader's simple yet sincere vocals. The band could handle swing, jump tunes or slow blues.

Robert Nighthawk (Guitar, vocals, 1909–67)

Robert Lee McCollum was born in Helena, Arkansas. He was taught guitar by his cousin, Houston Stackhouse, in 1930. He moved to St. Louis in 1934, now calling himself Robert McCoy, and first recorded in 1937 on acoustic guitar. He took the name Robert Nighthawk and used it professionally from the early 1940s. Nighthawk had converted to electric guitar by the time he recorded for Aristocrat/Chess from 1948–50. He was a master of the electric slide guitar and his work was influential on future slide stylists such as Muddy Waters and Earl Hooker.

Key Tracks

'R.M. Blues' Roy Milton
'Best Wishes' Roy Milton
'Prowling Nighthawk' Robert Nighthawk
'Harlem Nocturne' Johnny Otis
'Ma' Johnny Otis

Johnny Otis (Drums, vibes, vocals, b. 1921)

John Alexander Veliotes, born in Vallejo, California, started as a drummer and formed a big band in 1945. By 1947, Otis had switched to a seven- or eight-piece group. This was one of the earliest R&B combos to tour; the Johnny Otis Rhythm & Blues Caravan included vocalists Little Esther, Mel Walker and the Robins, and scored 10 entries on the R&B charts in 1950 alone. During the 1950s, Otis worked for record labels as an arranger and producer. He introduced Big Mama Thornton, produced vocalist Etta James and recorded with ill-fated singer Johnny Ace.

An elaborate publicity shot for the Johnny Otis Orchestra's single 'The Jelly Roll'.

ELDO
RECORDS
THE JELLY ROLL
JOHNNY OTIS

A-Z of Artists

Sammy Price (Piano, 1908–92)

Samuel Blythe Price was born in Honey Grove, Texas. His recording debut came in 1929. In 1938 he moved to New York and became the pianist for Decca Records blues sessions. In this capacity – in addition to making his own recordings – he accompanied Blue Lu Barker, Johnny Temple and Sister Rosetta Tharpe, among others. From 1948 Price played in France on a regular basis and made frequent recordings for European labels – as a piano soloist, with jazz bands and with blues singers.

Hal Singer (Tenor saxophone, b. 1919)

Harold Singer was born in Tulsa, Oklahoma. He worked with territory bands in the late 1930s and went to New York with Roy Eldridge in 1944. Singer worked around New York, playing on sessions for King and Savoy, during 1946–59. His own recording career began in 1948 and he had a number-one hit with 'Cornbread', the first big record of the honking R&B tenor style. He frequently toured with his own groups and with R&B shows during 1948–58, and by the late 1950s he was playing jazz as often as R&B. He relocated to Paris in 1965 and has recorded frequently for European labels.

'Sonny just mystified me. I mean how he did that I'll never know; I STILL don't – it's true! I played with Brownie years later and when I did I never tried to play like Sonny.'

Mark Hummel

Sonny Terry (Harmonica, vocals, 1911–86)

Saunders Terrell was born in Greensboro, Georgia and taught himself to play the harmonica at the age of eight. By 16 he had lost sight in both eyes. Terry played mostly in North Carolina from the late 1920s. He teamed up with Blind Boy Fuller in 1934 and recorded with him from late 1937 until Fuller's death. Terry was featured at the Spirituals To Swing concerts in New York in 1938 and 1939. He recorded for the Library of Congress in 1938 and made his commercial recording debut a few days later. He joined forces with Brownie McGhee in 1939 and was present on McGhee's recording of 'The Death Of Blind Boy Fuller' in 1941. The pair worked in New York with Champion Jack Dupree, Leadbelly and others on the folk-blues circuit of the 1940s. The Terry-McGhee team made dozens of duo albums from the mid-1950s through to the mid-1970s.

Harmonica player Sonny Terry (left) performs with longtime musical partner Brownie McGhee in 1969.

A-Z of Artists

Eddie 'Cleanhead' Vinson (Alto saxophone, vocals, 1917–88)

Edward L. Vinson Jr. was born in Houston, Texas. He studied saxophone in high school and played with the Chester Boone and Milt Larkin Orchestras, before touring with a show featuring Lil Green and Big Bill Broonzy in 1941. He joined the Cootie Williams Orchestra in 1942 and recorded hit vocals on 'Cherry Red Blues' and 'Somebody's Got To Go'. He formed his own group in 1945 and had a number-one Race Records hit with 'Old Maid Boogie'. Vinson's influences came from modern jazz, and he also had his own influence on the style, penning the Miles Davis hit 'Four'. Vinson continued to tour and record into the 1980s.

Dinah Washington (Vocals, 1924–63)

Ruth Lee Jones was born in Tuscaloosa, Alabama and raised in Chicago. She joined Lionel Hampton's band in 1943 and made her first recordings that year. Included were the hits 'Salty Papa Blues' and 'Evil Gal Blues'. She left Hampton in 1945 and signed with Mercury records in 1946. Her recorded output included all kinds of material – and she could handle it all. She had a number-one R&B hit in 1949 with 'Baby, Get Lost' – written by jazz critic Leonard Feather – and crossed over into pop music with 'What A Difference A Day Makes', which was a chart hit in 1959.

Key Tracks

'Cherry Red Blues' Eddie 'Cleanhead' Vinson
'Old Maid Boogie' Eddie 'Cleanhead' Vinson
'Evil Gal Blues' Dinah Washington
'What A Difference A Day Makes' Dinah Washington
'Ain't Nobody's Business Parts 1 & 2' Jimmy Witherspoon

Jimmy Witherspoon (Vocals, 1922–97)

Jimmy John Witherspoon was born in Gurdon, Arkansas. He joined the Jay McShann group in California in 1945. He recorded his own records in late 1947 and among them was 'Ain't Nobody's Business Parts 1 & 2', a huge Race Records hit. Witherspoon toured with his own group until 1952 and had another big hit with 'No Rollin' Blues'/'Big Fine Girl'. As a blues shouter, Witherspoon was influenced by Big Joe Turner; later in his life he developed a smoother, jazz-related ballad style.

Versatile R&B and jazz artist Eddie 'Cleanhead' Vinson lays down some vocals in the studio.

The Fifties

The 1950s was a big decade for blues, which began to spread still further and reach a wider and ever-expanding audience. In the wake of international triumph and the stirrings of empire, the US enjoyed a boom of babies, cars, television, and urban and suburban development, that trickled down to embolden a stronger movement for civil rights for black people, inspired immigration from Cuba, Puerto Rico and other Caribbean ports, and normalized the spread of its cultural products worldwide.

Europe, so much harder hit by the previous decade's war, was in a period of renewal, with the emergence of its first generation since the 1920s that could even imagine itself to be carefree. There were still conflicts, threats and dangers. The US brewed itself a Cold War with Communism as the bogeyman, Europe was divided by the Iron Curtain, and modernization had not yet arrived fully in Spain Portugal, Greece and southern Italy as it had in Great Britain, France, Scandinavia, West Germany and the Netherlands.

Key Artists

Ray Charles
Fats Domino
Muddy Waters

What did this mean to blues music? The musicians, backing themselves with loud combos and staunch beats, raised a shout that echoed through the songs of artists such as Bo Diddley, Chuck Berry, Ray Charles and Fats Domino and was taken up and reinterpreted by white teenagers, including one hip-shaking Elvis Presley. The blues had spread wildly and widely since its first recordings in the teens and twenties, and in the 1950s stepped out as an ambassador – and wherever it went, its call met with eager, imitative response.

Hysterical teenagers cheer Elvis Presley as rock'n'roll fever sweeps the US.

Separate but Not Equal

The US was at war in 1950, although the Truman administration referred to Korea as a 'police action'. Dwight Eisenhower was elected President in 1952, partly on his promise to 'go to Korea'. He fulfilled this promise and a truce was negotiated, which remains in place more than 50 years later.

Eisenhower embarked on a programme of highway development so that the country became more accessible by car, making it much easier for bands to travel. Vast super-highways such as Routes 80, 40 and 10 now went from coast to coast. He also worked to abolish segregation in Washington, DC; this proved slightly more difficult. The country was still largely segregated and the majority white population seemed worryingly comfortable with its racial separation. In 1954 the United States Supreme Court voted to overturn Plessy vs Ferguson, an 1896 ruling that 'segregation was in the natural order of things' and that 'separate but equal' was the law of the land. The Court, in a unanimous verdict, ruled that 'In the field of public education, the doctrine of separate but equal has no place'; this destroyed the legal basis for segregation. However, winning the hearts and minds of many US citizens would take a little longer.

'The blues had a baby and they named it rock'n'roll.'

Muddy Waters (song lyric)

It is significant that this decision came during a time of great glory for the blues. In 1954 Muddy Waters (1915–83) recorded his full band for the first time. The modern Chicago blues sound had arrived and artists such as Howlin' Wolf (1910–76), Sonny Boy Williamson II (Rice Miller, *c.* 1912–65), Jimmy Reed (1925–76) and Little Walter (1930–68) were beginning to have big records and reach a broader public. R&B, that sprawling, inclusive idiom that covered blues shouters, saxophone honkers and crooning vocal groups, was peaking. The biggest selling record of the year was by Guitar Slim (1925–59), and one by Big Joe Turner (1911–85) was fifth. Their success was largely driven by radioplay; in every major city there was now at least one radio station where black music was played every day. Stations such as WLAC in Nashville, with a clear channel signal, could reach as many as 38 states. Radio was colour-blind and was accessible to all; white teenagers were finding black radio stations in ever-increasing numbers. Record labels began to produce cover records, with white artists duplicating or sanitizing the arrangements of hit R&B records.

Black students enter a racially mixed school in Little Rock, Arkansas under armed escort.

The Role of the DJ

Celebrity disc jockeys were the key communicators in the world of rock'n'roll radio. One of the most famous was Alan Freed in New York, who insisted on playing the original versions of hit songs. He also insisted on calling the music that he played – whether by black or white artists – rock'n'roll, and is widely credited with coining the term.

The small labels that emerged from the carnage of the recording bans of the 1940s were now an industry unto themselves and they were flexing their muscles. Disc jockeys were paid by labels to play specific songs on the air, and black records began to cross over to the pop charts with greater frequency. Rock'n'roll allowed white artists such as Elvis Presley to flourish and be accepted into what had been a blacks-only idiom. Audiences, black and white, loved it.

The establishment, however, were not so enthusiastic, and rock'n'roll was attacked everywhere in the press. The old ASCAP-BMI wars were rekindled and the big record labels began to lose their dominance in the pop field. Before the end of the decade, the establishment seemed to be getting its way; rock'n'roll music, which had at first been so shocking, became bland and commercialized. The blues element, which had been such a key component of the early style, was receding (although still evident in the music of Chuck Berry and Bo Diddley) and R&B was finished. Furthermore, a number of the disc jockeys that had championed R&B – Alan Freed among them – were charged with accepting 'payola'.

Popular Melody

Elmore James – 'It Hurts Me Too' (1957)

Gospel Meets the Blues

Meanwhile, Ray Charles (1930–2004) was on to something different: he was beginning to secularize gospel music. Gospel performers, who had previously been shunned by their fans when they attempted to record 'the devil's music', were now routinely venturing into the blues and pop styles. Sam Cooke was one of the first performers to make the move; Johnny Taylor, Aretha Franklin and Lou Rawls would follow. The soul music that flourished in the next decade came alive in the mid-1950s and was gradually forging a place for itself.

Alan Freed, one of the first broadcasters to grant both black and white artists airplay.

WABC

Country Blues is Reintroduced

Country blues artists had been shunted aside in the onrushing march of everything else. Lightnin' Hopkins (1911–82) went almost five years without recording, and many performers had to earn a living elsewhere. From 1958, however, there was a revival of interest in folk music in the US, which included country blues artists. By the middle of the next decade, many black blues artists who had recorded in the 1920s were being tracked down, 'rediscovered', recorded and made into international stars.

This revival of the blues' popularity resulted in part from the introduction of the long-playing record. In 1950, 78 rpm was the dominant speed of records. The 45- and 331/3-rpm speeds, introduced in 1948, were slow to gain ground. Atlantic issued its first 45 single in 1951, while Chess did not have any blues LPs until 1958. By the end of the decade, however, 78 rpm had faded completely away and LPs were becoming more important.

Popular Melody

Howlin' Wolf – 'How Many More Years' (1951)

The Blues Spreads Overseas

Overseas markets were becoming more important for blues artists. The European tours of Big Bill Broonzy (1893–1958) and Muddy Waters in the 1950s would lead to the fully fledged, multi-artist tours of the 1960s. Champion Jack Dupree (1910–92) had settled in Europe; Mickey Baker (b. 1925) and Memphis Slim (1915–88) would follow. Blues artists were welcome all over the globe and European labels began to produce their own blues recordings, no longer content to license masters from the US.

B.B. King (b. 1925) kept working, averaging more than 300 dates a year from the mid-1950s. He was an artist whose popularity was almost unknown to white audiences, but a steady stream of hit singles and budget-priced LPs kept his name in front of the black public during the entire decade. Bobby Bland (b. 1930) made a breakthrough in 1957, while some stars from the early 1950s, such as Amos Milburn (1927–80) and Charles Brown (1922–99), dropped out of sight. Saxophone honkers such as Hal Singer (b. 1919), Sam 'The Man' Taylor and Big Al Sears were replaced by King Curtis, who assumed much of the New York studio work all by himself. Producers such as Leiber and Stoller, who also wrote songs, became important in guiding record dates.

Muddy Waters backstage in London; Waters' 1950s UK tours paved the way for the blues tours of the next decade.

Key Artist: Ray Charles

Ray Charles Robinson was born on 23 September 1930 in Albany, Georgia. Blind by the age of seven, he was educated at the Florida School for the Deaf and Blind in St. Augustine, where he studied piano and learned to read music in braille.

Shortly after his fifteenth birthday, he was expelled and left for Jacksonville, Florida to try to make a living from music. Within a few months, he was starting to play little jobs around the city. When he was at home, Ray would listen to country music, spirituals and blues on the radio; on his jobs, he heard singers such as Nat 'King' Cole and Charles Brown on the jukebox. Ray listened closely to these two singers and began to use them as his vocal models.

'I do jazz, blues, country music and so forth. I do them all, like a good utility man.'
Ray Charles

Over the next two years, Ray worked with a variety of different bands. In some cases he wrote arrangements, at other times he played alto sax or wrote songs. He travelled throughout Florida and got his first featured gig in Tampa, playing piano and singing with a combo modelled after that of Nat 'King' Cole.

In March 1948 Ray moved to Seattle, Washington on the advice of G.D. McKee, a guitarist with whom Ray had been working in Tampa. The pair quickly found plenty of work in their new surroundings, and within a few months had been signed by Downbeat Records. 'Confession Blues', one of Ray's tunes, became a hit in the spring of 1949. At this point Ray – who had been known as R.C. Robinson – became Ray Charles. The owner of Downbeat Records (now Swingtime), Jack Lauderdale, teamed Ray with his number-one act, Lowell Fulson and Ray became a part of Fulson's show, playing piano and singing in the band between 1950–52. The hit 'Baby, Let Me Hold Your Hand' brought Ray more attention, but Lauderdale had entered a dry spell and Charles's contract was sold to Atlantic Records.

A Shaky Start

Ray Charles's first recording session in his own name, in September 1952, was uneventful and follow-ups yielded only one minor hit ('It Should've Been Me'). Meanwhile, Charles was working

Right: Gifted pianist and entertainer Ray Charles.

as a solo artist, picking up musicians along the way. In the summer of 1954 he organized a band to back Ruth Brown on tour, after which the band continued on its own. In November, Ray was ready to call Atlantic Records.

'I Got A Woman', recorded on 18 November 1954, changed everything. The tune was based on a gospel song and, for the first time, all Charles's passion and fervour was captured on record. It was an R&B number one and Ray's biggest hit of the 1950s. His next session produced another number one, 'A Fool For You'. Ray Charles had arrived.

Ray Charles: 'The Genius'

Towards the end of the decade, Ray Charles spread his wings. He recorded jazz instrumentals, blues, gospel-inspired material and an album with a large orchestra, *The Genius Of Ray Charles* (1959). At the end of the decade, after more number ones with 'Drown In My Own Tears' and 'What'd I Say', Charles signed with ABC-Paramount. The deal included Ray's ownership of his own masters and complete artistic control. From this point, Ray Charles rarely looked back. He formed a big band, founded his own record label, Tangerine, and continued to have hits. He recorded a variety of jazz, pop, R&B, soul, and country & western material throughout the 1960s and 1970s, to varying degrees of success, but came back to prominence in the 1980s with a cameo in *The Blues Brothers* (1980) and a USA For Africa single 'We Are The World'. Charles, winner of 12 Grammys and a Lifetime Achievement Award, died on 10 June 2004. His album *Genius Loves Company* (2004), featuring duets with a variety of artists, was released posthumously to huge sales and recieved multiple awards, simultaneous with an Oscar-winning Hollywood biopic, *Ray* (2004).

Next Page: Charles in the 1980 film The Blues Brothers.

VISA

DANGER
NO SMOKING

Key Artist: Fats Domino

Antoine Domino Jr. was born on 26 February 1928 in New Orleans, Louisiana, the youngest of eight children. His father played violin and worked at the Fair Grounds Race Track in New Orleans. Young Antoine studied piano and credits Harrison Varrett, a former member of Papa Celestin's band, with giving him the advice and encouragement to keep going.

He practiced assiduously in his teens and was attracted to the music of boogie-woogie giants Meade 'Lux' Lewis and Albert Ammons, which he heard on jukeboxes, as well as the work of pianist/vocalists such as Charles Brown and Amos Milburn. He began playing parties and social functions at the age of 16 and the following year joined the combo of Billy Diamond, who christened him 'Fats'. In 1949, he began a regular gig at the Hideaway Club and started to draw crowds and get noticed. New Orleans bandleader Dave Bartholomew, who was serving as a talent scout for Imperial Records, brought the label's owner Lew Chudd to hear Fats at the Hideaway. Domino was signed; Bartholomew worked as producer and the two co-wrote songs together. In the first session, cut on 10 December 1949, Fats and Bartholomew's band recorded 'The Fat Man' – basically Champion Jack Dupree's 'Junker's Blues', dressed up with a new lyric from Bartholomew. It became a smash hit and climbed as high as number two on the *Billboard* magazine Race Records chart.

'When Fats plays that it's magic.... It's something just a little bigger than life, just the way Fats is.'

Allen Toussaint, on the introduction to 'Goin' Home'

A Signature Sound

Fats then formed a band modelled on Bartholomew's, which even included some of the same personnel. Much of Fats Domino's sound is based on his vocals and piano, plus tenor saxophone solos; the arrangements on his early records do not differ greatly from those of other blues bands, but the piano's distinctive sound and use of triplets became a Domino trademark after first appearing on 'Every Night About This Time' in 1950.

'Goin' Home' hit number one in 1952 and Fats continued his streak of bestselling singles. He was still working around New Orleans for the most part and recording with the same nucleus of players. He took time out to play piano on 'Lawdy Miss Clawdy' by Lloyd Price, another number-one hit (and yet

Right: Dave Bartholomew – bandleader, producer, composer, talent scout, trumpeter and Domino's mentor in the early days.

another lyric grafted on to the 'Junker's Blues' melody). The R&B coming out of New Orleans was beginning to sweep the country and Fats Domino was leading the way. The year 1953 found more hits with 'Please Don't Leave Me' and 'Goin' To The River'. Herb Hardesty took most of the tenor sax solos with Fats and began to tour with him, although later on Hardesty tended to split the solos with Lee Allen.

Rock'n'Roll?

Rock'n'roll really arrived in 1955 and Fats was at the head of the pack. He had three consecutive number-one hits with 'Ain't That A Shame', 'All By Myself' and 'Poor Me'. In 1956 he delivered three more: 'I'm In Love Again', 'Blueberry Hill' and 'Blue Monday'. The sound of Fats Domino's band changed little during this period; when people asked him about rock'n'roll, he would tell them that he called it R&B and that he had been playing it for years. Indeed, he still plays that way and little has changed in the 50 years since Fats Domino was the talk of the town. He has enjoyed so many hits that he is unable to play them all in any one show.

Next Page: New Orleans pianist and rock'n'roll superstar Fats Domino.

Key Artist: Muddy Waters

McKinley Morganfield was born in April 1915 in Rolling Fork, Mississippi and was raised by his grandmother Della Jones, a sharecropper on Stovall Plantation in Clarksdale. His education ended with the third grade and he remained illiterate throughout his life. He taught himself harmonica when he was about nine years old.

Morganfield was a farmer by the time he was 10. On weekends, he was able to hear music in local juke joints and on his grandmother's phonograph. He was 13 when he heard Leroy Carr's 'How Long Blues' and began to play along. He heard Charley Patton and also caught Big Joe Williams and the Mississippi Sheiks in Clarksdale. Within a few months, he was playing functions in the area; it was around this time that he acquired the nickname Muddy Waters.

'Muddy can really sing the blues … hollering, shouting, crying, getting mad – that's the blues.'

Big Bill Broonzy

In 1932, Muddy bought his first guitar. He became fascinated with Son House, who appeared frequently at area juke joints, and House taught the youngster how to fashion his first slide. Muddy also learned from Patton and his good friend Robert Lee McCollum, later Robert Nighthawk, and saw Robert Johnson play in 1937. Much later, Muddy would declare that his style was a mixture of House and Johnson influences, along with his own innovations.

From Stovall to Chicago

Muddy was recorded by Alan Lomax on Stovall Plantation in August 1941 and July 1942. In May 1943 he left Mississippi for Chicago and he began to work with Jimmy Rogers. He acquired his first electric guitar in 1945 and in April 1947 he recorded for Aristocrat Records. 'Gypsy Woman'/'Little Anna Mae', Muddy's first record, featured his vocal and guitar with Sunnyland Slim on piano and Big Crawford on bass. A second session in April 1948 produced 'I Can't Be Satisfied'/'I Feel Like Goin' Home', which was only a minor hit but helped Muddy to realize that he could be a successful entertainer. Leonard Chess, Muddy's producer and owner of Aristocrat (soon to become Chess Records), was rather conservative in choosing the supporting cast; Muddy was accompanied only by Crawford up to 1950

Right: Blues great Muddy Waters, whose illustrious recording career was an inspiration to countless blues artists.

and it was December 1951 before Little Walter, Rogers and Muddy were recorded together. The modern sound of the Chicago blues was beginning to take shape.

Otis Spann was introduced to Muddy by Rogers in 1952 and in 1954 Muddy, Walter, Rogers, Spann, Willie Dixon and drummer Fred Below went into the studio. The session produced 'I'm Your Hoochie Coochie Man', Muddy's biggest single, and 'Just Make Love To Me', 'I'm Ready' and 'Mannish Boy' followed in quick succession. The personnel in the band turned over with some regularity: Walter left in 1952; Pat Hare replaced Rogers in 1957; Dixon was used only on record dates, and there were several different drummers. Yet somehow the sound of the Muddy Waters band remained remarkably consistent.

Muddy Reaches New Audiences

In 1958 Muddy Waters was encouraged by British bandleader Chris Barber to tour England. It was his first opportunity to play before large white audiences – at home, his fans were mainly black and were dwindling in numbers due to the popularity of rock'n'roll. Despite some criticism for his use of amplification, Muddy's shows rocked skiffle-mad 1950s England and inspired Cyril Davis and Alexis Korner to branch out into the blues, thereby jump-starting the 1960s blues revival.

Muddy played New York's Carnegie Hall in 1959, and the following year he played the Newport Jazz Festival and was recorded live by Chess. The album was enormously important for Muddy's career. The song 'Got My Mojo Working' gained popularity through this performance and became his signature track. It had taken him just under 20 years to go from McKinley Morganfield, on Stovall's Plantation in Mississippi, to Muddy Waters, world-famous bandleader and recording artist. He continued to record, tour and collaborate throughout the rest of his career, which was filled with acknowledgements and awards befitting the man who was the source and inspiration of the modern blues sound. He died from heart failure on 30 April 1983.

Next Page: Muddy Waters' old home on Stovall Plantation, Clarksdale, Mississippi.

A–Z of Artists

Mickey Baker (Guitar, b. 1925)

McHouston Baker was born in Louisville, Kentucky. Originally a jazz player, he switched to blues after seeing guitarist Pee Wee Crayton. He began his recording career at Savoy in 1952 and became the first-call guitarist for R&B session work in New York. He teamed with vocalist Sylvia Vanderpool and, as Mickey & Sylvia, they had a huge hit with 'Love Is Strange' in 1956–57. He settled in Paris in 1961.

Dave Bartholomew (Trumpet, producer, composer, b. 1918)

Davis Louis Bartholomew was born in Edgard, Louisiana. He was one of the most prominent bandleaders in New Orleans in the mid-1940s. He recorded for DeLuxe, King and Imperial during the 1940s and 1950s, but is best known as the producer, bandleader and songwriting partner of Fats Domino, whom he produced at Imperial from 1949 into the 1960s. He also produced Smiley Lewis, the Spiders, Snooks Eaglin and dozens of other New Orleans R&B greats.

'[James Booker] would go and do his piano lessons … and then go and do all these great boogies and stuff…. He was so versatile as a teenager. And he just kept blossoming.'

Dr John

Bobby 'Blue' Bland (Vocals, b. 1930)

Robert Calvin Brooks was born in Rosemark, Tennessee. He began recording in 1951 and was associated with B.B. King, and others in Memphis. He signed with Duke Records in 1952 and was one of the most consistent hitmakers in the soul blues idiom from the late 1950s to the 1970s. He had R&B number ones with 'Further On Up The Road' (1957), 'I Pity The Fool' (1961) and 'That's The Way Love Is' (1963).

James Booker (Piano, organ, vocals, 1939–83)

James Carroll Booker III was born in New Orleans, Louisiana. He studied classical piano from the age of four and made his recording debut for Imperial at 14. He worked as a session musician in New Orleans from the mid-1950s and recorded for many labels, as well as playing and arranging for the Lloyd Price big band in the early 1960s. Despite some successful European tours, a narcotics addiction slowed his career development, but he is still remembered with deep admiration in his home town.

Bobby 'Blue' Bland performs a slow number at a crowded dance.

A–Z of Artists

Clarence 'Gatemouth' Brown (Guitar, violin, vocals, 1924–2005)

Clarence Brown Jr. was born in Vinton, Louisiana and raised in Orange, Texas. By the age of 10 he had learned guitar and violin. After the Second World War he settled in the Houston, Texas area. He made his recording debut in 1947 for Aladdin and signed with Peacock Records in 1949. Brown formed his own group, Gate's Express, in 1953 and it continued up until his death in 2005. He toured Europe in 1971 and became a frequent overseas traveller. He began to freelance his recording opportunities in the 1960s. On guitar, his signature tune 'Okie Dokie Stomp' exemplified his style of rapid, single notes. He used his violin more when playing other styles but it was also very effective on slow blues. He was one of the great modern Texas guitarists, along with T-Bone Walker and Albert Collins.

Nappy Brown (Vocals, b. 1929)

Napoleon Brown Goodson Culp was born in Charlotte, North Carolina. He sang with a gospel group, the Heavenly Lights, which recorded for Savoy, but was convinced to try blues material in 1954 and had several hits, including 'Don't Be Angry'. He returned to singing gospel in the 1960s but was rediscovered in the late 1970s by the blues community. He recorded several CDs for various labels in the 1980s and 1990s. He continues to tour and record.

Key Tracks

'Okie Dokie Stomp' Clarence 'Gatemouth' Brown
'Gate's Salty Blues' Clarence 'Gatemouth' Brown
'Don't Be Angry' Nappy Brown
'Teardrops From Your Eyes' Ruth Brown
'(Mama) He Treats Your Daughter Mean' Ruth Brown

Ruth Brown (Vocals, b. 1928)

Ruth Alston Weston was born in Portsmouth, Virginia. She was heard performing in Washington, DC, where she was recommended to Atlantic Records. Her 1950 R&B number one 'Teardrops From Your Eyes' was followed by four more, including '(Mama) He Treats Your Daughter Mean', and she was so successful that the fledgeling label became known as 'the house that Ruth built'. After a period away from music in the 1960s and 1970s, Brown re-emerged to great acclaim for work on radio, TV, stage and film.

Owing to the seemingly endless string of hits enjoyed by Ruth Brown on Atlantic Records, the then fledgling label came to be known as 'The House That Ruth Built'.

A-Z of Artists

James Cotton (Harmonica, vocals, b. 1935)

James Henry Cotton was born in Tunica, Mississippi and was inspired by hearing Sonny Boy Williamson II (Rice Miller) on the radio. He worked with his mentor from the late 1940s until 1953, when he made his recording debut for Sun Records. He joined Muddy Waters in 1954 and played with him, on and off, until 1966. He toured Europe with Muddy in 1961 and has been a frequent international traveller. He formed his own group in 1966 and continues to tour and record.

Floyd Dixon (Piano, vocals, 1928–2006)

Floyd Dixon was born in Marshall, Texas and was raised in Los Angeles from the age of 13. He made his recording debut aged 18 for Supreme Records and also recorded for Modern and Peacock before switching to Aladdin in 1950 and releasing his biggest record, 'Call Operator 210'. Dixon was a pianist and vocalist in the Charles Brown tradition.

Willie Dixon (Bass, vocals, songwriter, 1915–92)

Willie James Dixon was born in Vicksburg, Mississippi and moved to Chicago at the age of 11. He learned bass and made his recording debut with the Five Breezes in 1940. After the Second World War he formed the Big Three trio, with whom he worked until 1952. He wrote songs associated with Muddy Waters, Howlin' Wolf and Cream, among others. He joined forces with Memphis Slim in 1959 and toured internationally, and later formed his own band, the Chicago Blues All-Stars.

Key Tracks

'Cotton Crop Blues' James Cotton
'Hold Me In Your Arms' James Cotton
'Call Operator 210' Floyd Dixon
'I Just Want To Make Love To You' Willie Dixon
'Honky Tonk' Bill Doggett

Bill Doggett (Organ, piano, arranger, 1916–96)

William Ballard Doggett was born in Philadelphia, Pennsylvania. The band he led was taken over by Lucky Millinder in 1940 and Doggett stayed on as pianist and arranger. After working with the Ink Spots, he played with Louis Jordan's band from 1947–51. He was active as a studio pianist, organist and arranger until 1953, when he formed the first organ–tenor sax combo. His biggest hit, 'Honky Tonk', was recorded in 1956 for King and was an R&B number one. He continued to tour and record until his death.

Bassist, songwriter and producer Willie Dixon (centre) plays on a session at Chess Studios with J.B. Lenoir (far left).

PIANO
SAX
BASS
DRUMS

A-Z of Artists

Panama Francis (Drums, 1918–2001)

David Albert Francis was born in Miami, Florida. He worked around Florida with saxophonist George Kelly before going to New York in 1938. The following year he made his recording debut with Roy Eldridge, who named him after his choice of hats. Francis worked with Lucky Millinder from 1940–46 and Cab Calloway from 1947–52 but his reputation dates mainly from his session work in New York. He was the first-call drummer on R&B sessions throughout the 1950s and early 1960s, and was an important figure in changing the black swing beat to R&B.

Lowell Fulson (Guitar, vocals, 1921–99)

Lowell Fulson was born in Tulsa, Oklahoma and began his professional career in Oakland, California. He made his recording debut in 1946 and by 1950 he was a hitmaker for Swingtime Records with such songs as 'Every Day I Have The Blues' and 'Blue Shadows'. His band at this time featured a relatively unknown Ray Charles on piano. He switched to Chess in 1945 and had another hit with 'Reconsider Baby'; his final big record came in 1967 with 'Tramp'. Originally inspired by T-Bone Walker, Fulson managed to stay current with changing blues trends throughout his career.

Key Tracks

'Stomping At The Savoy' Panama Francis
'Just You, Just Me' Panama Francis
'Every Day I Have The Blues' Lowell Fulson
'Reconsider Baby' Lowell Fulson
'Just A Little Bit' Rosco Gordon

Rosco Gordon (Piano, vocals, 1928–2002)

Rosco Gordon was born in Memphis, Tennessee. He won an amateur contest in 1950 and was soon appearing on WDIA radio. He began recording with Sam Phillips in 1951; Phillips sold the master of 'Booted' to Chess Records and the master of 'No More Doggin'' to Modern. Gordon had two hits, on two different labels, at the same time in 1952. He had a further hit with 'Just A Little Bit' on Vee Jay in 1959. Gordon was out of music full-time after the 1960s. He moved to New York before forming his own record label and issuing 45-rpm singles in the 1980s. He was recorded by Stony Plain in 2000 and toured again for the last two years of his life. The loping rhythms of Gordon's music was influential on the development of ska and reggae music in Jamaica.

Eccentric blues pianist Rosco Gordon, whose music influenced early ska and reggae.

A-Z of Artists

Guitar Slim (Guitar, vocals, 1925–59)

Eddie Lee Jones was born in Greenwood, Mississippi. He sang in church as a child but had relocated to New Orleans by the age of 17, where he worked with Huey 'Piano' Smith in a small group until 1953. His recording debut was on Imperial in 1951, but his most important recordings were for Specialty during 1954–55 and Atlantic in 1956–58. Guitar Slim had only one hit, but it was an R&B number one: 'Things That I Used To Do', arranged by the pianist on the session, Ray Charles.

Slim was a flamboyant performer, noted for the wild colours of his suits and hair. He was famous for his 'walks': using a lengthy extension cord he would parade around a room or even out into the street, playing his guitar all the while as the sound continued to come out of his amplifier on stage.

Lightnin' Hopkins (Guitar, vocals, 1911–82)

Sam Hopkins was born in Centerville, Texas. His father and two brothers were musicians and he learned guitar from an early age. He met and played with Blind Lemon Jefferson at the age of eight. He accompanied his cousin, Texas Alexander, for much of the 1930s, drifting through Texas. He was discovered in Houston by Lola Cullum in 1946 and signed with Aladdin Records. His first record featured pianist Thunder Smith and with that release he became Lightnin' Hopkins. He recorded hundreds of songs from 1948–54, for a variety of different labels.

Key Tracks

'Things That I Used To Do' Guitar Slim
'Short-Haired Woman' Lightnin' Hopkins
'Lonesome Home' Lightnin' Hopkins
'Coffee Blues' Lightnin' Hopkins
'Hello Central' Lightnin' Hopkins

After a dry patch, Hopkins was 'rediscovered' during the folk blues revival of the late 1950s and from 1959 recorded dozens of albums for various labels. He toured constantly, became a regular on the festival circuit in North America and did considerable film and TV work. Lightnin' Hopkins' great gift was his ability to create songs from the flimsiest suggestion, and to play exquisite country blues guitar even though he lived in a big city for most of his life. He also had an extraordinarily fluid sense of song structure and time.

Texan blues legend Lightnin' Hopkins enjoys a cigarette in the studio.

A-Z of Artists

Earl Hooker (Guitar, vocals, 1930–70)

Earl Zebedee Hooker Jr., a cousin of John Lee Hooker, was born in Clarksdale, Mississippi. He learned guitar by the age of 10 and moved to Chicago in 1941. Hooker was inspired by Robert Nighthawk and at the end of 1940s returned south, where he played with Rice Miller and Ike Turner. He first recorded in 1952, and from 1959 recorded a series of singles for small Chicago labels. He recorded and toured internationally in 1965 and 1969. Hooker was a slide guitar player of great originality but was slowed by tuberculosis, which eventually killed him.

Big Walter Horton (Harmonica, vocals, 1918–61)

Walter Horton was born in Horn Lake, Mississippi. He taught himself harmonica at the age of five and was working the streets shortly thereafter. He moved to Chicago in 1940 but it wasn't until later in the decade that he began to be more active professionally. Horton replaced Junior Wells in the Muddy Waters band in 1953 and worked with Muddy for about a year. One of Chicago's finest harmonica players, he was particularly associated with Johnny Shines and Jimmy Rogers.

'When I heard Howlin' Wolf, I said, "This is for me. This is where the soul of man never dies."'

Sam Phillips

Howlin' Wolf (Guitar, harmonica, vocals, 1910–76)

Chester Arthur Burnett was born in White Station, Mississippi. Inspired by Charley Patton, Wolf earned his living as a farmer in the West Memphis, Arkansas area and was strictly a weekend performer until he was almost 40 years old. He got a radio spot in 1948 and the sound of that band, which was electric rather than acoustic, heightened interest in his work. He began to record in 1951 for Sam Phillips, who sold his masters to both Modern Records and Chess Records. Ultimately, Chess won out and Howlin' Wolf recorded for the label from 1952 until his death.

It was Wolf's intense, growling voice that dominated his performances – it was one of the great blues voices of all time. Unlike many of his blues peers, Wolf was a flamboyant entertainer who could rock the house. He was considered a leading light of the Chicago blues scene for many years.

Slide guitarist Earl Hooker, who played with Rice Miller and Ike Turner, among others.

A-Z of Artists

Elmore James (Guitar, vocals, 1918–63)

Elmore Brooks was born in Richland, Mississippi. He learned guitar at an early age and was playing functions by the age of 14. He often worked with Rice Miller from the late 1930s until he was drafted into the Navy in 1943. He rejoined Miller after the war and recorded 'Dust My Broom' at the tail end of a Rice Miller session for Trumpet Records in 1951, which it became a surprise hit.

James moved to Chicago, where he formed his own group, the Broomdusters, and recorded for Modern/Flair/ Meteor from 1952–56 and Fire/Fury/Enjoy in 1959–62. He was the premier electric slide guitarist of his era and his signature riff, used on 'Dust My Broom', was heard on many of his recordings and copied by countless imitators.

Etta James (Vocals, b. 1938)

Jamesetta Hawkins was born in Los Angeles, California. She moved to the San Francisco area, where she was discovered by Johnny Otis. She made her recording debut at the age of 16 for Modern, and had a number-one R&B hit with her first record, 'The Wallflower' (a.k.a. 'Roll With Me Henry'). She worked in rock'n'roll package tours throughout the 1950s before signing with Chess Records in 1960 and scoring another big record with 'At Last'. A versatile performer, Etta James can deliver the goods on low-down blues, rockers and tender ballads, and won a blues Grammy in 2005.

Key Tracks

'Dust My Broom' Elmore James
'Crossroads' Elmore James
'The Wallflower' Etta James
'At Last' Etta James
'Come On' Earl King

Earl King (Guitar, vocals, 1934–2003)

Earl Silas Johnson IV was born in New Orleans, Louisiana. He was influenced by Guitar Slim and made his recording debut for Savoy, as Earl Johnson, in 1953. Upon switching to Specialty in 1954, he became Earl King. Often associated with New Orleans blues pianist Huey 'Piano' Smith in the 1950s, King scored his biggest hit with 'Those Lonely, Lonely Nights' for Ace Records in 1955. A favoured songwriter among New Orleans R&B artists, King recorded for many small New Orleans labels over the years. He remained an active performer until shortly before his death.

Etta James, whose powerful voice suits a wide range of blues material.

A-Z of Artists

J.B. Lenoir (Guitar, vocals, 1929–67)

J.B. Lenoir was born in Monticello, Mississippi; his parents were farmers as well as musicians. He learned to play the guitar at the age of eight and left home in the early 1940s to work with Rice Miller and Elmore James, before settling in Chicago in 1949 and making his recording debut in 1951 for Chess Records. He worked around Chicago for most of the decade and recorded for a number of different labels. Lenoir toured Europe with the American Folk Blues Festival in 1965. He is best remembered for his original compositions – many of which explored topical themes – and his distinctive, keening falsetto vocals.

Little Walter (Harmonica, vocals, 1930–68)

Marion Walter Jacobs was born in Marksville, Louisiana. He taught himself harmonica at the age of eight and was working the New Orleans streets by the time he was 12. He worked in Helena, Arkansas and St. Louis before arriving in Chicago in 1946. He was encouraged by guitarists Tampa Red and Big Bill Broonzy and also met Jimmy Rogers. He made his recording debut in 1947 and joined forces with Muddy Waters the following year. He worked with Muddy until 1952 when his own Checker record, 'Juke', became an R&B number-one. Walter formed his own group with the Aces (David Meyers, Louis Meyers and Fred Below), and toured clubs and concert halls on R&B package tours. He continued to have hit records throughout the decade.

Key Tracks

'Mama Talk To Your Daughter' J.B. Lenoir
'Korea Blues' J.B. Lenoir
'My Babe' Little Walter
'Mardi Gras in New Orleans' Professor Longhair
'Tipitina' Professor Longhair

Professor Longhair (Piano, vocals, 1918–80)

Henry Roeland Byrd was born in Bogalusa, Louisiana and formed his first combo, Professor Longhair and the Four Hairs, shortly after the Second World War. His Atlantic sessions in 1949 and 1953 produced his signature songs 'Mardi Gras in New Orleans' and 'Tipitina'. As an ebullient and racy vocalist, and a pianist who employed a characteristic rhumba-boogie, Longhair is the link between older New Orleans pianists and the new arrivals of the 1950s. He enjoyed a comeback after appearing at the 1971 New Orleans Jazz & Heritage Festival, and returned to touring and recording until his death.

J.B. Lenoir performs in the UK during the 1965 American Folk Blues Festival tour.

A-Z of Artists

Earl Palmer (Drums, b. 1924)

Earl Cyril Palmer was born in New Orleans, Louisiana. As a member of Dave Bartholomew's band, he played drums on the first Fats Domino session in 1949. He recorded with a variety of artists that included Little Richard, Smiley Lewis, Bobby Mitchell, the Spiders and Shirley & Lee, and is generally credited with bringing the New Orleans street beat into the studio. He moved to Los Angeles in 1957 and continued to be a top studio drummer for many years.

Little Junior Parker (Harmonica, vocals, 1932–71)

Herman Parker Jr. was born in Bobo, Mississippi and worked with Howlin' Wolf in West Memphis. Parker was associated with B.B. King, Bobby Bland and Johnny Ace in the Memphis scene of the early 1950s. He recorded for Sun with his own group, the Blue Flames, in 1953 and signed with Duke Records in December of that year. Parker was a first-rate harmonica player but an even better singer. He was more of a crooner than a shouter and, as such, his blues ballads were always outstanding.

Piano Red (Piano, vocals, 1911–85)

Willie Lee Perryman was born in Hampton, Georgia. He was sometimes known as Dr Feelgood, and his older brother, Rufus, was known as Speckled Red. He worked mainly as a soloist in the Atlanta area before signing with RCA in 1950. His first record, 'Rockin' With Red'/'Red's Boogie' was a two-sided hit. His early records emphasized his piano, but later sessions were in more of an R&B groove, with horns and vocal groups. He continued to tour mostly in Europe, under the name Dr Feelgood, until his death.

Snooky Pryor (Harmonica, vocals, b. 1921)

James Edward Pryor was born in Lambert, Mississippi. He learned harmonica at the age of 14 and left home in 1937 to work as a musician. He settled in Chicago in 1940. After army service during the Second World War he got the idea of amplifying his harmonica, and was the first to develop that sound. He recorded for small Chicago labels throughout the 1950s but left music in the early 1960s, only to be 'rediscovered' in the 1970s.

Key Tracks

'The Fat Man' Earl Palmer
'Mystery Train' Little Junior Parker
'Rockin' With Red' Piano Red
'Red's Boogie' Piano Red
'Telephone Blues' Snooky Pryor

Sam Phillips, owner of Sun Records, for whom Little Junior Parker recorded 'Mystery Train' with his Blues Flames in 1953.

A-Z of Artists

Jimmy Reed (Guitar, harmonica, vocals, 1925–76)

Mathis James Reed was born in Dunleith, Mississippi. His friend Eddie Taylor taught him guitar and harmonica, but he rarely played professionally until he moved to Gary, Indiana in 1948. He recorded on harmonica with John Brim and, after failing an audition for Chess Records, recorded his own session for Chance Records in 1953. At this point, he reunited with Eddie Taylor.

Reed recorded for Vee Jay from 1953 until the label folded in 1965. From 1955–61 he had seven top 10 R&B hits ('Big Boss Man', 'Bright Lights, Big City' etc.). Reed's formula was simple: a lazy tempo with a boogie figure on the bottom, harmonica solos and his slurred, almost unintelligible vocals. He was the most popular Chicago bluesman, his records routinely making the pop chart, but credit must also go to his faithful guitarist Taylor and his wife, Mama Reed, who helped to write many of his songs.

Huey 'Piano' Smith (Piano, vocals, b. 1934)

Huey P. Smith was born in New Orleans, Louisiana and worked with Earl King and Guitar Slim in the early 1950s. He made his recording debut for Savoy in 1953 but his on-off tenure with Ace Records from 1955–64 was his most important. His group the Clowns had two huge R&B records in 'Rockin' Pneumonia And The Boogie-Woogie Flu' and 'Don't You Just Know It' in 1957–58. Smith was a fine songwriter, pianist and vocalist, and one of the bright stars of the New Orleans R&B scene of the late 1950s and early 1960s.

Key Tracks

'Big Boss Man' Jimmy Reed
'Bright Lights, Big City' Jimmy Reed
'Don't You Just Know It' Huey 'Piano' Smith
'Sunnyland Train' Sunnyland Slim

Sunnyland Slim (Piano, vocals, 1906–95)

Albert Luandrew was born in Vance, Mississippi. He was self-taught as a pianist and spent the period from 1925–39 in Memphis, playing functions and small clubs. He went to Chicago to find work outside music, but instead fell in with the local blues crowd and worked with Tampa Red, Jump Jackson and Muddy Waters. He began recording in 1947 and recorded for more than two dozen small labels around Chicago. A solid, workman-like performer, Slim was the patriarch of the Chicago blues scene in his later years.

Jimmy Reed (right), whose urban Chicago sound was a big influence on the British blues bands of the 1960s.

A-Z of Artists

Rufus Thomas (Vocals, 1917–2001)

Rufus Thomas Jr. was born in Cayce, Mississippi and raised in Memphis, Tennessee. He worked with tent and minstrel shows throughout the 1930s. He recorded for Sun Records in the early 1950s and had the label's first hit with 'Bear Cat' in 1953; he also worked as a disc jockey at WDIA, Memphis. He began recording for Stax in 1959 and had big R&B hits with humorous dance songs such as 'Walkin' The Dog' and 'Do The Funky Chicken'. Billed as the 'World's Oldest Teenager', Rufus Thomas was an ambassador for Memphis blues and is the father of 1960s soul siren Carla Thomas.

Big Mama Thornton (Harmonica, vocals, 1926–84)

Willie Mae Thornton was born in Montgomery, Alabama. She settled in Houston, Texas in 1948 and began recording for Peacock in 1951. She toured with Johnny Otis in 1952–53 and recorded her number-one R&B hit, 'Hound Dog', with his band. The record, famously covered by Elvis Presley, enabled her to branch out on her own. After leaving Peacock in 1957, she settled in the San Francisco area and worked as a solo artist. She recorded albums for Arhoolie, Mercury and Vanguard in the 1960s and 1970s.

Sonny Boy Williamson II (Rice Miller) (Harmonica, vocals, *c.* 1912–65)

Alex Ford 'Rice' Miller was born in Glendora, Mississippi. He taught himself the harmonica at the age of five and by his early teens had left home to sing and play as 'Little Boy Blue'. He worked streets, clubs and functions through Mississippi and Arkansas during the 1930s, often playing with Robert Johnson, Elmore James and Robert Lockwood Jr. In 1941 he began a radio programme, *King Biscuit Time*, on KFFA in Helena, Arkansas and billed himself as Sonny Boy Williamson.

Sonny Boy started recording for Trumpet in 1951. He switched to Checker in 1955 and had a big R&B hit with 'Don't Start Me To Talkin''. He toured Europe with the American Folk Blues Festival in 1963 and recorded with the Yardbirds. He was an outstanding harmonica player and also had a fantastic blues voice.

Key Tracks

'Walkin' The Dog' Rufus Thomas
'Do The Funky Chicken' Rufus Thomas
'Hound Dog' Big Mama Thornton
'Ball And Chain' Big Mama Thornton
'Don't Start Me To Talkin'' Sonny Boy Williamson II

Sonny Boy Williamson II (Rice Miller) tours with the 1963 American Folk Blues Festival.

The Sixties

The cultural momentum of the 1950 spilled directly into the 1960s amid significant social and political change. Most blues was issued as disposable 45-rpm singles, but that changed mid-decade, after Columbia Records released the first collection of Robert Johnson recordings from the 1930s, and Chess Records put out LP compilations of hits by Muddy Waters, Howlin' Wolf, Sonny Boy Williamson, Little Walter et al.

In that format, the blues hit the UK with a bang and resonated with many young musicians; this resulted in the birth of bands such as the Beatles, the Rolling Stones and the Yardbirds, all of whom based their early material on American blues and soul records – broadening the music's popularity in the UK and encouraging the US to listen to itself again. Between the British Invasion and the folk-music movement, interest in the blues of all eras was rekindled, and rock'n'roll was soon stretching the traditional form into psychedelic shape. The blues also informed the newly emerging rock sound, and in the hands of artists such as Jimi Hendrix it continued to explore new musical avenues.

Key Artists

Buddy Guy
Albert King
B.B. King

Transformation was again the cultural watchword, as assassinations shook the US, civil rights became undeniable and a war in Asia provoked unrivalled discontent. The music of different nations, such as Brazil, began to influence many popular styles in the West, while new instruments and studio techniques allowed musicians options beyond imagination; fusions of all styles, from anywhere and everywhere, foreshadowed the shape of things to come.

Vietnam War protesters burn draft cards. Social issues such as the war began to divide the generations in the 1960s.

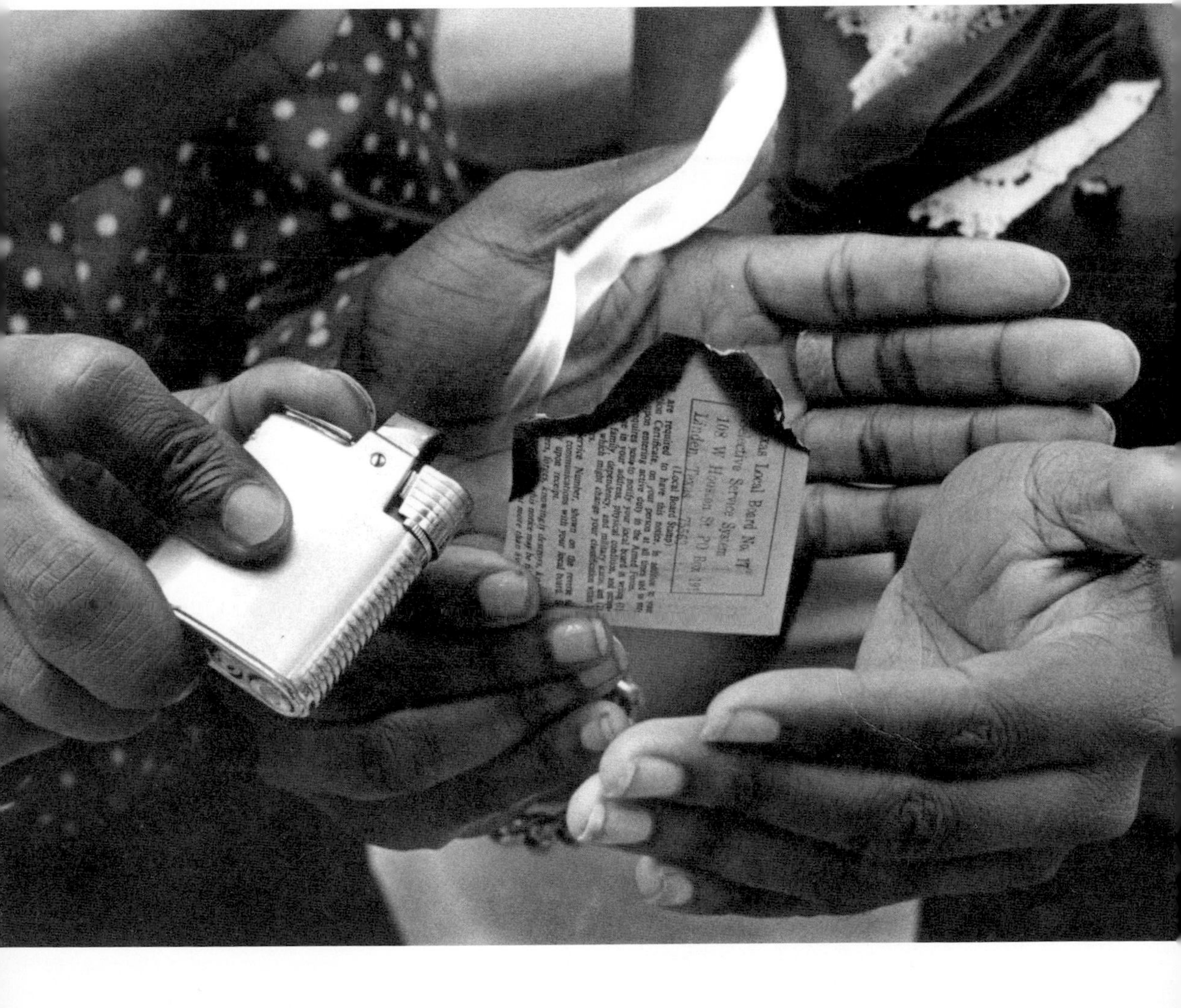
Local Board No.
Service System
108 W Houston St PO Box
Linden
(Local Board Stamp)

The Blues is Reborn

The seeds for the blues explosion of the 1960s were planted in the previous decade; rock'n'roll resulted from the fusion of African-American blues and R&B with white folk and country music, which was then sped up and amplified in keeping with the pace and technology of the prosperous 1950s.

The rock'n'roll revolution did not win everyone over, however; an older generation of folk enthusiasts still pursued their acoustic passions, while some younger listeners began to investigate the roots of the new music. In America, these fans played a crucial role in launching the decade's blues revival. Collectors of 78-rpm discs, such as Gayle Dean Wardlow, travelled to rural southern towns looking for prized acetate recordings by bluesmen of the 1920s and 1930s, and began to turn up surprising bonuses in the form of the artists themselves. Musicologist Alan Lomax (1915–2002), musician John Fahey and Bob Jones, a young hand at the Newport Folk Festival, were all in the thick of rediscovering a whole host of bluesmen and -women previously only embodied by scratched discs. Thus the blues boom of the 1960s truly began.

'Wolf loved it when he heard the Rolling Stones and Eric Clapton play his songs.... He said, "Hubert, them white boys is gonna make me famous. Then maybe we can make us some money."'

Hubert Sumlin

The old records were reissued as vinyl LPs. The old musicians were dusted off and began to tour. Some, including Son House (1902–88), hadn't held a guitar in years and had to be re-taught some of their own numbers. Others, such as Mississippi John Hurt (1893–1966) and Rev. Gary Davis (1896–1972), emerged with their virtuosity intact. Although Robert Johnson (1911–38) had long been dead, his *King Of The Delta Blues Singers* collection was issued in 1961, and his razor-edged guitar virtuosity and keening vocal style fired the imaginations of many budding guitarists – Eric Clapton and Keith Richards included, who both went on to cover Johnson songs ('Cross Road Blues' and 'Love In Vain' respectively).

Mississippi John Hurt, one of the old bluesmen to be 'rediscovered' in the 1960s.

The Great Festivals

The Newport Folk Festival, established in 1959, helped to propel old blues artists back into the public eye and also drew contemporary blues artists such as John Lee Hooker (1917–2001) and Muddy Waters (1915–83). However, the watershed year for blues at Newport was 1966, when Lomax organized a bill that included Howlin' Wolf (1910–76), Son House, Skip James (1902–69) and Bukka White (1906–77).

Newport was the catalyst for the cross-pollination of blues and the singer-songwriter-based original music that was beginning to redefine the folk idiom. Bob Dylan, who had started out with traditional blues numbers, began to take on increasingly modern elements of the genre. Dylan's electric performance that summer ensured that folk music was no longer a purely acoustic medium.

Europe also caught festival fever. In 1962, German fans Horst Lippmann and Fritz Rau organized the American Folk Blues Festival. The main difference between this and Newport was electricity. Although Waters and Wolf played amplified sets at Newport, traditionalists such as Pete Seeger and Lomax booked mostly acoustic acts – hence why Dylan's electric debut caused such a stir. By 1962 there was a new, younger audience emerging that would permanently change the face of blues music.

Popular Melody

Cream – 'Crossroads' (1968)

Alexis Korner (1928–84) was the first white British musician to really seize electrified blues and make it his own. He couldn't find a club in London that would book his group Blues Incorporated, so he opened one. It became a magnet for future English blues players – Mick Jagger, Keith Richards, John Mayall and Eric Clapton were among those who haunted the Ealing establishment. When the Rolling Stones, the Yardbirds and the Animals began to make hits, the sound of the blues echoed back across the Atlantic. For many young Americans this music seemed novel – but not all. In Chicago, Mike Bloomfield, Paul Butterfield and Charlie Musselwhite had absorbed the blues in the ghetto clubs where black artists reigned seven nights a week. Meanwhile, in New York, Jimi James & the Blue Flames were holding down a residency at Greenwich Village's Café Wha?; here audiences could catch the group's incendiary guitarist and frontman before he was swept off to England by former Animals bassist Chas Chandler and renamed Jimi Hendrix.

Howlin' Wolf performs at London's Marquee club with Chris Barber's band in 1964.

Closing the Cultural Gap

New York was home to the seminal R&B label Atlantic Records, which – like Chess and other independent blues recording companies – fuelled the imaginations of young white players and listeners with its releases by African-American artists. Although Atlantic had nurtured R&B, it also released sides by blues musicians including T-Bone Walker (1910–75), Guitar Slim (1926–59) and Freddie King (1934–76). More importantly, Atlantic was the distributor of Stax Records, which produced classics by Albert King (1923–92) and Booker T. and the MGs, and was in the vanguard of soul music.

Although the 1960s was an era of prosperity in the US, it also brought great cultural upheaval. The accelerating Vietnam War caused a rift between generations. For teenagers and twenty-somethings, embracing the music of a cultural group that was actively protesting for civil rights – African-Americans – was part of the package. It was not much of a leap to also embrace the people who made that music, and the blues became a bridge between races that led to common ground.

Popular Melody

Albert King – 'Born Under A Bad Sign' (1967)

The English bluesmen were also sending a message. Much of the success of *Blues Breakers* (1966), the debut album from John Mayall's band, hung on the dazzling playing of guitarist Eric Clapton; this indicated that audiences were ready to listen to blues in a different way. Clapton adopted the techniques of Buddy Guy (b. 1936), Freddie King, B.B. King (b. 1925) and Albert King, and pushed them to a new level of virtuosity. After Clapton, who went on to form the improvisational blues rock supergroup Cream, the blues became associated with the sound of the guitar – particularly that of flattened blue notes and bent, vibrato-coloured strings, teased from an electric instrument. If Clapton did not seal the deal as far as virtuoso electric blues guitarists were concerned, the arrival of Jimi Hendrix did. Hendrix was the musical embodiment of the 1960s – a young black man who became a cultural superstar by pushing the limits of musical freedom. Established bluesmen, including B.B. King and Albert King, suddenly found themselves playing alongside rock stars before racially mixed audiences at large festivals and important venues. The blues seeped throughout the cultural terrain, making the 1960s the greatest period of growth and popularity the genre had experienced since it first emerged on recordings in the 1920s and 1930s.

A publicity poster for the 1965 American Folk Blues Festival.

Lippmann+Rau present
AMERICAN
FOLK
BLUES
FESTIVAL '65
A
documentation
of the
authentic
blues
with the
best blues artists
of america
in concert
John Lee Hooker
Roosevelt
Sykes
J.B. Lenoir
Buddy Guy
Big Walter
Shakey Horton
CHICAGO
BLUES
Big Mama
Thornton
Eddie Boyd
Mississippi
Fred
Mc Dowell
Lonesome
Jimmy Lee
Doctor Ross
Freddie Below

Key Artist: Buddy Guy

'When I first heard of the electric guitar, I thought somebody was bullshittin' me,' says George 'Buddy' Guy. 'We lived so far in the country I didn't even know what an acoustic guitar was until my mother started getting mail-order catalogs'. In 2007, Guy, who was born in Lettsworth, Louisiana on 30 July 1936, stands at the pinnacle of modern electric blues.

Guy's first instruments were one-stringed contraptions that he made from screen wire, nails and paint cans, before he graduated to a battered acoustic bartered for by his father. He first heard an electric six-string played by Lightnin' Slim at a general store near the plantation where his family sharecropped, and the sound took root. After witnessing Guitar Slim's fiery live act in a Baton Rouge club, Guy's interest in becoming a baseball player vanished. He moved to Baton Rouge himself and began playing professionally, until he earned enough money for a bus ticket to Chicago in 1957.

Chicago Blues

The Windy City was less than welcoming. Guy failed to find work even though Chicago's blues scene was at its peak, heightened by Howlin' Wolf, Muddy Waters and many other stars, as well as the presence of the Chess, United and Cobra labels. Frustrated and starving, Guy resolved to return home, but Waters intervened and took him under his wing. Guy then became a regular session player and recorded singles for Chess and Cobra. He supported Waters on the 1963 classic *Folk Singer* and fell into a partnership with vocalist and harmonica player Junior Wells, with whom he recorded *Hoodoo Man Blues* (1965) and *Southside Blues Jam* (1967) on Delmark. Guy became known for his great live delivery (hanging from rafters and playing with his teeth), his gospel-style testifying and a guitar vocabulary built on explosive dynamics, off-the-neck bends, subtle chromatic lines and uninhibited improvisation.

'He is a consummate blues musician. He's living history.'

Eric Clapton

Guy's reputation reached further than he imagined. His playing influenced guitarists as widespread as Eric Clapton and Jimi Hendrix. Equally impressed, musicologist Samuel Charters produced Guy's first solo albums for the Vanguard label, including the brilliant *A Man & The Blues* (1968), still widely

Right: Electric blues star Buddy Guy performs at London's Marquee club in 1965.

considered to be Guy's masterpiece. In 1970 Guy and Wells were invited to tour with the Rolling Stones but their fame was fleeting. Guy spent the 1980s without a contract, playing clubs including his own, the Checker-board Lounge. He later opened Legends in downtown Chicago.

At the Zenith

It took another acolyte, Texan guitarslinger Stevie Ray Vaughan, to propel Guy to the top of the contemporary blues world, where he remains, second only to B.B. King. Vaughan's tireless support won Guy a contract with Silvertone Records, resulting in 1991's *Damn Right, I've Got The Blues*. The disc, which includes cameos by Jeff Beck, Mark Knopfler and Eric Clapton, received significant airplay and thrust Guy back to the festival and outdoor amphitheatre circuit, where he continues to play today. Several subsequent CDs found Guy aiming for pop crossover breakthroughs, but their diminishing sales figures indicated that they were eroding his standing among his listeners.

Once again, a prominent fan interceded. Producer Dennis Herring took the reins for 2001's *Sweet Tea*, using vintage amplifier tones and songs culled primarily from the catalogue of modern Mississippi juke blues master Junior Kimbrough. The raw-sounding venture restored Guy's momentum, which he maintained by joining Herring again for 2003's *Blues Singer*, an acoustic country blues homage to Muddy Waters' *Folk Singer* (1964) that returned Guy to his rural roots.

Next Page: Musicologist Sam Charters, who produced Guy's early albums.

THE LEGACY OF THE BLUES SAMPLER
from the series of recordings by today's blues artists
THE LEGACY OF THE BLUES vol.12
A series of recordings by the great blues artists
THE LEGACY OF THE BLUES

From the series of recordings by today's blues artists
THE LEGACY OF THE BLUES SAMPLER
A series of recordings by the great blues artists
SUNNYLAND SLIM
TWELVE GREAT BLUES

Key Artist: Albert King

Albert King's late 1960s and early 1970s recordings for the Stax label remain cornerstones of modern blues. Tunes like 'Born Under A Bad Sign' and 'I'll Play The Blues For You' are also an antidote to the over-the-top playing indulged in by so many contemporary blues guitarists. For King, a six-foot-four, 250-pound man possessed of a big, mellow voice and an equally proportional guitar tone, each carefully chiselled note took on the resonance of a life experience.

Born Albert Nelson on 25 April 1923 in Indianola, Mississippi, near the birthplace of B.B. King, Albert King was raised on a plantation in Arkansas, where he occasionally heard Howlin' Wolf perform at parties and roadhouses. He taught himself guitar and began playing local juke joints in 1939. King travelled north and sang lead tenor with the Harmony Kings gospel quartet around South Bend, Indiana for several years before arriving in Chicago, where he played drums with Jimmy Reed, Jackie Wilson, Brook Benton and others.

'Well, if you listen to the Blues guitar players today, about ninety per cent of what they are playing is Albert King'.

Carl Weathersby

Guitar Prowess

As a guitarist, King's technique was evolving. He graduated from acoustic to electric guitar, playing in a single-note style based on that of B.B. King, whose surname he also borrowed. These B.B. approximations can be heard on his early singles for the Parrot and Bobbin labels, including his first national hit, 'Don't Throw Your Love On Me So Strong', from 1961. By the time King signed to Stax Records in Memphis in 1966, he had developed his own

Albert King, whose clear, sparse sound was a welcome departure.

brawny style. In the late 1950s he had purchased the Gibson Flying V guitar that became his signature instrument. The left-handed musician turned it upside down, tuned it to an open E-minor chord and turned his amplifier's volume up. The resulting sound – round-toned, deliberately squeezed from each string and full of melismatic bent notes – was the soulful equivalent of his gospel-honed voice.

The Stax Years

Featuring a roster of artists and session players that included Booker T. & the MGs, Isaac Hayes and the Memphis Horns, King's Stax singles and albums brought blues into the soul era. The spread of FM radio, along with Eric Clapton's incorporation of King's licks and a cover of his 'Born Under A Bad Sign' into Cream's repertoire, introduced King to white listeners. In 1964 King was invited to open a series of shows for Janis Joplin and Jimi Hendrix at San Francisco's Fillmore Auditorium, which solidified his reputation with the rock audience.

King's popularity remained strong until the late 1970s, which was an especially difficult time for blues, as arena rock captured the commercial airwaves and disco claimed clubs that had patronized live music. However, thanks to an association he made with a young guitarist and fan named Stevie Ray Vaughan at the Austin, Texas club Armadillo World Headquarters, King would again experience something of a renaissance. Vaughan continually sang King's praises after his own ascent to blues and rock stardom in the early 1980s, and invited King to open many important shows. In 1983 they appeared together on Hamilton, Ontario television station CHCH. The ensuing jam and conversation eventually became the CD *Albert King With Stevie Ray Vaughan* (1999).

Although King never regained the level of commercial success he'd achieved with Stax in the 1960s, he toured regularly, playing clubs and blues festivals until he suffered a fatal heart attack in Memphis on 21 December 1992. His body lies beneath a large tombstone at the Paradise Gardens Cemetery in Edmonson, Arkansas bearing a bronze plaque with the epitaph 'I'll play the blues for you'.

King, still brandishing a trademark Gibson Flying V guitar, performs at the Hammersmith Odeon, London in 1983.

Key Artist: B.B. King

When the great Mississippi musician Riley King left the cotton fields to seek his fortune in Memphis in 1946, he had $2.50 in his pocket and a battered guitar in his hand. Today, his name is synonymous with the blues.

King is probably the most influential guitarist of the past 50 years, with a lush, sustained tone and singing vibrato that has had a vast impact on generations of players across all genres. The soaring phrases of his warm, Delta-accented voice cut right to the emotional core of the blues. Yet his ascendance to the zenith of the blues world has never altered his friendly, downhome nature.

'Well B.B. was like a hero. You listen to the way that band swings on Live At The Regal, it's just like a steam roller.'

Mick Fleetwood

King was born on a plantation near Indianola on 16 September 1925. He had a difficult childhood, with the intimidations of Jim Crow compounded by his mother's death when he was 10 years old. King was already playing gospel when he left for Memphis to stay for a time with his cousin, bluesman Bukka White. With his bold voice and charisma, and a distinctive guitar style influenced by Lonnie Johnson and T-Bone Walker, King began to win talent shows. In 1948 he secured a daily 10-minute spot on radio station WDIA, which he used to sell patent medicines like Pepticon while also plugging his area gigs. King chose 'The Beale Street Blues Boy' as his radio moniker, which was then abbreviated to 'B.B.' for 'Blues Boy'. The next year he made his debut recordings for the local Bullet label, then signed with Los Angeles-based Modern Records. King's first hit was 'Three O'Clock Blues' (1951), still a staple of the nearly 200 shows he plays each year.

Dynamic guitarist B.B. King, perhaps the most influential blues artist of the post-war era.

I AM A
GUITAR
NAMED
LUCILLE
PLEASE
HANDLE
WITH CARE
THANKS

Playing the Chitlin Circuit

King spent most of the 1950s and 1960s expanding his touring base. Initially, he worked at roadhouses within a few hours of Memphis. At a show in Twist, Arkansas in December 1949, he nearly lost his life when he rushed into a burning club to rescue his Gibson L-30 guitar. From that day he has named each of his guitars 'Lucille', after the woman who allegedly started the fire.

When more hit records, including 'You Upset Me Baby' and 'Please Love Me', allowed King to demand $800 a show, he began touring widely in the South. At first he was supported by Memphis bandleader Bill Harvey's group, travelling in a Cadillac and two station wagons to the small theatres and auditoriums where the New York City-based booking agency Universal Attractions secured him shows. In 1955, King assembled his own B.B. King Orchestra and got a loan for his first bus – a used Aero that he dubbed 'Big Red'. His touring route began to include northern African-American population centres, such as Chicago, Los Angeles and Harlem.

King cut many of his finest numbers during this period, 'Sweet Sixteen', 'Rock Me Baby' and 'How Blue Can You Get' among them. The influence of Louis Jordan, another of King's musical heroes, can be heard on many of these sides. In 1962 he switched to ABC-Paramount Records and made the concert album *Live At The Regal* (1964), recorded in a Chicago theatre before a wildly enthusiastic crowd. Although most white fans were listening to acoustic blues at the time, a new generation of musicians began to sing his praises. Eric Clapton, Mike Bloomfield, Jimi Hendrix and Johnny Winter helped King to reach the rock audience. His star rose, and then soared when the song that would become his signature, 'The Thrill Is Gone', hit number 15 on the American pop charts in January 1970.

Recognition is Achieved

Since then King has been the blues' top traditional performer, recording several excellent albums including *Indianola Mississippi Seeds* (1970), *Live In Cook County Jail* (1971) and *Now Appearing At Ole Miss* (1980). He made his home in Las Vegas, which remains his base, but graduated to international touring, playing dozens of countries. King was inducted into the Blues Foundation's Hall Of Fame in 1984 and the Rock And Roll Hall Of Fame in 1987. He also received a Grammy Award for Lifetime Achievement that year. In 1989 he recorded the smash 'When Loves Comes To Town' with U2, which introduced King to a new generation of rock fans.

King in London with his trusty guitar, Lucille.

A-Z of Artists

The Animals (Vocal/instrumental group, 1962–68)

This R&B-influenced UK rock group from Newcastle comprised powerful blues singer Eric Burdon (vocals), Hilton Valentine (guitar), Chas Chandler (bass), Alan Price (keyboards) and John Steel (drums). They backed visiting US bluesmen before releasing their US and UK number-one hit 'House Of The Rising Sun' in 1964. A string of blues- and R&B-influenced smashes followed. After the band split, Chandler went on to manage Jimi Hendrix while Burdon recorded with War and Night Shift.

Mike Bloomfield (Guitar, vocals, 1943–81)

Bloomfield apprenticed in Chicago with legends such as Muddy Waters and Howlin' Wolf, as well as among his peers Paul Butterfield, Charlie Musselwhite and Elvin Bishop. He played with the Paul Butterfield Blues Band, Bob Dylan and organist Al Kooper, helped to form Electric Flag and briefly played in KGB. From the late 1970s, he made virtuoso, instructive recordings until his death in 1981.

The Blues Project (Vocal/instrumental group, 1965–71)

The Blues Project was formed around respected session musicians Tommy Flanders (vocals), Danny Kalb (guitar), Steve Katz (guitar, vocals), Al Kooper (organ, vocals), Andy Kulberg (bass, flute) and Roy Blumenfeld (drums). This experimental band quickly rose to the apex of the New York City music scene. They recorded three albums, including the excellent debut *Live At The Café Au Go Go* (1966), before Kooper and Katz departed to form Blood, Sweat & Tears.

Key Tracks

'House Of The Rising Sun' The Animals
'Don't Let Me Be Misunderstood' The Animals
'East-West' Mike Bloomfield
'Two Trains Running' The Blues Project
'All These Blues' Paul Butterfield Blues Band

Paul Butterfield Blues Band (Vocal/instrumental group, 1963–67)

Harmonica player and singer Butterfield conditioned his band – Jerome Arnold (bass), Elvin Bishop and Mike Bloomfield (guitars), Sam Lay (drums, vocals) and Mark Naftalin (keyboards) – in black Chicago clubs. They backed Dylan's electric debut at the 1965 Newport Folk Festival and helped to usher blues into the psychedelic era. After the departure of Bloomfield, Butterfield changed his sound for *The Resurrection Of Pigboy Crabshaw* (1967), considered to be the band's last blues album.

The Animals' albums were largely hard R&B, lacking the pop of their hit singles.

mono
Columbia
EMI
– THE GREATEST RECORDING ORGANISATION IN THE WORLD
the animals

A-Z of Artists

Canned Heat (Vocal/instrumental group, 1966–present)

Comprising Bob Hite (vocals, harmonica), Al Wilson (guitar, harmonica, vocals), Henry Vestine (guitar), Larry Taylor (bass) and Fito De La Perra (drums), this Los Angeles band's heyday was between 1966–70, when covers of the Memphis Jug Band's 'On The Road Again' and Henry Thomas's 'Goin' Up The Country' propelled them up the charts. A teaming with John Lee Hooker, *Hooker 'N Heat* (1971), is a highlight in a long slide to the oldies circuit, which began with the fatal overdose of Wilson in 1970 and included the death of Hite in 1981.

Clifton Chenier (Accordion, vocals, 1925–87)

This Opelousas, Louisiana native cut his teeth on French dance tunes flavoured by Creole blues, as played by his musical forebear Amédée Ardoin. Chenier invented the zydeco style by adding elements of R&B, country and rock'n'roll, combined with a swinging beat. He enjoyed a string of hit singles, including his career-making 1955 US hit 'Eh, Petit Fille'. Chenier's son C.J. joined his band in 1978, and today C.J. carries on his father's musical tradition, updated with a twist of funk. Clifton's blues guitarist cousin Roscoe Chenier also regularly tours.

Albert Collins (Guitar, vocals, 1932–93)

Collins's highly original and bold, chiselled tone earned the Texan his nickname 'The Iceman'. The moniker was abetted by a string of chilly-themed, early 1960s instrumental hits that incorporated R&B rhythms, including the million-selling 'Frosty', 'Sno Cone' and 'Thaw Out'. Although his cousin was Lightnin' Hopkins, Collins's agressive playing style was primarily influenced by T-Bone Walker and Gatemouth Brown.

'When I see him I thank God I don't play guitar.'

Kim Wilson

He crossed over to the mainstream in the late 1960s, when he moved to California and was adopted by San Francisco's psychedelic rock scene. Nonetheless, he achieved his greatest popularity after signing with Alligator Records in 1978, playing the Montreux Jazz Festival and winning a Grammy for 1985's *Showdown!*. Collins was still among the top attractions in blues when he died from cancer in 1993.

Los Angeles band Canned Heat covered a selection of 1920s and 1930s blues tracks.

A-Z of Artists

Cream (Vocal/instrumental group, 1966–68)

In 1966, Eric Clapton (guitar) joined Jack Bruce (bass, vocals, harmonica) and Ginger Baker (drums) to form Cream, the first rock supergroup. These virtuosos fused blues, rock and jazz-like improvisation into a sound that became so popular it altered modern blues from a primarily vocal style into a music dominated by the electric guitar. Their albums *Fresh Cream* (1966), *Disraeli Gears* (1967) and *Wheels Of Fire* (1968) remain dramatic examples of modern blues reinterpretation.

Snooks Eaglin (Guitar, vocals, b. 1936)

Glaucoma and a brain tumour left Eaglin blind at the age of 19 months, but his unorthodox fingerpicking style and a sensibility based on the Crescent City's Caribbean rhythms made him the king of New Orleans guitar. He first performed gospel in churches, before turning to blues and recording his debut album, *New Orleans Street Singer* (1959). Eaglin's music became more sophisticated through associations with Dave Bartholomew and Professor Longhair, and he remains a vital performer.

Fleetwood Mac (Vocal/instrumental group, 1968–present)

Many fans who love Fleetwood Mac's string of 1970s hits are unaware of their earlier blues explorations. The band came into being when guitarist Peter Green, drummer Mick Fleetwood and bassist John McVie broke away from John Mayall's Bluesbreakers. In 1968, with Jeremy Spencer on second guitar, Fleetwood Mac debuted on Blue Horizon. A third guitarist, Danny Kirwan, joined in time for the band to gig in Chicago with Willie Dixon and Otis Spann. Their original tunes and covers of blues classics (e.g. 'I Need Your Love So Bad') testified to the band's aptitude.

In 1970, after the release of the album *Then Play On*, Green was replaced by keyboardist Christine Perfect. The blues content of Fleetwood Mac's music dwindled as they began to lean towards mainstream rock. By the time the band achieved superstar status in 1975, their blues days were over. The band has survived several personnel changes and breakups, remaining a popular concert draw.

Key Tracks

'I Feel Free' Cream
'White Room' Cream
'That's All Right' Snooks Eaglin
'Albatross' Fleetwood Mac
'Man Of The World' Fleetwood Mac

Guitarist Peter Green (centre) gave Fleetwood Mac a blues sound in the band's early days.

A-Z of Artists

John Hammond Jr. (Guitar, harmonica, vocals, b. 1942)

The son of A&R genius John Hammond, this New York City native left home at the age of 19 to perform professionally. He remains primarily an acoustic player, in the tradition of the classic Delta musicians. Hammond cut a fine series of LPs during 1964–76, encapsulated on 2000's *Best Of The Vanguard Years*. He notably joined Mike Bloomfield and Dr John for *Triumvirate* (1973).

Slim Harpo (Harmonica, guitar, vocals, 1924–70)

Born James Moore in Lobdell, Louisiana, Harpo developed an upbeat style playing juke joints and parties before signing to Excello Records in 1955, where he was instrumental in defining the label's 'swamp-blues' sound. He had a profound influence on 1960s rockers including Van Morrison, the Kinks and the Rolling Stones, who covered Harpo's 'I'm A King Bee' and 'Shake Your Hips'. Harpo died from a heart attack in Baton Rouge, Louisiana.

'Jimi to me was one of the great explorers if you will of the so-called Delta blues....'

B.B. King

Jimi Hendrix (Guitar, vocals, 1942–70)

This left-handed Seattle, Washington native taught himself to play by flipping over a $5 acoustic guitar and copying licks from blues, R&B and rock'n'roll records. Hendrix apprenticed on the R&B circuit, backing up Little Richard among others, and mastered techniques from the stuttering ninth chords of James Brown sideman Jimmy Nolen to the epic string-bending of Albert King. His solo career ignited when he was discovered at Greenwich Village's Café Wha? by Animals bassist Chas Chandler, who became his manager and moved Hendrix to London. The Jimi Hendrix Experience was formed and the group's debut LP *Are You Experienced?* (1967) became an international smash, fortified by Hendrix's flamboyant performing style. Throughout Hendrix's three brief years as an international pop star, his music became increasingly experimental, but even his incendiary version of the 'Star-Spangled Banner', recorded live at Woodstock and full of feedback explosions, showed his unswerving devotion to blues tonality.

Slim Harpo, whose 'I'm A King Bee' was covered by the Rolling Stones on their debut album.

A-Z of Artists

Janis Joplin (Vocals, 1943–70)

Influenced by Bessie Smith, Joplin became a rock star while in San Francisco's Big Brother & the Holding Company, and enjoyed a meteoric solo career before her untimely death from a heroin overdose. Nonetheless, she was perhaps the most commanding female blues singer of the modern era. Joplin's raw emotional expression and fiery presence overruled complaints about her straying intonation both in concert and on albums like Big Brother's *Cheap Thrills* (1968) and *Pearl* (1971).

Freddie King (Guitar, vocals, 1934–76)

Freddie King was born in Gilmer, Texas and learned guitar from his mother at age six. He moved to Chicago in 1950, earning a reputation with his gritty approach. His 1950s recordings for the Cobra label were not released, but King made his mark after signing with Cincinnati's Federal/King Records in 1960. His Federal/King sides included the oft-covered instrumentals 'Hideaway' and 'San-Ho-Zay', as well as 'Have You Ever Loved A Woman', subsequently made famous by Derek & the Dominos. Waning interest in blues left him without a contract in 1965, but King was soon accepted by white rock audiences. He played clubs and festivals and recorded for major labels until his heart failed after a Dallas concert.

Key Tracks

'Ball And Chain' Janis Joplin
'Hideaway' Freddie King
'How Long Blues' Alexis Korner's Blues Incorporated

Alexis Korner's Blues Incorporated (Vocal/instrumental group, 1962–67)

Alexis Korner (guitar, piano, vocals), born in Paris in 1928, was considered to be the father of electric British blues. When he and Cyril Davies (harmonica, vocals) formed Blues Incorporated in 1962 with Dick Heckstall-Smith (saxophone), Andy Hoogenboom (bass), Ken Scott (piano) and Charlie Watts (drums), their amplified line-up met with resistance. So Korner and Davies opened their own venue, the Ealing Rhythm & Blues Club. Jack Bruce and Ginger Baker replaced Hoogenboom and Watts, and the group began a residency at the Marquee Club. Their debut, the live *R&B From The Marquee* (1962), was the first British blues album. Yet commercial success evaded Korner, as the Rolling Stones, Bluesbreakers and others ascended. Korner remained musically active until his deathin 1984.

Guitarist and blues promoter Alexis Korner (right) with harmonica player Cyril Davies and drummer Charlie Watts (seated behind) in Blues Incorporated.

A-Z of Artists

Sam Lay (Drums, vocals, b. 1935)

Shuffle master Lay was an important figure in the racial integration of 1960s blues. He was born in Birmingham, Alabama and moved to Chicago, where he played with Little Walter, Howlin' Wolf and other Chess Records artists. He joined the Paul Butterfield Blues Band for its first two albums and played on Bob Dylan's *Highway 61 Revisited* as well as Dylan's electric debut at Newport in 1965. Lay leads his own band today and has also recently recorded with the Siegel-Schwall Band.

Sammy Lawhorn (Guitar, 1935–90)

Respected sideman Lawhorn began a nine-year stint with Muddy Waters' band in 1956 after working with harmonica players Sonny Boy Williamson II and Willie Cobbs, among others. Waters fired the Little Rock, Arkansas native in 1973 for excessive drinking. By then his razor-edged tone and imaginative soloing had already left an indelible mark on the blues. Lawhorn subsequently played on sides by James Cotton, Junior Wells and Koko Taylor.

Key Tracks

'I Get Evil' Sam Lay
'You Don't Love Me' Sammy Lawhorn
'If Walls Could Talk' Little Milton
'Feel So Bad' Little Milton
'Steady Rolling Man' Robert Lockwood Jr.

Little Milton (Guitar, vocals, 1934–2005)

Born in Inverness, Mississippi, the country music Milton Campbell heard in radio broadcasts from the Grand Ole Opry shaped his soulful sound as much as gospel and blues. After regional success, he signed to Checker in 1961 and cut the classics 'If Walls Could Talk', 'Feel So Bad' and 'Grits Ain't Groceries', among others. He was a major artist on the chitlin circuit, recording for Jackson, Mississippi's Malaco Records.

Robert Lockwood Jr. (Guitar, harmonica, vocals, 1915–2006)

This curmudgeonly survivor is thought to be the only musician given lessons by Robert Johnson. But Lockwood, who was raised in Helena, Arkansas, also assimilated jazz chords and swinging rhythms to become one of the most sophisticated guitarists to emerge from the Delta. After decades as a sideman and songwriter, Lockwood resided in Cleveland, Ohio, where until his death in 2006 he led a big band, and travelled the world playing solo in Johnson's style.

Highway 61 Revisited, *Dylan's sixth studio effort and most influential album, featured the drumming talents of Sam Lay.*

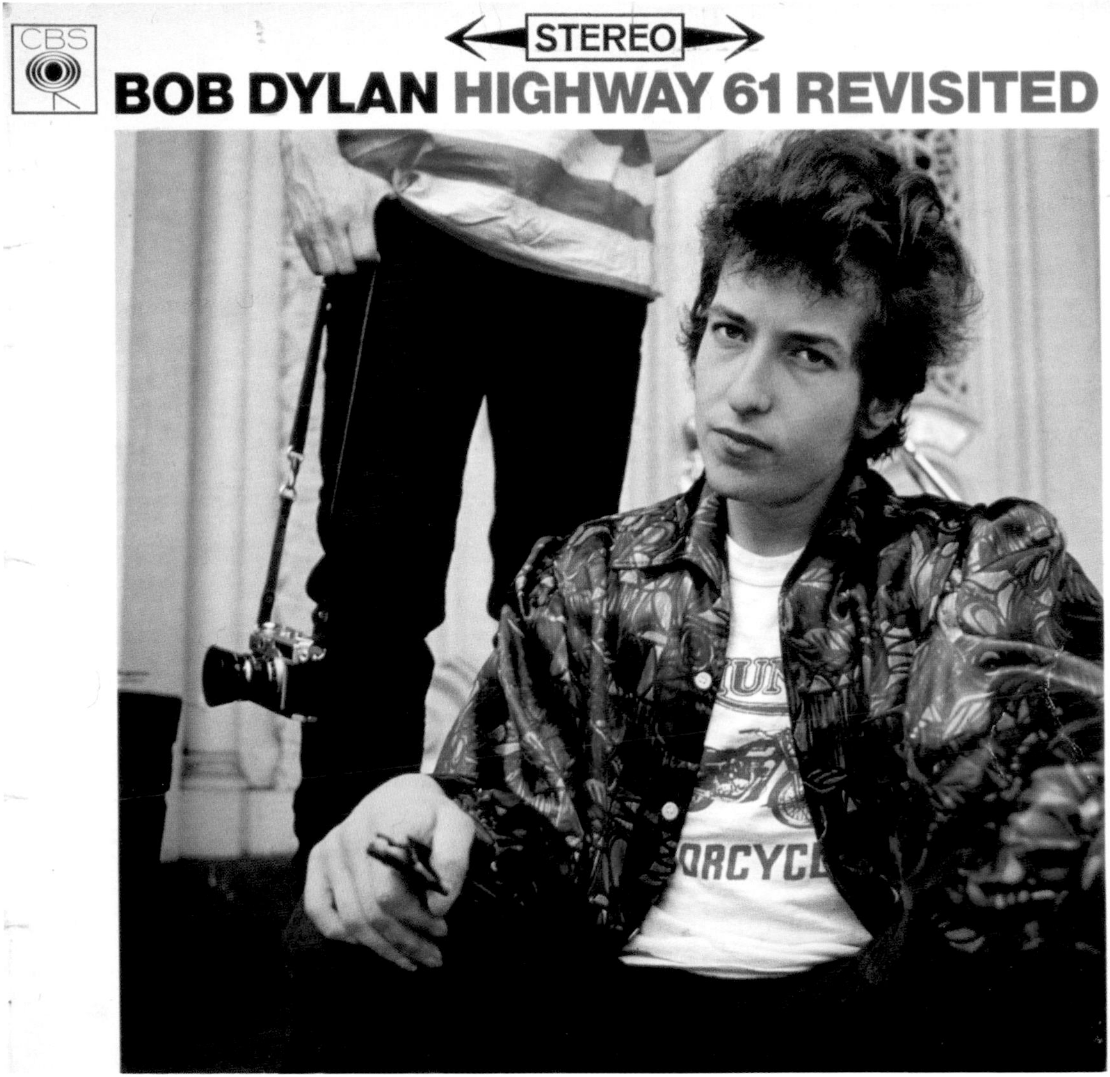
CBS
STEREO
BOB DYLAN HIGHWAY 61 REVISITED

A-Z of Artists

Magic Sam (Guitar, vocals, 1937–69)

Along with peers Otis Rush and Buddy Guy, Mississippi native Samuel Maghett pioneered the ghetto-born mix of soul singing and guitar pyrotechnics that defined Chicago's west side sound. 'Easy Baby' and 'All Your Love', cut for Cobra in the 1950s, are his signature tunes, but his Delmark LP *West Side Soul* (1967) is a classic example of raw, open-hearted emotional expression. He died unexpectedly of a heart attack just as his career was gaining momentum.

John Mayall's Bluesbreakers (Vocal/instrumental group, 1963–present)

Talented bandleader John Mayall (vocals, piano, organ, harmonica), born in Macclesfield, Cheshire in 1933, is largely responsible for igniting the popularity of British blues as well as the careers of famed guitarists Eric Clapton, Peter Green and Mick Taylor. Mayall's 1966 debut album *Blues Breakers* established the reputation of Clapton and also featured John McVie (bass) and Hughie Flint (drums). The album reached number six on the UK charts. It remains the seminal British electric blues album and began a streak of Bluesbreakers classics, including *A Hard Road* (with Green, 1967) and *Crusade* (with Taylor, 1967). Mayall began a parallel solo career with the underrated *The Blues Alone* (1968) that peaked the next year, following his relocation to California. He continues to perform with a version of his Bluesbreakers and remains one of the few white blues performers whose songwriting equals that of his heroes Muddy Waters and J.B. Lenoir.

Key Tracks

'Easy Baby' Magic Sam
'All Your Love' Magic Sam
'Room To Move' John Mayall's Bluesbreakers
'Hard Road' John Mayall's Bluesbreakers
'Pinetop's Boogie Woogie' Pinetop Perkins

Pinetop Perkins (Piano, guitar, b. 1913)

Belzoni, Mississippi's Perkins performed throughout the Delta until 1949, when he relocated to Chicago to play with Robert Nighthawk and Earl Hooker through the 1950s. In 1969 he replaced Otis Spann in Muddy Waters' band. Perkins stayed until 1980, when he, Calvin Jones (bass), Jerry Portnoy (harmonica) and Willie Smith (drums) left Waters to form the Legendary Blues Band. Perkins still works as a solo artist and with the Muddy Waters Tribute Band.

Blues Breakers, the debut album from John Mayall's band, featured the stunning guitar work of Eric Clapton and put British blues on the musical map.

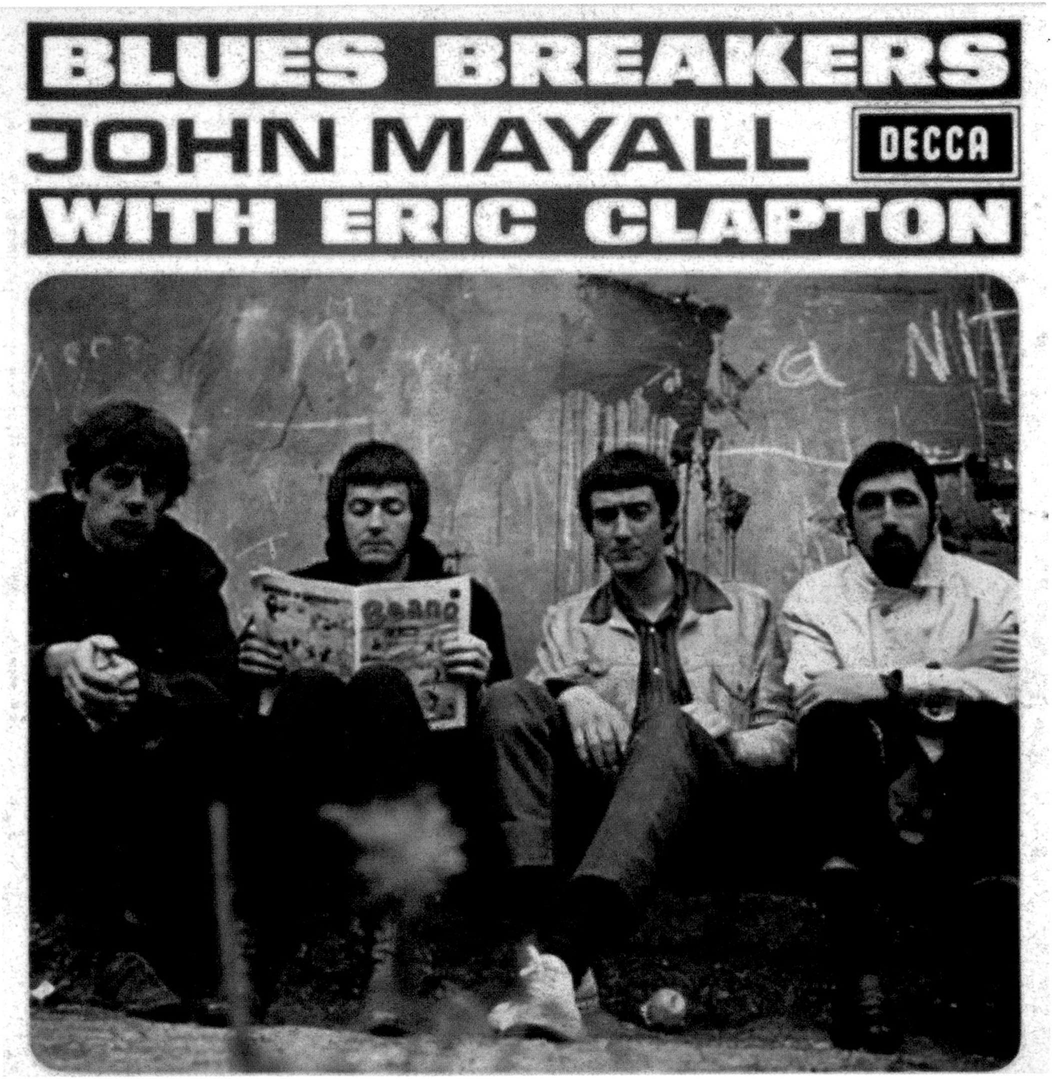
BLUES BREAKERS
JOHN MAYALL
DECCA
WITH ERIC CLAPTON

A-Z of Artists

Yank Rachell (Mandolin, guitar, harmonica, violin, vocals, 1910–97)

Rachell and fellow Brownsville, Tennessee musicians Sleepy John Estes and Hammie Nixon played throughout the mid-South in the 1920s, eventually relocating to Memphis. Rachell and Estes partnered with pianist Jab Jones, recording for Victor as the Three J's Jug Band. During the 1930s and 1940s, Rachell played with John Lee 'Sonny Boy' Williamson. In 1962 he reunited with Estes and Nixon, recording and touring as Yank Rachell's Tennessee Jug-Busters on Chicago's Delmark label.

Rolling Stones (Vocal/instrumental group, 1962–present)

One of the most successful bands of all time, the Rolling Stones' original line-up comprised Mick Jagger (vocals, harmonica), Brian Jones and Keith Richards (guitars), Bill Wyman (bass) and Charlie Watts (drums). Named after a Muddy Waters song, the band were heavily influenced by blues and R&B and on their early albums recorded many cover versions that helped to bring blues music to a wider audience, particularly in the UK. Although the Stones' self-penned material also showed soul, pop and psychedelic influences, the blues were never far away and the band released the heavily blues-influenced *Beggars Banquet* in 1968.

Key Tracks

'My Baby's Gone' Yank Rachell
'Moonshine Whiskey' Yank Rachell
'Satisfaction' The Rolling Stones
'I Can't Quit You Baby' Otis Rush

Following the loss of Jones, who drowned in 1969, and the addition of Mick Taylor, from John Mayall's Bluesbreakers, the Stones released three more blues rock masterpieces: *Let it Bleed* (1969), *Sticky Fingers* (1971) and *Exile On Main Street* (1972). Now minus Wyman and Taylor, and with Ronnie Wood on guitar, the Stones continue to roll.

Otis Rush (Guitar, vocals, b. 1934)

Rush, who was born in Philadelphia, Mississippi, was – along with Buddy Guy and Magic Sam – part of the defining trinity of Chicago's west side sound. His 1950s Cobra Records singles 'All Your Love (I Miss Loving)' and 'I Can't Quit You Baby' became standards. Rush is undoubtedly a genius, with a big soulful voice and an unpredictable command of the guitar, but music-business troubles and his own erratic personality have impeded his career.

Keith Richards (far right) of the Rolling Stones was among the many to be influenced by the 1961 release of Robert Johnson's King Of The Delta Blues.

A-Z of Artists

Siegel-Schwall Band (Vocal/instrumental group, 1964–present)

College mates Corky Siegel (harmonica, piano) and Jim Schwall (guitar) started out as a duo. They softened the electric blues they heard in Chicago with acoustic guitar and folk-music leanings. They expanded – adding Jos Davidson (bass, vocals) and Russ Chadwick (drums) – and made their debut album for the Vanguard label in 1966. They disbanded in 1974, but reformed in 1988 and released the live *Siegel-Schwall Reunion Concert*.

Otis Spann (Piano, vocals, 1930–70)

The finest post-war blues pianist, Spann learned to play at churches and parties around his Jackson, Mississippi birthplace. From 1952 until his death, he was house keyboardist at Chess Records, recording with Muddy Waters, Bo Diddley, Sonny Boy Willliamson, Howlin' Wolf, Little Walter and others. Although Spann made a clutch of fine solo recordings, including the first Candid release, *Otis Spann Is The Blues* (1960) and duets with Robert Lockwood, he is best known as Waters' music director.

Taj Mahal (Guitar, banjo, bass, harmonica, mandolin, piano, vocals, b. 1942)

Henry Saint Clair Fredericks' concept of the blues was formed partly by his West Indian father's diverse record collection. Since Taj Mahal's eponymous debut in 1967, followed in 1968 by a role in *The Rolling Stones' Rock And Roll Circus*, he has challenged purists by employing the sounds and beats of Caribbean, African, Latin and American folk styles. He remains a tireless performer and champion of earlier artists.

Key Tracks

'I Like It Where We Walked' Siegel-Schwall Band
'Got My Mojo Working' Otis Spann
'Hungry Country Girl' Otis Spann
'Corinna' Taj Mahal
'Goin' Home' Ten Years After

Ten Years After (Vocal/instrumental group, 1967–present)

This UK rock band from Nottingham, comprising Chick Churchill (keyboards), Alvin Lee (guitar, vocals), Ric Lee (drums) and Leo Lyons (bass), emerged as a vehicle for Alvin Lee's speed-demon playing. Their sound was most notably captured on the Woodstock soundtrack in an 11-minute version of 'Goin' Home'. The classic line-up lasted until 1975, when Alvin Lee left, however the band reformed in 1989.

Otis Spann, house pianist for Chess Records, pictured at London's 100 Club, 1969.

A-Z of Artists

Johnny 'Guitar' Watson (Guitar, piano, vocals, 1935–96)

The self-proclaimed 'Gangster of Love', Watson learned piano from his father in Houston, Texas but became known for his terse, stinging guitar, which influenced Frank Zappa and has been sampled by rappers. Etta James patterned her early singing after Watson's declarative vocals, best immortalized along with his wicked instrumental prowess on King and Federal singles from 1953 to 1963, including 'Motorhead Baby' and 'Space Guitar'. He suffered a fatal heart attack onstage in Japan.

Junior Wells (Harmonica, vocals, 1934–98)

Amos Blackmore grew up in west Memphis, Arkansas under the sway of Sonny Boy Williamson II and began recording as a teenager in Chicago, playing with the innovative Four Aces before joining Muddy Waters' band. Wells created a personal style influenced by James Brown. In the mid-1960s he began a long association with guitarist Buddy Guy (who played on Wells's masterful 1965 debut LP *Hoodoo Man Blues*, Delmark Records), which lasted until Wells's death from cancer in 1998.

Key Tracks

'Motorhead Baby' Johnny Guitar Watson
'Space Guitar' Johnny Guitar Watson
'Hoodoo Man Blues' Junior Wells
'Lawdy! Lawdy!' Junior Wells
'For Your Love' The Yardbirds

Yardbirds (Vocal/instrumental group, 1963–68)

The Chicago blues-inspired Yardbirds, featuring Keith Relf (vocals, harmonica), Eric Clapton and Chris Dreja (guitars), Paul Samwell-Smith (bass) and Jim McCarty (drums), took over the Rolling Stones' residency at London's Crawdaddy Club and backed Sonny Boy Williamson II on tour in 1963. Clapton left after the release of their debut album in 1963 and was replaced by Jeff Beck; a succession of pop hits followed. Guitarist Jimmy Page joined in 1966 and after Beck departed, Page and Dreja formed the New Yardbirds (an ensemble which would eventually develop into Led Zeppelin). A version of the Yardbirds reformed after their 1992 induction into the Rock And Roll Hall Of Fame and continues to tour.

Johnny 'Guitar' Watson, whose stinging guitar style complemented his declarative vocals.

The Seventies

Of the entire twentieth century, the 1970s were the years of catching one's breath. Superficially, the promise of the 1960s had faded or failed, the victim of wretched excess and just plain bad taste. America's war in Vietnam sputtered to an end, international relations elsewhere seemed to stalemate in détente and economically the world suffered from stagflation: exhaustion beset with mixed signals.

Blues also reached some sort of crossroads. Several of the music's elders were still active, but their best days were behind them and their appearances often amounted to little more than valedictory trots. North American and European blues festivals sought these veterans as if they were holy men, by their presences condoning the appropriation of their lifelong works. A younger wave of true bluesmen had emerged from Chicago's south side, but they did not gain much notoriety or respect. Meanwhile, however, the torch was kept alight in more mainstream musical circles by blues-influenced rock artists such as Led Zeppelin.

Key Artists

Allman Brothers Band
Dr John

Looking back, great music of the period is identifiable, but at the time such pop genres as progressive rock and disco seemed relatively content-free. The best blues and roots music existed beneath the radar, if not exactly underground. Part of the problem was media-related: FM radio programmed with imagination, but many recording companies had over-extended their investments without adequate gain. The mood was largely: May the 1970s end! What's next?

The early 1970s was a prosperous time for some black blues artists, who were booked on package tours such as the American Blues Legends, presented by Big Bear music.

Big Bear Music
Presents
AMERICAN BLUES
LEGENDS 73
HOMESICK JAMES
SNOOKY PRYOR
ASHBOARD WILLIE
OOGIE WOOGIE RED
LIGHTNIN´SLIM
HISPERING SMITH
UESDAY 20TH FEBRUARY
100 CLUB
OXFORD ST
LONDON
AMERICAN
BLUES LEGENDS
73

Crossing Over

In the 1970s, it could be said that the blues took a back seat to its own influence. The root sensibilities and typical three-chord structures of the blues could be detected in the music of hundreds of artists, yet musicians who could genuinely claim the blues as their own territory were all but obscured from the public eye.

The cross-pollination of blues and rock elements continued as the sounds of the British scene crossed the Atlantic Ocean to re-inspire Americans. The Rolling Stones, the Yardbirds, Cream, John Mayall's Bluesbreakers and a number of other British groups motivated younger artists like Johnny Winter (b. 1944), the Allman Brothers Band and ZZ Top to develop their own distinctive hybrids. Although Duane Allman and ZZ Top's Billy Gibbons had little in common when it came to guitar techniques, both ranked among the most popular, influential players of the time. By mid-decade, their blues-enriched sounds were hotly competing with disco on the American music market.

Across America, so many styles were formulated in so many regions that it was difficult to differentiate between them all. In Austin, Texas, while guitarist Jimmie Vaughan and the Fabulous Thunderbirds were starting down the road to stardom in 1974, little brother Stevie Ray Vaughan (1954–90) was putting together his first band. Around the same time, Roy Buchanan (1939–88) was rocking the house in Washington, DC, Johnny Copeland (1937–97) was club-hopping in New York City and down in New Orleans Dr John (b. 1940) blended traditional jazz, Creole music, blues and voodoo weirdness.

'The stuff they're doin' now – the disco and everything else – it's taken from the blues. The music they call "soul music", you know, it's the blues. So disco is not soul; rock'n'roll is not soul. The blues is soul.'

John Lee Hooker

The west coast of the US boasted an innovative recording-studio blues community. In Los Angeles Ry Cooder (b. 1947) and Taj Mahal (b. 1940), who had played together in the Rising Sons, represented the global side of things as they tied together diverse threads of the blues, jazz, country, gospel and African and Hawaiian music. Elsewhere in town, a young guitarist and singer named Bonnie Raitt (b. 1949) was turning heads with her slide abilities.

Slide guitarist Ry Cooder was a key figure on the 1970s Los Angeles blues scene; his music reflected influences from other cultures, including Africa and Hawaii.

Hard Times

Despite this resurgence of interest in the idea of the blues, many influential players found themselves pushed out of the marketplace altogether and the musicians who inspired the British Invasion now found themselves unable to make a living.

At the start of the decade, the Rolling Stones had toured with Buddy Guy (b. 1936), Junior Wells (1934–98) and Bonnie Raitt, temporarily expanding the blues audience. But by 1979, many of their fans were unaware of the primal southern roots of the Stones' beloved music. A number of desperate blues artists retreated into drug and alcohol abuse, further complicating their declines in popularity.

A few stalwarts kept their careers afloat. B.B. King (b. 1925) seemed to be an unstoppable force in the 1970s: he kicked off the decade with the tremendous hit 'The Thrill Is Gone', collaborated several times with Bobby 'Blue' Bland (b. 1930), and released no fewer than 10 new records before the decade's end. Beloved worldwide and constantly busy, King was a beacon of hope that the bluesmen's stars would someday rise again. He has remained a pre-eminent blues musican into the twenty-first century, guesting with rock stars and appearing in commercials.

Muddy Waters (1915–83) was moderately active at the time, although it was not until Johnny Winter produced Waters' Hard Again in 1977 on Columbia Records that he reclaimed a sizeable portion of his prior high profile. Arthur 'Big Boy' Crudup (1905–74) – an R&B legend who had influenced Elvis Presley – and Albert King (1923–92) experienced rejuvenation in the early 1970s through music festivals and new recording opportunities. And, thanks to a contract with Leon Russell's Shelter label, Freddie King (1934–76) also kept relatively busy until his death in 1976. Howlin' Wolf had not performed much outside of a regular gig at Chicago's 1815 Club due to chronic health problems. His last performance was with B.B. King at the Chicago Amphitheatre in November 1975, two months before his death.

Popular Melody

B.B. King – 'The Thrill Is Gone' (1970)

Chicago's 1815 club, run by Eddie Shaw (centre, with Frank Weston and Mike Rowe), was an important blues venue in the 1970s.

EDDIE'S PLACE
The NEW
1815 Club
Home of the
BLUES
Budweiser
IN BOTTLES
EDDIE'S

The Rock Influence

Around the middle of the decade, some British artists veered away from the blues and headed deeper into mainstream rock. The phenomenon was not universal, as illustrated by the success of Eric Clapton, John Mayall and Rory Gallagher (1949–95), all three of whom stayed relatively faithful to the blues. But other influential British blues artists either faded away or irreversibly changed course.

Led Zeppelin was born from the ashes of the Yardbirds when guitarist Jimmy Page put together a 'ghost band' to honour the group's contracts. Its young fans loved the power of Page's sizzling guitar, Robert Plant's banshee voice, John Paul Jones's virtuoso bass licks and John Bonham's thunderous drums, but knew little about the blues covers in Led Zeppelin's set lists. As the band assumed the throne of heavy-metal monarchy, fewer of its songs drew from the blues.

Popular Melody

Led Zeppelin – 'In My Time Of Dying' (1975)

Rising Again

A number of promising enterprises arose to keep the blues flame flickering. *Living Blues*, one of the most purist magazines devoted to the music, published its first issue in 1970. It became the principal voice for blues artists. Also, in 1971, when producer Bruce Iglauer failed to get Delmark Records to sign Hound Dog Taylor (1917–75), he inaugurated his Alligator label specifically to document Taylor's music. Alligator was soon one of the most active blues imprints, issuing albums by artists including Albert Collins (1932–93) and Son Seals (1942–2004).

One of the greatest blessings to grace the blues came in 1977, when comedians Dan Aykroyd and John Belushi unveiled their Blues Brothers characters on TV's *Saturday Night Live*. The skit was intended to spoof white blues enthusiasts, but many in the show's audience missed the joke and fell in love with them. In 1980 their first feature film employed authentic blues and R&B artists as the Brothers' backing band and showcased performances by Aretha Franklin, Ray Charles (1930–2004), James Brown and Cab Calloway (1907–94), capturing the breadth of inspiration, influence and inherent entertainment imperatives of the blues. This ignited a widespread revival of interest in urban blues. The blues had survived its toughest decade, and its future was looking brighter.

Led Zeppelin's 1975 album Physical Graffiti *included some tracks that relied heavily on traditional blues songs, suggesting that the band never completely abandoned its blues roots.*

LED ZEPPELIN
P
H
Y
S
I
C
A
L
G
R
A
F
F
I
T
I

Key Artist: Allman Brothers Band

Few groups made as powerful an impression on American blues music in the early 1970s as the Allman Brothers Band. Its blend of blues, jazz, rock and country elements was a predominant sound on nascent FM radio and influenced countless bands that followed in their wake. The Allman Brothers Band have endured tragedies, periods of obscurity and personnel shifts to remain active in the new century.

Guitarist Duane Allman (1946–71) and his brother, organist/vocalist Gregg Allman (b. 1947), grew up in Daytona Beach, Florida. Their first band, the Escorts, aped the Rolling Stones and the Beatles. They moved further into hard blues and soul with the Allman Joys and the Hour Glass, the latter of which recorded two albums for Liberty Records. In the late 1960s Duane worked as a studio guitarist in Muscle Shoals, Alabama, the famed breeding ground of latter-day soul. He made his name backing King Curtis, Wilson Pickett and Aretha Franklin while framing his own approach to R&B, soul and blues. In 1969 manager Phil Walden urged Allman to put together a band of his own. He hired bassist Berry Oakley, guitarist Dickey Betts and selected two drummers: Butch Trucks and Jai Johanny Johanson, a.k.a. Jaimoe. A long jam session proved the concept's viability, and eventually Gregg Allman was brought in on vocals and organ.

'Writing a good instrumental is very fulfilling because you've transcended language and spoken to someone with a melody.'

Dickey Betts, Allman Brothers Band

The Allman Brothers Band initially toured Georgia and Florida to build upon its blues-rock template. It first recorded in 1969 for Walden's label, Capricorn. The album did not sell well at first but impressed many of those who did hear it. The Allmans settled in Macon, Georgia, where they worked more acoustic guitar and jazz flavourings into their sound. Duane Allman kept active as a sideman, working with Boz Scaggs, Otis Rush and Johnny Jenkins. He also teamed with Eric Clapton in Bonnie & Delaney, and later Derek & the Dominos.

Triumph and Tragedy

The group's fame spread on the strength of its second album, the hit tune 'Midnight Rider' and the powerful jam sessions that coloured their live concerts. While the musicians were capable of playing

Right: Gifted guitarist Duane Allman, who worked as a session musician and touring sideman in addition to his exquisite slide playing with the Allman Brothers Band.

in odd keys and time signatures, their music was still accessible and rock-based enough to maintain its popular momentum.

In March 1971 the band played a series of shows at the Fillmore East, which were documented on its third album. Polydor Records churned up momentum for the record, which turned Duane Allman into America's newest guitar hero. But shortly after *At Fillmore East* was certified gold in October, Duane was killed in a motorcycle accident. Almost exactly one year later, following the success of the follow-up recording, *Eat A Peach*, Berry Oakley also died in a motorcycle crash. Rather than dissolve the group, Gregg Allman and Dickey Betts opted to press on. The first two albums were reissued as a double-LP set, and the next record moved away from the blues underpinnings for a more country-tinged flavour. 'Ramblin' Man' became another huge hit for the band.

Around 1974 the group started to fall apart. Gregg Allman's tumultuous marriage to rock singer Cher, his solo career and problems with substance abuse made it hard for the band to stay consistent. Two years later the Allman Brothers Band broke up, with Betts going solo and the other members forming Sea Level. In 1978, cleaned up and ready to roll, Allman reformed the band but faced the spectre of irrelevance as New Wave and punk had staked their claims to rock radio. The band struggled through the 1980s, issuing moderate-selling albums that skirted its prior glory. In 1989 the band reinvented itself again by bringing in guitarist Warren Haynes and bassist Allen Woody, whose skills were well beyond anything the Allmans had presented in years. The next album, *Seven Turns* (1990), proved that the band's rock-blues-country fusion was still viable 30 years on. The Allman Brothers Band soon returned to prominence, selling out arenas and concert halls as it has continued to do into the twenty-first century.

Next Page: The Allman Brothers Band, whose unique blend of blues and other musical styles began to dominate the 1970s American blues scene.

Key Artist: Dr John

Malcolm John 'Mac' Rebennack Jr., a.k.a. 'Dr John the Night Tripper', was born in New Orleans in November 1940. The singer and pianist began his professional career while he was still a teenager. He backed local favourites including Joe Tex and Professor Longhair on guitar and keyboards, produced and arranged sessions at Cosmio Studio, also frequented by Allen Toussaint, and issued a few singles of his own as Mac Rebennack. A hand injury caused him to abandon the guitar in the mid-1960s, and soon he migrated to Los Angeles for studio work.

The Dr John persona emerged in the late 1960s, as Rebennack began to formulate his 'voodoo music', a unique fusion of blues, jazz, R&B and rock elements. His rough, drawling voice, combined with horn licks, deep blues, Mardi Gras funk and electric psychedelia, gave Dr John an instantly recognizable sound. In live performances he draped himself and the stage with coloured beads, feathers, furs and exotic props, conducting a religious/musical ritual of sorts.

'When I first came up, the blues I was playing was almost bebop orientated – very hip.... Now it's going back beyond that to some kind of roots....'

Dr John

His stage theatrics were an amazing blend of authentic voodoo tradition and modern New Orleans hokum, perfectly complementing his otherworldly music; this was exemplified by 'I Walk On Gilded Splinters' and the title track of his debut album *Gris Gris* (1968), which Dr John had recorded during studio time left over from a Sonny and Cher session on which he had worked. This album and its follow-up, *Babylon* (1969), were especially heavy on voodoo symbolism and social commentary, often with the sounds layered so densely that the lyrics were hard to discern. In tuneful, often swinging, sometimes sultry pieces, he drew from the standard New Orleans repertoire of jazz, Cajun, Creole and R&B tunes. He quickly integrated the electric piano and keyboards into his signature sound and challenged his generation of guitarists with the mock-heroic 'Lonesome Guitar Strangler'. His approach to music was so unusual and fresh that he built a small but loyal cult following. In the meantime, he also worked in support of artists such as Canned Heat, Jackie DeShannon, B.B. King, Buddy Guy, Albert Collins and John Sebastian.

Right: A youthful Dr John back when he was still known as Mac Rebennack.

In the Right Place

In 1972, on *Dr John's Gumbo*, he garnered more attention by interpreting New Orleans standards, including 'Iko Iko' and 'Junko Partner', which had wider public appeal than his prior psychedelic fusions. The following year he broke out on to the mass market with an unlikely hit; on 'Right Place, Wrong Time', Dr John was backed by the Meters, New Orleans' premier funk and soul band. The public ate up the infectious rhythms and his rasping voice, placing the tune high on the charts. It was the most substantial hit of his career and did well enough to seal his legacy.

He attempted to duplicate the winning formula without success on his next few recordings, and even tried a venture into disco. He made an appearance on the Band's *Last Waltz* show in 1977, but a collaboration with guitarists Mike Bloomfield and John Hammond did not draw much attention. He rose to prominence again in 1981 with an acclaimed solo acoustic album that showed off his authentic New Orleans piano style. His debt to pianists such as Professor Longhair and Huey 'Piano' Smith became clearer once the voodoo trappings were removed.

Other Zones

More experiments followed for Dr John: a recording of jazz and pop standards, then another jump into New Orleans history, interpretations of Duke Ellington and several career retrospectives. His more innovative pursuits were followed by rote-sounding returns to his comfort zone, giving Dr John a rather patchy discography during this period. In 1990 Dr John dug deeper into jazz in the trio Bluesiana Triangle, with saxophonist David 'Fathead' Newman and bebop drummer Art Blakey. At his most ambitious, Dr John collaborated with members of alternative rock bands like Portishead, Squeeze, Primal Scream and Supergrass, upon whom his murky early recordings had been a surprising influence. In 2000 he signed with Blue Note Records and founded his own reissue label, Skinji Brim. His 2001 album, *Creole Moon*, was well-received and saw him continuing to experiment with a melange of musical styles, including jazz, blues and funk.

Next Page: Eccentric New Orleans bluesman Dr John (far left) with his band at London's Roundhouse.

A-Z of Artists

Luther Allison (Guitar, vocals, 1939–97)

Luther Allison was an impressive electric bluesman whose guitar playing at times recalled Jimi Hendrix. After his brother taught him basic guitar techniques, Allison backed artists such as Muddy Waters, Jimmy Dawkins and Howlin' Wolf in Chicago clubs. Early records on Delmark and triumph at the Ann Arbor Festival led to Allison signing with Motown. He lived in France from 1984–94 and died of cancer in the midst of a strong comeback. His son Bernard carries on the family tradition.

Carey Bell (Harmonica, vocals, b. 1936)

Carey Bell is one of Chicago's most distinctive harmonica players. He began playing with pianist Lovie Lee in Mississippi at the age of 13 and moved to Chicago at 20. Sonny Boy Williamson II and Little Walter were key influences on his harmonica style, while tenures with Willie Dixon and Muddy Waters increased his profile in the business. Bell has led over a dozen sessions since his debut in 1969.

Roy Buchanan (Guitar, vocals, 1939–88)

Roy Buchanan's use of harmonics and his melodic sense were incomparable. Raised on gospel and R&B, he performed with Johnny Otis, Johnny 'Guitar' Watson and Ronnie Hawkins' Hawks as a young man. A 1971 PBS documentary, *The Best Unknown Guitarist In The World*, together with adulation from the likes of John Lennon and Eric Clapton, kick-started Buchanan's rise. He retired in frustration for several years but returned in 1985. Sadly, Buchanan committed suicide while jailed for public drunkenness.

'J.J. Cale was so great at making records, I think he really is one of the giants and such a major influence, not just as a writer/performer, but as a producer.'

Michael Messer

J.J. Cale (Guitar, vocals, b. 1938)

Cale gigged around his native Tulsa, Oklahoma before moving to LA in 1964. He issued his first record in 1971, after Eric Clapton's hit with Cale's 'After Midnight'. Cale is still known to many only through covers of his songs and has always preferred to stay in the background; this is reflected in his music as he places his vocals way down in the mix, thereby drawing the listener's attention into the record.

J.J. Cale was influential on the 1970s blues scene but has always shied away from the limelight.

A-Z of Artists

Ry Cooder (Guitar, mandolin, vocals, b. 1947)

Cooder is one of America's most versatile musicians, equally at home with blues, rock, jazz and various ethnic musics. In the mid-1960s he played guitar with Taj Mahal (in the Rising Sons) and Jackie DeShannon, then did studio work with Paul Revere & the Raiders. Especially gifted as a slide guitarist, he has filled that role on sessions with the Rolling Stones, Captain Beefheart, Little Feat, Randy Newman and other artists.

Cooder has also performed on and/or composed a large number of film scores, including *Performance* (1970), *Paris, Texas* (1984), *Streets Of Fire* (1984), *Cocktail* (1988) and *Steel Magnolias* (1989). On his first album, made in 1970, Cooder interpreted classic blues and folk songs as re-envisioned by arranger Van Dyke Parks. Since that time he has delved into jazz, Hawaiian music, Tex-Mex, Indian sitar music and other styles. Cooder gained particular acclaim for the 1997 album Buena Vista Social Club, made with various legendary Cuban musicians, and the subsequent documentary film of the same title.

Key Tracks

'If Walls Could Talk' Ry Cooder
'Little Sister' Ry Cooder
'All For Business' Jimmy Dawkins
'It Serves Me Right To Suffer' Jimmy Dawkins
'Welfare Blues' Jimmy Dawkins

Jimmy Dawkins (Guitar, vocals, b. 1936)

Guitarist Jimmy Dawkins came from Mississippi to the west side of Chicago in 1955, formed a friendship with Luther Allison and slowly built a good reputation with his slow-burning expressiveness. He made his first recording, the award-winning *Fast Fingers*, in 1969 for Delmark Records and followed up with the equally serious *All For Business* (1973). In 1970 Dawkins toured and recorded in Europe with Clarence 'Gatemouth' Brown and Otis Rush. He has been a sideman with many key artists.

Guitarist Jimmy Dawkins on a 1972 European tour.

A-Z of Artists

Robben Ford (Guitar, vocals, b. 1951)

Robben Ford was born into a musical family on the coast of northern California. His father, Charles, was a guitarist who encouraged Robben to teach himself the instrument at the age of 13. Ford has two musical brothers, drummer Pat and harmonica player Mark. Influenced by Mike Bloomfield, Robben and Pat played in the Charles Ford Band in the late 1960s and were hired by Charlie Musselwhite in 1974.

Robben Ford split his allegiances between playing blues with Jimmy Witherspoon, contemporary jazz with Tom Scott and Miles Davis, rock with Joni Mitchell and George Harrison, and leading his own bands. In 1977 his electric backing band, Yellowjackets, became a jazz group in its own right. Ford has continued to skirt the line between jazz and blues. In 1990 he rejoined his brother Pat in the Ford Blues Band, and he formed his acclaimed Blue Line in 1992.

Key Tracks

'Miss Miss' Robben Ford
'Everyday I Have The Blues' Robben Ford
'Alright Now' Free
'Fire And Water' Free
'Heavy Load' Free

Free (Vocal/instrumental group, 1968–73)

Fronted by charismatic Paul Rodgers, Free was a catalyst in the popular shift from blues-dominated rock to heavy-metal forms. Rodgers left Brown Sugar to form Free with guitarist Paul Kossoff, whose playing on the hit 'All Right Now' sealed its popularity in 1970. Not long thereafter, tensions and drug abuse began to weaken the band. By 1973, Rodgers and drummer Simon Kirke had moved on to Bad Company; Kossoff died of heart failure in 1976.

Blues, jazz and rock guitarist Robben Ford, pictured at the 2003 Yellowjackets reunion.

SON

A-Z of Artists

Rory Gallagher (Guitar, vocals, harmonica, 1949–95)

Irish blues musician Rory Gallagher fell in love with Delta and Chicago blues as a child. In 1969 he formed the band Taste, receiving moderate acclaim, and a year later he released his own eponymous album to very good reviews. Gallagher became a very popular touring artist in the US and Europe and issued 14 albums in his lifetime, all with a strong flavouring of his personal blues sensibility.

Director Tony Palmer's documentary *Irish Tour* captures Gallagher performing live in 1974, while the live albums from the 1970s also successfully represent his energy and subtlety. He performed and recorded with Muddy Waters and Albert King at the height of his career, holding his own with the masters. Aside from a four-year hiatus in the 1980s, Gallagher stayed active as a touring musician until his death at the age of 46, following a failed liver transplant.

Hot Tuna (Vocal/instrumental group, 1970–present)

Jefferson Airplane's Jorma Kaukonen (guitar, vocals) and Jack Casady (bass) – together with drummer Bob Steeler – formed Hot Tuna in San Francisco in order to satisfy their interest in acoustic blues. After an eponymous debut album, the group went electric, added fiddler Papa John Creach and expanded its range to become a staple of the jam-band scene spearheaded by the Grateful Dead. Many line-ups later, Kaukonen and Casady soldier on, blending acoustic blues songs from the 1920s and 1930s with the occasional electric performance.

'I've done songs in all the different styles … train blues, drinking blues, economic blues…. The music can be very traditional, but you can sort of creep into the future with the lyrics.'

Rory Gallagher

J.B. Hutto (Guitar, vocals, 1926–83)

The highly theatrical Joseph Benjamin 'J.B.' Hutto sang in the Golden Crowns Gospel Singers as a child and made his first records with his backup band, the Hawks, in 1954. Hutto then left the music business but returned, rejuvenated, 10 years later. He toured with various incarnations of the Hawks until Hound Dog Taylor's death in 1976, when Hutto briefly took over Taylor's band the Houserockers. He continued to perform with the New Hawks until his own passing.

J.B. Hutto graces the cover of a 1976 issue of Living Blues.

living blues

nov.-dec. 1976 no. 30 75¢

A-Z of Artists

Led Zeppelin (Vocal/instrumental group, 1968–80)

In 1968, after all the original members had left the Yardbirds, guitarist Jimmy Page had custody of the band's name and contracts. John Paul Jones, who had produced some of Page's side work, joined on bass, and Page hired singer Robert Plant away from Hobbstweedle. Drummer John Bonham, a friend of Plant's, rounded out the New Yardbirds to fulfil standing contractual obligations. After Keith Moon, drummer with the Who, quipped that their audacious, harder blues sound would 'go over like a lead zeppelin', the quartet took on a new name.

The group's love of the blues was explicit in its altered cover versions Led Zeppelin's self-titled debut album in 1969 was heavy on blues tunes with a psychedelic energy. As Led Zeppelin rose to superstardom it moved further away from the blues but never abandoned it completely. Bonham's death in 1980 effectively brought the premier heavy metal band to an end.

Louisiana Red (Vocals, harmonica, guitar, b. 1936)

Iverson Minter, a.k.a. Louisiana Red, rose from childhood tragedy to build an impressive career. His mother had died and his father had been murdered by the Ku Klux Klan by the time Red was five years old. He first recorded for Chess in 1949, prior to his military service, and then played with John Lee Hooker before leading his own bands. Louisiana Red is a gifted guitarist, influenced by Elmore James and Muddy Waters.

Key Tracks

'Stairway To Heaven' Led Zeppelin
'Black Dog' Led Zeppelin
'Rollin' Stone' Louisiana Red
'This Little Letter' Louisiana Red
'Givin' It Up For Your Love' Delbert McClinton

Delbert McClinton (Harmonica, vocals, b. 1940)

McClinton gigged around Fort Worth as a young man, playing with local acts like the Rondells. He moved to Los Angeles in the early 1970s, playing and writing songs with Glen Clark, but returned to Texas in 1975. As both a performer and songwriter, McClinton smoothly crosses the dividing lines between blues, country, rock and soul. He has enjoyed important collaborations with Roy Buchanan, Bonnie Raitt, Tanya Tucker, B.B. King, Vince Gill and others.

Louisiana Red first recorded for Chess in 1949 and is equally at home on harmonica and guitar.

A-Z of Artists

Matt Murphy (Guitar, vocals, b. 1927)

Matt 'Guitar' Murphy came up in Memphis, playing with Howlin' Wolf, Little Junior Parker and Bobby 'Blue' Bland before gaining serious attention with Memphis Slim's band from 1952 to 1959. In the 1960s Murphy contributed to sessions by Sonny Boy Williamson II, Chuck Berry and Otis Rush, and was a crowd favourite while performing on the 1963 American Folk Blues Festival tour. Murphy's appearance in *The Blues Brothers* film in 1980 helped to seal his place in blues history.

Charlie Musselwhite (Harmonica, vocals, guitar, b. 1944)

Charlie Musselwhite has an exceptionally fluid and melodic harmonica style that places him head and shoulders above most competitors. He debuted on record in 1967 and has remained faithful to the Chicago style in his own projects and in supporting work for Elvin Bishop, Big Joe Williams, John Hammond Jr., Junior Watson and others. Musselwhite also gave brothers Robben and Pat Ford their start in the blues business in 1974. He staged a comeback in 2004 with a highly promoted album.

Key Tracks

'Matt's Guitar Boogie' Matt Murphy
'Talkin' 'Bout My Friends' Charlie Musselwhite
'Christo Redemptor' Charlie Musselwhite
'Your Love Is Like A Cancer' Son Seals
'Sitting At Home Alone' Hound Dog Taylor

Son Seals (Guitar, vocals, drums, 1942–2004)

In 1973 dynamic guitarist Frank 'Son' Seals became one of the most exciting artists signed to Alligator Records. His choppy technique and hard-hitting vocals on songs such as 'Your Love Is Like A Cancer' combine to create an extremely powerful sound. In 2000 Seals recorded *Lettin' Go* for Telarc, with Hammond organist Al Kooper of Blood, Sweat & Tears and guitarist Trey Anastasio of the jam band Phish.

Hound Dog Taylor (Guitar, vocals, 1915–75)

Many guitarists might sound as if they have extra fingers, but Theodore 'Hound Dog' Taylor, who did not become a full-time musician until he was well past 40, actually had an extra digit on each hand. Producer Bruce Iglauer founded the Alligator label in 1971 expressly to record the guitarist's energetic, raw almost to the point of primitive, 'house-rockin'' style. Taylor and his backing duo, the Houserockers, were among the label's hottest stars for four years until Taylor's death from cancer.

Hound Dog Taylor, for whom producer Bruce Iglauer set up Alligator Records in 1971.

A-Z of Artists

Koko Taylor (Vocals, b. 1935)

Singer Koko Taylor (née Cora Walton) earned the title 'The Queen of Chicago Blues' due to her no-nonsense, brazen vocal style. She writes much of her own material, songs that resonate with womanly power and assert her claim to blues royalty. Taylor grew up singing gospel in Memphis and switched to the blues after moving to Chicago in 1953. Bassist Willie Dixon signed her to Chess Records and wrote her big hit 'Wang Dang Doodle' in 1964. In 1975 Taylor moved to Alligator, becoming one of the label's biggest stars. She was managed by her husband, Pops Taylor, who died in 1989 after an auto accident in which Koko was also severely injured. Since her comeback in 1990 she has toured the world constantly, appearing at all the major blues and jazz festivals.

Johnny Winter (Guitar, vocals, harmonica, b. 1944)

Johnny Winter is a Caucasian albino from Texas who reshaped the face of the blues in the 1970s. A phenomenal guitar technician, he rose to prominence in Texas bars and local studios. On his first album for Imperial Records, Winter explored psychedelic blues with middling success. Shortly thereafter he signed with Columbia, for whom he recorded between 1969 and 1974. His group Johnny Winter And, with guitarist Rick Derringer, had a hit with 'Rock And Roll Hoochie Koo'. Winter is a great interpreter of classic material, covering blues and rock'n'roll tunes by Chuck Berry, B.B. King, Bob Dylan, the Rolling Stones and Van Morrison. He is also a gifted producer, working with Muddy Waters in the 1970s on such projects as *Hard Again* (1977).

Key Tracks

'Wang Dang Doodle' Koko Taylor
'What Kind Of A Man Is This?' Koko Taylor
'Rock And Roll Hoochie Koo' Johnny Winter
'La Grange' ZZ Top
'Jesus Just Left Chicago' ZZ Top

ZZ Top (Vocal/instrumental group, 1970–present)

ZZ Top is a perennial blues trio from Houston, Texas, as well known for their sunglasses, furry guitars and long beards as for their signature boogie beats. Guitarist Billy Gibbons, bassist Dusty Hill and drummer Frank Beard specialize in hard, shuffling electric blues, usually tinged with humour and double entendres. Hits like 'La Grange', 'Jesus Just Left Chicago', 'Tush', 'Legs' and 'Sleeping Bag' have kept the band in the studio and on the road since 1970.

Powerful blues singer Koko Taylor, who recorded for Chess Records before signing with the 1970s-founded Alligator label.

The Eighties

As the end of the twentieth century approached, the United States – its culture included – entered a rare period of recapitulation, retrieval and, ultimately, renewal. The election as President of ageing Ronald Reagan, ex-movie star and California governor, introduced unexpected neo-conservatism, an ideology that looked back to a rosy, though mythical, Golden Age.

Declaring 'It's morning in America', Reagan spoke for ways of life that had little to do with blues (or jazz, rock, classical and the newly surging rap/hip hop styles). Blues reacted in its own way, by returning to the past. It was aided by the advent and institution of a whole new recording format, the compact disc.

Key Artists

Robert Cray
Stevie Ray Vaughan

The CD, a palm-sized digital medium developed by German BMG and Japanese Sony corporations and introduced in 1983, re-energized the teetering recording industry as music devotees rushed to replace favourite LPs with the wondrous new product. New digital techniques also allowed for old and poor-quality recordings to be re-mastered, leading to a cleaner, brighter sound and the 'rediscovery' by the listening public of many artists that had fallen out of favour. Reissues of blues and jazz classics outnumbered but also financed new albums by younger artists. Those younger artists, however, also looked back to the glories of the 1950s and early 1960s for inspiration, polishing the past up to streamlined sheen. The new bluesmen still sang of love's pangs, but more often at white college fraternity parties than for black and hipster crowds in low-rent venues.

By the 1980s' end, home computers had transformed how people lived; Communism, the Iron Curtain and the USSR itself were gone, and the global economy had a running start into the contemporary era.

A mural in Austin, Texas, which boasted a lively blues scene during the 1980s.

GREETINGS FROM
AUSTIN
Capitol
OF TEXAS
RELICS
GALLERY ENTRANCE
VINTAGE
NEON

Stevie Ray Vaughan Arrives

Texas was a hotbed of rockin' blues in the mid- to late 1970s. Austin-based bands such as the Cobras, featuring guitar sensation Stevie Ray Vaughan (1954–90), and the Fabulous Thunderbirds, formed by Stevie Ray's older brother Jimmie Lee Vaughan, were gathering strong regional followings with their tough brand of roots-oriented roadhouse blues. These potent groups spearheaded a 1980s blues-rock boom that paralleled the trend towards blues rock sparked in the late 1960s.

The Fabulous Thunderbirds went on to build a national following in the 1980s in the wake of their major crossover success with 1986's *Tuff Enuff* (the title track was released as a single with accompanying video and received heavy play on MTV). Stevie Ray Vaughan went on to form his own band, Double Trouble, which quickly became one of the most popular bands in Texas and by 1982 began to receive national recognition. Stevie Ray's appearance with Double Trouble at the Montreux Jazz Festival in the summer of 1982 caught the attention of pop star David Bowie; he recruited the flashy Texan to lay down stinging lead-guitar tracks on his 1982 album *Let's Dance*, bringing Vaughan further into the public eye. Legendary record producer John Hammond (1910–86), who had significantly influenced the careers of everyone from Charlie Christian (1916–42) and Billie Holiday (1915–59) to Bob Dylan and Bruce Springsteen, signed Stevie Ray to a contract with Epic; his 1983 debut, *Texas Flood*, became an unqualified hit, crossing over to the pop market and earning two Grammy nominations.

'Ironically, very little [blues today] comes from the radio. It seems to come from other outlets, like commercials and films.'

Roy Rogers

The combined successes of the Vaughan brothers invigorated the blues-rock genre and also led to a renewed appreciation of blues-rock pioneers such as Lonnie Mack (b. 1941), Johnny Winter and Roy Buchanan (1939–88), all of whom signed with Chicago-based Alligator Records in the mid-1980s. The momentum that the Vaughan brothers had created paved the way for 1990s blues-rock players, including Kenny Wayne Sheppard, Jonny Lang, Coco Montoya, Tinsley Ellis (b. 1957), Sonny Landreth, Chris Duarte, Bryan Lee, Little Jimmy King, Larry McCray, Charlie Sexton and British blues-rock guitar hero Gary Moore.

The Vaughan brothers Jimmie Lee (left) and Stevie Ray were key figures on the circuit.

Key Artist: Robert Cray

Although Robert Cray's clean, good looks, precise guitar lines and slick presentation earned him some knocks from critics early on in his career (hardcore blues aficionados tended to dismiss him as 'blues lite' for yuppies), he later gained their respect for his smart songwriting and razor-sharp guitar licks, along with an intensely passionate vocal style reminiscent of the great 1960s R&B singer O.V. Wright.

Born on 1 August 1953 in Columbus, Georgia, Cray moved around frequently until the age of 15, when his family finally settled in Tacoma, Washington. Inspired by Texas guitarslinger Albert Collins (who played at Cray's high-school graduation), he taught himself to play guitar and formed his first band in 1974 with bassist Richard Cousins. After playing around the Pacific Northwest during the 1970s, even joining Collins's backing band on a few West Coast gigs, Cray's band made its recording debut in 1980 with *Who's Been Talkin'* (on Tomato Records). That first album set the tone for Cray's recording career, reflecting an equal allegiance to blues and R&B in his faithful covers of O.V. Wright's 'I'm Gonna Forget About You', Freddie King's 'The Welfare (Turns Its Back On You)' and the Willie Dixon-penned title track. But it was Cray's originals 'Nice As A Fool Can Be' and 'That's What I'll Do' that pointed to a future direction for this talented singer, songwriter and guitarist.

'I walked into a record store, and they were playing Robert Cray's new record ... the music just grabbed me ... I said, "Man, it's time for me to get back into this music!".'

Joe Fonda

Singer, songwriter and razor-sharp guitarist Robert Cray lets rip onstage during a 1987 UK tour.

Cray followed up with two solid outings on the High Tone label – 1983's *Bad Influence*, which contained the chilling original 'Phone Booth', and 1985's *False Accusations* – before finally breaking through to mainstream acceptance following the release of his superb 1986 Mercury Records debut, *Strong Persuader* (containing his hit original song 'Smoking Gun'). In 1985 Cray appeared on a guitar summit meeting, the aptly-named *Showdown!* (Alligator Records), with fellow blues six-stringers Albert Collins and Johnny 'Clyde' Copeland.

A Southerly Direction

During the 1990s, Cray took more of a southern soul direction on recordings such as 1990's *Midnight Stroll*, 1992's *I Was Warned* and 1995's *Some Rainy Morning* (all on Mercury), while continuing to blossom as a songwriter with a knack for minor-key confessionals. In 1999 he collaborated with drummer Steve Jordan, who produced and played on the Memphis-flavoured *Take Your Shoes Off* (Rykodisc). Also appearing on that retro-soul outing was drummer-producer Willie Mitchell of Hi Records fame; he co-wrote and also created the horn arrangements for the opening track, which has the distinct feel of an early 1970s Al Green number. Elsewhere on the album, Cray offers faithful renditions of Mack Rice's '24-7 Man' and Solomon Burke's 'Won't You Give Him (One More Chance)'.

Time Will Tell

Cray has continued to expertly blend relaxed, good-feeling southern soul and urgent blues on 2001's Stax/Volt-flavoured *Shoulda Been Home* (again produced in Memphis by drummer Steve Jordan) and 2003's *Time Will Tell* (Sanctuary), his thirteenth recording as a leader. That most recent release is easily his most ambitious to date and is in some ways uncharacteristic of his style. Not only does it contain two stridently anti-war songs in 'Survivor' and 'Distant Shore', it also features Cray in an odd turn on electric sitar, playing with the Turtle Island String Quartet on 'Up In The Sky', a psychedelic number that sounds like an outtake from *Prince's Around The World In A Day* (1985). Regardless of the context, however, Cray remains a commanding vocal presence and an assertive six-stringer. After 30 years of constant gigging, he has become one of the seasoned veterans on the contemporary blues scene.

Cray (right) with blues legend B.B. King in 1992.

Key Artist: Stevie Ray Vaughan

The premiere torch-bearer for the blues-rock boom of the 1980s, Texan guitar wizard Stevie Ray Vaughan galvanized a generation of players and fans alike with his pyrotechnic licks and flamboyant stage presence. Connecting deeply with both the psychedelic, 'voodoo chile' mystique of Jimi Hendrix and the down-home roadhouse grittiness of his biggest guitar influence, Albert King, Vaughan fashioned a sound that reached out and grabbed listeners with its combination of raucous rock-fuelled abandon, string-bending intensity, gut-level directness and real-deal, bluesy authority.

His meteoric rise to fame during the mid-1980s, over the course of four recordings and countless gigs, was fuelled by self-destructive cocaine-and-alcohol binges that led to a physical collapse and subsequent rehabilitation in 1987. Stevie Ray ultimately mustered the courage to overcome his addictions, returning to the scene in 1988 with a clean bill of health and a renewed sense of conviction. He continued touring and recording and was at his peak when he died in a tragic helicopter crash after a concert in the summer of 1990.

'I've said that playing the blues is like having to be black twice. Stevie Ray Vaughan missed on both counts, but I never noticed.'

B.B. King

Born in the Oak Cliff area of Dallas, Texas on 3 October 1954, Stevie Ray Vaughan grew up under the influence of his older brother Jimmie, an accomplished blues and R&B guitar player and vintage record collector. Stevie Ray got his first guitar at the age of seven and began copying licks from brother Jimmie's records by the likes of Lonnie Mack, Albert King, Freddie King, B.B. King, Buddy Guy, T-Bone Walker, Otis Rush and Jimmy Reed. Stevie Ray idolized Jimmie and closely followed his progress through a succession of early bands, including the Swinging Pendulums, the Chessmen and Texas Storm. Stevie Ray formed his own band, Blackbird, in 1970.

In 1971, aged 17, he dropped out of high school to concentrate on music. On New Year's Eve of 1971, Stevie Ray and his Blackbird bandmates all moved to Austin and began working on the thriving blues scene there. In 1973 Steve Ray joined the Nightcrawlers and by the end of 1974 was playing his first gig with Paul Ray's popular Cobras. After leaving the Cobras in July 1977 he formed his own Triple Threat

Right: Stevie Ray Vaughan – the greatest guitar virtuoso since Jimi Hendrix – who died tragically young in a helicopter crash.

Revue, featuring singer Lou Ann Barton, guitarist W.C. Clark, drummer Freddy 'Pharoah' Walden and keyboardist Mike 'Cold Shot' Kindred. After Triple Threat imploded due to inner bickering between Vaughan and Barton, Stevie Ray formed Double Trouble in May of 1978. The band built a strong regional following for the next few years, culminating in a triumphant appearance at the Montreux International Jazz Festival on 17 July 1982. Pop stars Jackson Browne and David Bowie were in the audience at that galvanizing performance; Browne later offered his studio to record Double Trouble, while Bowie hired Stevie Ray to play on his recording *Let's Dance* (1983), considerably elevating his profile.

A Brilliant Career

Vaughan and Double Trouble were signed to an Epic Records contract by legendary producer and talent scout John Hammond. Stevie Ray's 1983 debut, *Texas Flood*, was an immediate hit and led to a triple award from *Guitar Player* magazine for Best New Talent, Best Electric Blues Guitar Player and Best Guitar Album, as well as W.C. Handy Blues Awards for Entertainer of the Year and Blues Instrumentalist of the Year. Stevie Ray's virtuoso playing and Hendrix-inspired mystique (for a generation of young fans who missed out on the 1960s, he provided a bridge to Jimi through his faithful covers of 'Voodoo Chile [Slight Return]' and 'Third Stone From The Sun', replete with wild guitar-thashing stage antics) helped to fuel subsequent successes with 1984's *Couldn't Stand The Weather* and 1985's *Soul To Soul*. Following an extensive tour in 1986, which yielded the double LP *Live Alive* and culminated in an onstage collapse in London, Vaughan entered a rehabilitation hospital in Georgia. After taking a year out he returned to the scene, re-energized and with a new outlook on life. By the end of 1988, he had begun writing the material that would make up the bulk of 1989's *In Step*, which went gold (500,000 copies sold) within six months of its release and later won a Grammy Award for Best Contemporary Blues Recording. Vaughan co-headlined a 1989 tour of America with rock guitarist Jeff Beck, and in the spring of 1990 he recorded an album with his brother Jimmie entitled *Family Style*.

Next Page: Vaughan's well-travelled guitar case.

An Untimely Death

On 26 August 1990 Stevie Ray and Double Trouble played a gig at the Alpine Valley Music Theater in Easy Troy, Wisconsin. The concert culminated with an all-star encore jam featuring special guests Eric Clapton, Buddy Guy, Jimmie Vaughan and Robert Cray. After the concert, Vaughan boarded a helicopter bound for Chicago; minutes after its 12:30 a.m. takeoff, the helicopter crashed into hills, killing the

blues guitar hero instantly. At his funeral in Dallas, Stevie Wonder sang 'Amazing Grace' at the gravesite. Jimmie and Stevie Ray's *Family Style* was released posthumously in October 1990 and won two Grammy Awards for Best Rock Instrumental ('D/FW') and Best Contemporary Blues Recording. Other posthumously released recordings by Stevie Ray Vaughan include 1992's *In The Beginning*, which documents a 1980 concert by Double Trouble, and 2000's four-CD boxed set *SRV*.

A-Z of Artists

Marcia Ball (Piano, vocals, b. 1949)

One of the leading exponents of the Professor Longhair school of piano playing, East Texas-born 'Long Tall' Marcia Ball was also greatly influenced by R&B divas Irma Thomas and Etta James, and zydeco king Clifton Chenier. Her infectious blend of modern Texas roadhouse blues, boogie-woogie and Louisiana swamp rock is best exemplified on a series of Rounder recordings, including 1984's *Soulful Dress*, 1986's *Hot Tamale Baby* and 1989's *Gator Rhythms*. Ball still tours continuously and is an annual attraction at the New Orleans Jazz & Heritage Festival.

Rory Block (Guitar, vocals, b. 1949)

An interpreter of classic country blues, Block took guitar lessons from Rev. Gary Davis, Mississippi John Hurt and Son House before moving to California and working on the folk-blues coffeehouse circuit. She recorded for small labels before signing with Rounder Records and debuting with 1982's *High Heeled Blues*. She is featured in the Robert Mugge film *Hellhounds On My Trail* (2000), celebrating Robert Johnson's posthumous entry into the Rock And Roll Hall Of Fame. Her most recent recordings are 2003's *Last Fair Deal* and 2004's *From The Dust* (both on Telarc Blues).

Key Tracks

'Soulful Dress' Marcia Ball
'Walkin' Blues' Rory Block
'Since You Been Gone' Rory Block
'Come On In' The Blues Band
'Flatfoot Sam' The Blues Band

The Blues Band (Vocal/instrumental group, 1979–present)

Blues aficionados Paul Jones (vocals, harmonica), Dave Kelly (vocals, guitar), Tom McGuiness (guitar), Gary Fletcher (bass) and Hughie Flint (drums) formed the Blues Band in 1979, purely for their own enjoyment. Initial success on the pub and club circuit swiftly led to greater things and their first album was released in 1980. Flint was replaced in 1981 by Rob Townsend and the band has continued to perform and record prolifically. Ex-Manfred Mann star Jones also plays an important role in keeping the blues alive as Britain's premier blues DJ.

A major influence on Marcia Ball, Zydeco accordionist Clifton Chenier plays at London's Albert Hall in 1969.

A–Z of Artists

Cephas & Wiggins (Vocal/instrumental group, 1978–present)

The W.C. Handy Award-winning duo patterned itself after Sonny Terry & Brownie McGhee. Guitarist John 'Bowling Green' Cephas (b. 1930) and 'Harmonica' Phil Wiggins (b. 1954) began performing together in 1978. They toured the globe on a US State Department tour and recorded throughout the 1980s, while their most recent recordings are 1996's *Cool Down*, 1999's *Homemade* and 2003's *Somebody Told The Truth*. They remain the leading exponents of the Piedmont blues style.

Eddy Clearwater (Guitar, vocals, b. 1933)

Mississippi-born Eddy Harrington left the South in 1950 and established himself on Chicago's west side as a Chuck Berry imitator named Guitar Eddy. He later took the stage name Eddy 'The Chief' Clearwater, a nickname he got from his penchant for wearing Native American headdresses His tough, slashing, southpaw guitar attack is best documented on 1980's Rooster Blues debut, *The Chief*.

Johnny 'Clyde' Copeland (Guitar, vocals, 1937–97)

The Houston guitarist played with bluesman Joe 'Guitar' Hughes before forming his own band in the late 1950s. Relocating to New York in 1974, Copeland debuted on Rounder Records with 1977's *Copeland Special*. In 1985 he recorded a guitar summit meeting with Albert Collins and Robert Cray (*Showdown!*) and in 1986 recorded *Bringin' It All Back Home*, an adventurous hybrid of African music and blues. He continued this fusion on his last recording – 1996's *Jungle Swing* (Verve), featuring jazz pianist Randy Weston. Singer Shemekia Copeland is his daughter.

Key Tracks

'Chicken' Cephas & Wiggins
'A Minor Cha Cha' Eddy Clearwater
'Sufferin' City' Johnny 'Clyde' Copeland
'Smoking' Ronnie Earl

Ronnie Earl (Guitar, b. 1953)

New York City native Ronald Horvath began playing in Boston blues clubs during the 1970s, and in 1980 replaced Duke Robillard in Roomful of Blues. After eight years with the band, he struck out on his own with the Broadcasters, which prominently showcased his passionate Magic Sam meets T-Bone Walker guitar style. One of the jazziest of blues guitarists, he combines finesse and fire on his best outing, 1987's *Smokin'* (on Black Top Blues).

Guitarist Eddy Clearwater has a distinctive playing style that combines the blues with elements of Chuck Berry's hit songs.

A-Z of Artists

Fabulous Thunderbirds (Vocal/instrumental group, 1974–present)

Fusing straight blues, early rock'n'roll and classic R&B, the Texas roadhouse band – formed by guitarist Jimmie Vaughan and harpist/vocalist Kim Wilson – built a cult following in the 1970s and early 1980s, before breaking through commercially in 1986 with *Tuff Enuff*. While the band's early Chrysalis recordings appealed mainly to blues and rock'n'roll purists, their late 1980s output for Epic, including 1987's *Hot Number*, brought wider recognition and helped to absorb rock fans into the blues arena.

Lil' Ed & The Blues Imperials (Vocal/instrumental group, 1975–present)

This Chicago native learned slide guitar from his uncle, renowned bluesman J.B. Hutto. During the early years of the Blues Imperials, flamboyant frontman Ed Williams continued working at his day job in a local car wash, but by the early 1980s the band had established a substantial regional following. Their 1986 Alligator Records debut, *Roughhousin'* is a prime example of their raucous, rough-edged party music.

Key Tracks

'She's Tuff' Fabulous Thunderbirds
'Wrap It Up' Fabulous Thunderbirds
'Old Oak Tree' Lil Ed & the Blues Imperials
'Memphis' Lonnie Mack
'Wham' Lonnie Mack

Lonnie Mack (Guitar, vocals, b. 1941)

Mack's 1964 debut album, *The Wham Of That Memphis Man* – full of lightning-fast licks, vibrato-drenched lines and whammy-bar techniques on his Flying V guitar – captured the imagination of a young Stevie Ray Vaughan growing up in Dallas. Two decades later, Vaughan would produce Mack's 1985 comeback album on Alligator Records, *Strike Like Lightning*. The Indiana native followed up with two offerings on Alligator, before moving to Epic with *Road Houses & Dance Halls* (1988).

Magic Slim (Guitar, b. 1937)

Born Morris Holt in Grenada, Mississippi, Slim began playing on Chicago's west side in the mid-1960s. In 1976, when Hound Dog Taylor passed away, Slim took over his Sunday afternoon gig at Theresa's on the south side. Slim's band the Teardrops was featured on the 1970 Alligator anthology series *Living Chicago Blues*. Throughout the 1980s, Slim recorded for the Alligator and Rooster Blues labels, highlighting his stinging licks and gruff vocals.

Blues-rock artists such as Lonnie Mack enjoyed renewed fame following the Vaughans' success.

A-Z of Artists

Bonnie Raitt (Guitar, vocals, b. 1949)

During the 1960s, while attending college in Cambridge, Massachussetts, Raitt learned the ropes firsthand from slide masters Son House and Mississippi Fred McDowell. She began appearing on the folk and blues festival circuit in the late 1960s, sometimes encouraging elderly, rediscovered blues legends (such as Sippie Wallace) to join her onstage, and in 1971 recorded her self-titled debut for Warner Bros., featuring bluesmen Junior Wells and A.C. Reed. Her blues sensibility has graced gold-selling and Grammy-winning recordings from the 1980s to the present.

Roy Rogers (Guitar, vocals, b. 1950)

An exponent of acoustic and electric blues, California-based slide guitarist Rogers played with John Lee Hooker's Coast To Coast band from 1982–86, before releasing his debut recording as a leader, *Chops Not Chaps* (1986). He followed up with 1988's *Slidewinder* and in 1990 produced Hooker's Grammy-winning comeback album *The Healer*. Rogers maintained an acoustic duo in the 1990s with harmonica maestro Norton Buffalo. He is also featured in the Robert Mugge film *Hellhounds On My Trail* demonstrating Robert Johnson's slide-guitar techniques.

'Roy [Rogers] is one of the most authentic interpreters of modern blues. He's a real master man who has spent so much time getting in touch with and really honing in on his craft.'

Bonnie Raitt

Roomful Of Blues (Vocal/instrumental group, 1967–present)

The nine-piece, horn-based outfit from Westerly, Rhode Island was formed by guitarist Duke Robillard and pianist Al Copley and has been a swinging institution in the Northeast since 1967. The band concentrates on jump blues, boogie-woogie and slow blues numbers. Roomful's self-titled debut on Island Records in 1979 began a rich recorded legacy, which has included Grammy-nominated collaborations with blues greats Big Joe Turner, Eddie 'Cleanhead' Vinson and Earl King. Roomful released its eighteenth album, *Standing Room Only* (Alligator), in 2005.

Harmonica ace Junior Wells showed his style to full effect on Bonnie Raitt's debut album in 1971.

A-Z of Artists

George Thorogood & The Destroyers (Vocal/instrumental group, 1973–present)

Thorogood's Delaware-based band drew inspiration from Elmore James and Hound Dog Taylor. Guitarist/vocalist Thorogood moved the band to Boston in 1974 and gained popularity on the blues circuit there, leading to its 1978 self-titled debut. The 1979 album *Move It On Over* was a commercial breakthrough and the band's popularity was further enhanced after opening a Rolling Stones tour in 1981. The band continue to play no-nonsense, rocking boogie into the twenty-first century.

Joe Louis Walker (Guitar, vocals, b. 1949)

A passionate singer, Walker came up in the 1960s on the San Francisco blues scene. In 1975 he began singing on the gospel circuit until he formed his own band, the Boss Talkers in 1985. He recorded some strong albums during the 1980s for the High Tone label, such as his 1986 debut *Cold Is The Night*. Walker continued to turn out consistently good recordings in the 1990s and remains active.

Walter 'Wolfman' Washington (Guitar, vocals, b. 1943)

This New Orleans guitarist started out accompanying R&B singers, but as a leader in the 1970s he developed a strong local following and gradually crossed over to wider audiences. He debuted on Rounder Records in 1986 with the funky *Wolf Tracks*, following up with 1988's *Out Of The Dark* and 1991's *Wolf At The Door*. After recording for other labels, Washington returned to Rounder with 1998's *Funk Is In The House*. He continues to tour worldwide with his band, the Roadmasters.

Key Tracks

'Bad To The Bone' George Thorogood & The Destroyers
'Cold Is The Night' Joe Louis Walker
'Are You The Lady' Walter 'Wolfman' Washington

Katie Webster (Piano, organ, 1939–99)

This Texas native was active on the southern Louisiana swamp-blues scene in the late 1950s and early 1960s, recording for various regional labels. She spent the 1970s and early 1980s playing her unique brand of boogie-woogie piano around Louisiana before being 'discovered' by Alligator Records in 1987. She debuted in 1988 with *Swamp Boogie Queen* and followed up with two strong offerings, *Two-Fisted Mama!* (1990) and *No Foolin!* (1991), before suffering a stroke in 1993.

George Thorogood's energetic guitar playing and gruff vocals gave his band an enduringly popular down'n'dirty blues-rock sound.

The Contemporary Era

By definition, a contemporary era defies summary. No one living in it has the conclusive perspective to discern the prevailing character of our times, even though we all know what we're going through, and can hear what we hear.

The reductive view is: Americans, after a burst stock-market bubble and terrorist attacks, live in uncertainty, tinged with denial. Newly unified Europe, with the UK at some slight distance, is quite possibly on the rise. The large and small states of the former Soviet Union are in disarray, Japan's economy stands still and China has become a production behemoth despite political isolation. Africa remains beset with under-development and internal conflicts. South and Central America, the Caribbean, the South Pacific, including Australia, and Canada exist almost unto themselves. Nice places to visit, they're heard from now and then.

Blues in the contemporary era, on the other hand, is known everywhere. The music seems artistically robust, though no more fiscally secure than usual. As time marches on, the conditions of blues music's birth are beginning to fade into history, and the blues' fundamental assertions are at times obscured by aggressive and ironic attitudes, digital electronics and the unforgiving beat. Simultaneously, however, thriving blues scenes exist in many cities and the influence of the blues continues to underlie many forms of popular music currently being performed and recorded. The hunt for unreleased original blues material is ongoing, and the re-mastering and repackaging of older blues recordings remains a profitable sector of the music industry. If blues is beginning to reach the end of its creative development, it is at least being lovingly and painstakingly prepared, we hope prematurely, for museum display. The future of blues music is unpredictable. The contemporary era is what's happening now.

Key Artists

Corey Harris
Paul Rishell & Annie Raines
Chris Thomas King
Otis Taylor
Hubert Sumlin

Mali musician Ali Farka Toure, one of the most prominent artists of modern contemporary blues, found widespread fame following a 1994 collaboration with guitarist Ry Cooder.

Hard Times for Musicians

We are now in one of the most exciting yet frustrating periods of the blues' long history. The music has become a living continuum, with artists whose ages range from early teens to late-eighties performing everything from field hollers and fife-and-drum band songs to Delta slide guitar, barrelhouse piano, Chicago, Texas and jump blues, blues rock, blues rap and even more experimental hybrids.

A worldwide decrease in album sales has occurred in all genres, but the blues' already slim margin has been hit especially hard. At the turn of the millennium, blues CDs accounted for little more than two per cent of overall sales, and since then, that figure has fallen to less than one per cent. Without the emergence of a major crossover artist to spark interest in the music within the mainstream, as Stevie Ray Vaughan (1954–90) did in the 1980s, there is little immediate hope for reversal.

Furthermore, the reissue explosion means that contemporary artists who are lucky enough to hold recording contacts find themselves competing against the likes of Muddy Waters and Robert Johnson for sales, press and airplay. In the US in particular, they do so in an environment that has also been shaken by the closings of many clubs and music shops, declining spending on live entertainment, and commercial radio programming that has been narrowed to the lowest common denominator. Internet radio has been a bright spot in the marketplace, with UK programmes such as Paul Jones's BBC Radio 2 show bringing blues to a worldwide audience.

'If an art form doesn't evolve, it dies. If blues wants to survive, it's got to do something fresh and it's got to reach the youth.'

Otis Taylor

John Lee Hooker (1917–2001) once said 'When they bury me, they're gonna bury the blues aside of me'. Indeed, as influential labels withdrew from the market, his words seem like they might have been frighteningly prophetic. Even a chart-topping collaboration between rock star Eric Clapton and the blues' reigning performer B.B. King, *Riding With The King* (2000), failed to produce a trickle-down of interest in other artists. Likewise, the high-profile public television series *Martin Scorsese Presents: The Blues* had little effect on overall attention for the genre or on record sales. Both of those events came in 2003, proclaimed the 'Year of the Blues' by the US Congress in order to celebrate the music's centennial.

The late, great John Lee Hooker, whose notion that the blues would die with him seems frighteningly prophetic.

Unswerving Dedication

As John Lee Hooker and many others among the style's elder statesmen have repeated over the decades until it has become a cliché, the blues will never die. The ever-silver lining of the style is its durability and strength, born of its roots in struggle and spirituality.

Corey Harris (b. 1969), who was featured in the Scorsese-directed episode of *Presents: The Blues,* has dedicated himself to exploring every traditional avenue of the genre and spoke not just for himself when he declared in mid-2004, 'It's a sacrifice for me to do this music, but I'm dedicated to its sounds and words and I take my path in it very seriously'. Harris made that statement after a long day at the carpentry job he must work to support his family when he is at home, despite his international standing as a performer. If anything unites the majority of artists who continue to perform and record blues music today, it is their unswerving dedication to the genre no matter the economic consequences.

Traditional Artistry Thrives

There are musicians, such as the New Englanders Duke Robillard (b. 1948) and Ronnie Earl (b. 1953), who can play with the linear eloquence of swinging, single-note guitar soloist T-Bone Walker. Others, including Doug MacLeod, who records for the Netherlands' Black and Tan Records, and Louisiana Red (b. 1936), an expatriate American living in Germany, evoke the raw complexity of the Texas acoustic virtuoso Blind Lemon Jefferson (1897–1929) or the early Delta masters Charley Patton (1891–1934) and Son House (1902–88). Regardless of approach, what the finest of today's traditional blues artists share is a drive for mastery combined with personal expression. Some are astonishingly eclectic, dipping into every font of the blues with grace and authenticity. A sterling example is Paul Rishell (b. 1950) & Annie Raines (b. 1969), a guitar and harmonica duo from Massachusetts that won the Blues Foundation's W.C. Handy Award for Acoustic Blues Album of the Year in 2000 for *Moving To The Country*. Their repertoire embraces the ballads of Patton, the gospel of Washington Phillips and the laconic playfulness of the Memphis Jug Band, but also extends past that early-twentieth-century music to include Little Walter instrumentals and the Chicago ghetto blues of Magic Sam (1937–69) as well as their own songs.

Popular Melody

Otis Taylor – 'Hands On Your Stomach' (2001)

Corey Harris, who appeared in Scorsese's 2003 episode of Presents: The Blues *entitled* From Mississippi To Mali, *has dedicated himself to keeping the blues alive.*

Keeping The Blues Alive

Otis Taylor (b. 1948) follows tradition even further back, albeit with modern instrumentation. Using digital effects and electric banjos in Appalachian folk tunings, he is able to evoke the sounds of ancient African instruments such as the kora and the n'jarka.

Then Taylor, who may be the finest blues lyricist to emerge since Sonny Boy Williamson II (1899–1965) and Willie Dixon (1915–92), ups the ante by returning the blues to the realm of visceral protest music. His song 'My Soul's In Louisiana', about a lynching, is a blood-chilling example of his art. Then there are artists who focus on a single type of blues with laser precision. English harmonica virtuoso Paul Lamb (b. 1955), who fronts the Kingsnakes, and his US counterpart Kim Wilson, who performs both as a solo artist and with his Fabulous Thunderbirds, are at the forefront of this camp, playing first-generation-style electric blues so authentic that it sounds as if it has been transported from a Chicago steelworkers' bar of the late 1950s.

Blues rock, the brushfire ignited by Cream in the 1960s and swept to all corners of the planet by the likes of Fleetwood Mac, Led Zeppelin, the Rolling Stones and other pioneering British bands, has by now existed long enough to fall into tradition's camp. Many artists who played in those groups, including Peter Green, Robert Plant and Mick Taylor, are still at the style's forefront. Newcomers Walter Trout (b. 1951), the Black Crowes and Government Mule have carved their place in the subgenre, but overall rock's relationship to blues has become increasingly distant in the past two decades – despite the late crown-prince of grunge Kurt Cobain's penchant for Leadbelly (he covered 'Where Did You Sleep Last Night' and 'They Hung Him On A Cross' with his band Nirvana).

Popular Melody

Chris Thomas King – 'Tha Real' (2002)

Some of the most interesting musicians in contemporary blues are those nudging it towards its future. Blues industry pundits agree that the music must find a younger audience to gain sales and avoid further marginalization. The blues-pop blendings of Keb' Mo' (b. 1951) and Eric Bibb (b. 1951), popular as they are, do not speak to the under-25 or even the under-35 crowd in the same way that John Mayall's Bluesbreakers, to say nothing of the Rolling Stones, did in the 1960s.

Guitarist Otis Taylor blends the roots of blues music with 1960s-style psychedelic sounds.

New Directions in Blues

A new breed of daring artists are banking their hopes on infusing blues with the electronic rhythms and blunt vocal cadences of hip hop. Foremost among them is Chris Thomas King (b. 1964), who grew up playing traditional electric blues in his father's juke joint in Baton Rouge, Louisiana, but whose imagination was inflamed by the potent words and music of this comparatively new urban sound.

Inspired by hip hop's anti-authority stance, King has also delved into the realms of protest music with his stories of hard ghetto life and racial discrimination. Like other rappers, he uses sampling as part of his palette, but on his albums he often samples the likes of Delta pioneer Son House. King may become a true touchstone for this hybrid. Other mainstream rappers, notably Arrested Development and Michael Franti of the group Spearhead, have explored blues themes with more satisfying results.

Several years ago King started his own record label dedicated to the blues. Among his signings is England's Nublues, a group that blends acoustic textures with singing, rapping, sampling and turntable manipulation. There are other smart hybridizers at work, too. The North Mississippi Allstars, for example, have built a niche within the jam-band audience for their live blend of Delta sounds, 1970s blues rock, rap and bursts of electronic noise. Jazzmen James 'Blood' Ulmer (b. 1941) and Olu Dara took a deeper trip at the end of the 1990s. Ulmer began collaborating with Vernon Reid, the guitarist in Living Coloür, while Dara traded cornet for guitar. Both began exploring blues and their native Mississippi roots, without relinquishing their improvisational impulses, in acclaimed albums that have won broad acceptance in Europe. Out on the very horizon, a few dedicated experimenters are pushing blues further into the digital age while still honouring its deepest traditions. Foremost among them may be Elliott Sharp (b. 1951), who spent years at the front of avant-garde rock before returning to blues in the early 1990s with his group Terraplane.

Key Albums

Greens From The Garden Corey Harris
Respect The Dead Otis Taylor
About Them Shoes Hubert Sumlin

All of these artists and many others guarantee that the future of the blues will be bright. However, whether the style will again enjoy the kind of prominence, economic success and wide appeal that it did in the 1930s, 1960s and, briefly, the 1980s, remains to be seen.

Elliott Sharp has helped to modernize the blues.

A-Z of Artists

Lurrie Bell (Guitar, vocals, b. 1958)

Bell grew up among Chicago legends, including his harmonica-playing father Carey Bell. The self-taught guitarist was 17 when he joined Willie Dixon's band and 19 when he toured with Koko Taylor. He had already built a reputation for wiry, envelope-pushing improvisations when he formed Sons of Blues with Billy Branch in the mid-1970s. He has since recorded several solo albums, including 1995's superb *Mercurial Son*, but his career has been interrupted periodically by homelessness and health issues.

Eric Bibb (Guitar, vocals, b. 1951)

Folk-bluesman Bibb blends deep roots with pop influences, occasionally incorporating African and Afro-Cuban sounds. He was born in New York City, where his father, Leon, performed in musical theatre and on the folk scene. His uncle was John Lewis of the Modern Jazz Quartet, while Odetta, Pete Seeger and Paul Robeson were among his family's friends. Bibb's finest album to date, 2004's *Friends*, features Odetta, Guy Davis, Martin Simpson, Harry Manx and his role model Taj Mahal.

Elvin Bishop (Guitar, vocals, b. 1942)

This Tulsa, Oklahoma native's return to his roots as a blues player has been characterized by barnstorming live sets in the Chicago electric tradition. Bishop, who became a charter member of the Paul Butterfield Blues Band in the 1960s, stopped making music for nearly a decade following his Elvin Bishop Group's US number-three pop hit 'Fooled Around And Fell In Love' in 1976.

Key Tracks

'Kiss Of Sweet Blues' Lurrie Bell
'For You' Eric Bibb
'Fooled Around and Fell In Love' Elvin Bishop
'Don't You Lie To Me' Elvin Bishop
'I Put My Baby Out' Billy Branch

Billy Branch (Harmonica, vocals, b. 1951)

Branch began playing harmonica at the age of 10, before polishing his onstage technique in Chicago with Big Walter, James Cotton, Junior Wells and Carey Bell. In 1975 he became a sideman for Willie Dixon and then formed Sons of Blues with Lurrie Bell (guitar). Branch continues to front the band and is a respected blues educator. He also appears in the Robert Mugge-directed concert film *Hellhounds On My Trail: The Afterlife Of Robert Johnson* (1999).

Blues harpist Billy Branch (right), with guitarist Kenny Neal.

A-Z of Artists

R.L. Burnside (Guitar, vocals, 1926–2005)

Rural 'R.L.' Burnside was inspired to learn guitar by his north Mississippi neighbours Fred McDowell and Ranie Burnette, as well as John Lee Hooker records. He first recorded in the 1960s, but his career ignited after he appeared in the documentary *Deep Blues* (1991) and released *Too Bad Jim* (1994) on Fat Possum, a label based in Burnside's birthplace of Oxford, Mississippi. Along with Junior Kimbrough, this potent rhythm and slide guitarist and singer was responsible for the 1990s juke-blues revival.

John Campbell (Guitar, vocals, 1952–93)

Campbell, who was born in Louisiana and grew up in Texas, combined the traditional approach of Lightnin' Hopkins with his own swampy, electrified New Orleans hoodoo spiritualism. His debut, the Ronnie Earl-produced *A Man & His Blues* (1988), is a superb summation of his acoustic roots, but its two electric follow-ups, *One Believer* (1991) and *Howlin' Mercy* (1993), which introduced rock flourishes, had him poised for a commercial breakthrough when his heart failed.

Shemekia Copeland (Vocals, b. 1979)

This Harlem-born daughter of Texas bluesman Johnny 'Clyde' Copeland apprenticed onstage with her father. She emerged as a solo artist in 1997, beginning a run of albums that made her one of the most popular artists in contemporary blues. Nevertheless, it wasn't until 2002's Dr John-produced *Talking To Strangers* that the quality of Copeland's songs matched that of her powerful shouter's voice and live charisma.

Key Tracks

'Hard Time Killing Floor' R.L. Burnside
'R.L.'s Story' R.L. Burnside
'When The Levee Breaks' John Campbell
'Talking To Strangers' Shemekia Copeland
'Hell Or High Water' Tinsley Ellis

Tinsley Ellis (Guitar, vocals, b. 1957)

Blues rocker Ellis grew up in Florida and emerged in the 1980s from Atlanta, Georgia, where he led the Heartfixers, whose albums include a disc featuring blues shouter Nappy Brown. Ellis blends the dynamic technique of B.B. King, Freddie King, Albert King, Otis Rush and Magic Sam with the Cream-era pyrotechnics of Eric Clapton. His evolution as a songwriter and musical pluralist, incorporating elements of funk and soul, is captured best on 2000's *Kingpin*.

Blues singer Shemekia Copeland is the daughter of Texas bluesman Johnny 'Clyde' Copeland.

A-Z of Artists

Corey Harris (Guitar, vocals, b. 1969)

Harris was discovered on the streets of New Orleans playing acoustic blues. Soon after his debut, 1995's *Between Midnight And Day*, the Denver, Colorado native began incorporating rock, Afro-Cuban, Afro-Caribbean and African influences into his repertoire, creating a distinctive fusion. The electric *Mississippi To Mali* (2004), a collaboration with musicians from Mississippi and Africa, tied to his appearance in a similarly titled 2003 Martin Scorsese documentary, capture his soulful versatility.

Michael Hill (Guitar, vocals, b. 1952)

Hill's Blues Mob earned an international cult following with a gritty, aggressive style well-tailored to Hill's lyrics, which often focus on urban social issues. Born in the south Bronx, Hill began playing blues after hearing Jimi Hendrix and Cream. In 1993 he formed Blues Mob and recorded *Bloodlines*, the first of five strong albums that fuse his rock-fuelled instincts with pop, African and Caribbean flourishes.

Junior Kimbrough (Guitar, vocals, 1931–98)

David 'Junior' Kimbrough, from Holly Springs, Mississippi was a leader of the 1990s juke blues revival and had also played a part in creating the 'Sun sound' by influencing early rockers in the 1950s, including Charlie Feathers. Kimbrough's approach was rooted in traditional African drum groups and he functioned much like a drum master, establishing the band's rhythms on his guitar. His later recordings include *All Night Long* (1993).

Key Tracks

'Wild West' Corey Harris
'Hard Blues For Hard Times' Michael Hill
'All Night Long' Junior Kimbrough
'Trouble Will Soon Be Over' Chris Thomas King

Chris Thomas King (Guitar, bass, keyboards, drums, vocals, b. 1964)

Multi-talented King began in the footsteps of his father – Baton Rouge, Louisiana juke bluesman Tabby Thomas. King has mastered traditional electric and acoustic blues. He also performs and records rock- and rap-blues hybrids. He played Lowell Fulson in the Ray Charles biopic *Ray* (2004) and Blind Willie Johnson in *The Soul Of A Man*, the Wim Wenders-directed episode of *Martin Scorsese Presents: The Blues*. In 2002 Chris Thomas King established his own New Orleans-based label, 21st Century Blues.

Chris Thomas King combines his blues roots with hip hop influences and often samples standard blues records.

A-Z of Artists

The Kinsey Report (Vocal/instrumental group, 1984–present)

Gary, Indiana's Kinsey brothers formed the Kinsey Report to support their father, Lester 'Big Daddy' Kinsey, and in 1985 they recorded *Bad Situation*. Led by Donald (guitar, vocals), who had been a sideman for Albert King and Bob Marley, the brothers signed with Alligator Records and released *Edge Of The City*, the first of three snarling, blues-rock albums, in 1987. Big Daddy Kinsey went on to make fine solo recordings, including 1993's *I Am The Blues*, until his death from cancer in 2001.

Paul Lamb & The Kingsnakes (Vocal/instrumental group, 1989–present)

English harmonica virtuoso Lamb (b. 1955) initially learned to play from recordings, but was mentored by Sonny Terry after they met at the World Harmonica Championships when Lamb was 15. He performed with other blues legends, including Buddy Guy and Junior Wells, before forming the five-piece Paul Lamb & the Kingsnakes in 1989. They released the first of their nine albums in 1990 and play nearly 300 dates annually, faithfully recreating the sound of late 1950s Chicago blues.

Keb' Mo' (Guitar, vocals, b. 1951)

Songwriter Kevin Moore spent the 1970s and 1980s in his native Los Angeles, playing studio sessions and in mainstream funk and blues bands. Committing himself to blues, he travelled to the Mississippi Delta to study with the late guitarist Eugene Powell. Moore then combined blues with pop hooks and instrumental sweetening, and has released eight easy-listening, semi-acoustic albums, including his eponymous 1994 debut and the 1996 Best Contemporary Blues Grammy-winner *Just Like You*.

Key Tracks

'Come To Me' The Kinsey Report
'Mad About My Baby' Paul Lamb & the Kingsnakes
'Just Like You' Keb' Mo'
'Come On In My Kitchen' Keb' Mo'
'Gone To Hell' John Mooney

John Mooney (Guitar, vocals, b. 1955)

Born in East Orange, New Jersey, Mooney grew up in Rochester, New York, where he joined Joe Beard's group at 15 and studied slide with Delta giant Son House. In 1976 he moved to New Orleans, where he began to concoct an electric style that blended Crescent City funk rhythms with traditional blues, gelling on his 2000 album *Gone To Hell*.

Blues-rock group the Kinsey Report, pictured in London during a 1993 UK tour.

A-Z of Artists

Neville Brothers (Vocal/instrumental group, 1977–present)

The Neville Brothers – Art (keyboards, vocals), Aaron (percussion, vocals), Charles (saxophone, vocals) and Cyril (percussion, vocals) – have been one of New Orleans' foremost musical families since 1954. Art led Allen Toussaint's house band (the Meters) from the late 1960s, before convening his brothers into a unit in 1976. They released the successful *Fiyo On The Bayou* in 1981 and since then have made consistently good albums including *Yellow Moon* (1989), produced by Daniel Lanois. Their album *Walkin' In The Shadow Of Life* (2004) focuses on family ties, cultural heritage and spiritual identity.

Lucky Peterson (Keyboards, guitar, bass, drums, trumpet, vocals, b. 1963)

Born Judge Kenneth Peterson in Buffalo, New York, this child prodigy keyboardist had played on *The Ed Sullivan Show* by the age of six. His father is soul bluesman James Peterson. At 17, Lucky became Little Milton's bandleader and then played with Bobby Bland. In 1988 he focused on guitar and began a solo career that has become increasingly experimental, culminating in the racial themes and heavy rock and funk of 2003's visceral *Black Midnight Sun*, produced by Bill Laswell.

Paul Rishell & Annie Raines (Vocal duo, 1993–present)

This Cambridge, Massachusetts-based duo embrace vintage music styles with absolute authenticity. Brooklyn-born Rishell (b. 1950, vocals, guitar) discovered traditional blues in the 1960s and played with Son House and Johnny Shines. He began leading bands and performing solo in 1975, releasing his debut *Blues On Holiday* in 1990. He then met Raines (b. 1969, harmonica, mandolin, vocals), whose influences included Little Walter and Sonny Boy Williamson I. Their first recording together was 1996's *I Want You To Know*, while *Moving To The Country* (2000) won a W.C. Handy Award for Acoustic Blues Album of the Year.

Key Tracks

'Yellow Moon' Neville Brothers
'1-2-3-4' Lucky Peterson
'Black Midnight Sun' Lucky Peterson
'Moving To The Country' Paul Rishell & Annie Raines
'Twist It Babe' Paul Rishell & Annie Raines

The Neville Brothers worked as the house band for Allen Toussaint before going their own way in the 1970s.

A-Z of Artists

Duke Robillard (Guitar, vocals, b. 1948)

Robillard's grasp of blues and jazz has kept him in demand since he founded Roomful of Blues in 1967. He was born in Woonsocket, Rhode Island and was influenced by Bill Doggett, T-Bone Walker and many others. He left Roomful in 1979 for a stint with rockabilly singer Robert Gordon and then ignited his solo career, which he interrupted in 1990 to join the Fabulous Thunderbirds. In the late 1990s he began producing albums for Ruth Brown, Jay McShann, Eddy Clearwater and others.

Mighty Mo Rodgers (Keyboards, vocals, b. 1942)

Maurice Rodgers grew up sneaking into chitlin circuit clubs in his native Chicago and nearby Gary, Indiana. His distinctive songwriting combines funky arrangements with explorations of the metaphysics of the blues, notably on his 1999 debut *Blues Is My Wailin' Wall*. He began performing in the mid-1960s in Los Angeles with T-Bone Walker, Albert Collins and others; his sound is influenced by the Memphis Stax stable of stars.

Bobby Rush (Guitar, bass, harmonica, b. 1940)

Rush's mix of vaudeville stage antics and soul-blues grooves has made him the king of the modern chitlin circuit. Born in Homer, Louisiana, Rush moved with his family to Chicago in 1953. He emerged from the west side blues scene in the 1960s and his career took off with 1971's 'Chicken Heads', after which he spent the next two decades touring and recording. Increasing press coverage and a starring role in an episode of 2003's *Martin Scorsese Presents: The Blues* series have introduced him to a wider audience.

Key Tracks

'I Still Love You Baby' Duke Robillard
'Blues Is My Wailing Wall' Mighty Mo Rodgers
'Chicken Heads' Bobby Rush

Saffire – The Uppity Blues Women (Vocal/instrumental group, 1984–present)

Formed in Virginia by virtuoso Ann Rabson (piano, guitar, vocals) and her guitar student Gaye Adegbalola, Saffire burst out internationally in 1990 with the release of their eponymous debut. Andra Faye replaced original bassist Earlene Lewis in 1992. The band has a knack for framing contemporary songs with twists of novelty humour, written from a feminist perspective in traditional acoustic settings.

Mighty Mo Rodgers is a gifted songwriter who has absorbed both blues and soul influences.

RD-600 Roland

A-Z of Artists

Elliott Sharp (Guitar, bass, reeds, programming, vocals, b. 1951)

Cleveland, Ohio-born Sharp is on the cutting edge, combining his experience as an improviser with deep tradition. Sharp's earliest gigs were with blues bands. After 20 years of sophisticated experimentation with other forms, he formed his own blues band, Terraplane, in 1994. Sharp's playing pushes the envelope of blues tonality and incorporates digital programming and other unconventional elements. It is best heard on 2004's *Do The Don't,* which features guest guitarist Hubert Sumlin.

Kim Simmonds (Guitar, harmonica, piano, vocals, b. 1947)

Simmonds emerged as the leader of early British blues-rock band Savoy Brown in 1965. Although the Welsh-born guitarist's group grew louder and heavier into the 1970s, he never lost his interest in the acoustic country blues. Savoy Brown soldiers on, but in 1997 Simmonds began a parallel solo career with the all-acoustic *Solitaire*, and continues to perform and record in that vein.

Angela Strehli (Vocals, b. 1945)

This raw-edged songstress emerged from the same Austin, Texas scene that yielded Stevie Ray Vaughan, with her 1986 debut *Stranger Blues*. Strehli, who was born in Lubbock, perfected her slow phrasing and dynamic attack at the famed Antone's nightclub, learning from visiting artists Muddy Waters, Otis Rush, Albert Collins and Albert King. In recent years Strehli has incorporated more 1940s and 1950s R&B influences into her music.

Key Tracks

'Please Don't' Elliott Sharp
'Struck By Lightning' Kim Simmonds
'Solitaire' Kim Simmonds
'Blue Highway' Angela Strehli
'Back Door Man' Hubert Sumlin

Hubert Sumlin (Guitar, vocals, b. 1931)

Sumlin's distinctive riffs are all over Howlin' Wolf's classic Chess recordings; Wolf plucked the Greenwood, Mississippi innovator from a band he had started with James Cotton, and Sumlin became an integral part of Wolf's sound. After Wolf's death in 1976, Sumlin joined Eddie Shaw in his Wolf Gang band and went solo 1980, but excessive drinking kept his performances patchy. However, Sumlin sobered up in the late 1990s and has since recorded several successful solo albums, including 2005's brilliant *About Them Shoes.*

Howlin' Wolf's erstwhile guitarist Hubert Sumlin plays a gig at London's Borderline club in 2000.

A-Z of Artists

Otis Taylor (Guitar, banjo, mandolin, harmonica, vocals, b. 1948)

Colorado's Otis Taylor is the most inventive blues songwriter to emerge in recent decades. The Chicago native revives the genre's role as protest music, often telling stories of lynchings and racial injustice. His use of archaic Appalachian banjo tunings, droning progressions and digital delay creates a sound that reflects the blues' African roots and echoes 1960s psychedelia. It is a wise, timeless combination, best captured on his potent albums *Respect The Dead* (2002) and *Truth Is Not Fiction* (2003).

Susan Tedeschi (Guitar, vocals, b. 1970)

Tedeschi was introduced to blues and gospel via her parents' record collection. While singing in the Berklee College of Music gospel choir, she performed at blues jams around her native Boston and formed her own group. Her international debut, 1998's *Just Won't Burn*, earned her a Grammy nomination and sold 700,000 copies. She seemed poised for a crossover career until the follow-up, 2002's far superior, soul-steeped *Wait For Me*, failed to generate much attention outside blues circles.

Ali Farka Toure (Guitar, gurkel, n'jarka, vocals, 1939–2006)

Toure based his distinctive style on the music of his native Mali and on American blues and R&B – in particular John Lee Hooker, whose simple yet inimitable hypnotic drones are echoed in Toure's songs. Five earlier albums had made Toure a cult favourite when his 1994 Grammy-winning collaboration with slide guitarist Ry Cooder, *Talking Timbuktu*, elevated him to *éminence grise* of the world music scene.

Key Tracks

'Ten Million Slaves' Otis Taylor
'Tired Of My Tears' Susan Tedeschi
'Diaraby' Ali Farka Toure
'Go The Distance' Walter Trout

Walter Trout (Guitar, vocals, b. 1951)

In a BBC radio poll, blues rocker Trout was ranked number six among the top 20 guitarists of all time. Not bad for an Ocean City, New Jersey native who worked for decades as a sideman with John Lee Hooker, Big Mama Thornton, Canned Heat and John Mayall before forming his own band in 1990. Since then he has recorded a dozen albums, heavy on guitar, and earned an international reputation for his fiery live performances.

Susan Tedeschi, whose 1998 album Just Won't Burn *earned her a Grammy nomination.*

STYLES OF THE BLUES

One of the great things about blues music is its simplicity; its recognizable 12-bar structure, often repetitive lyrics and familiar instrumentation create an instantly accessible sound that has a powerful emotional effect on the listener. However, the inventiveness of countless performers over the years has sent the blues in many different directions and has transformed it into the wide-ranging genre that it has become.

This section of *Blues: The Complete Story* examines the various styles of blues music that have arisen from musicians delivering their own take on the standard blues formula. A number of factors can inform the development of music: in some cases the very landscape in which the musicians live may provide a key influence (consider the beautiful yet desolate music inspired by the Mississippi Delta); in other cases the cultural mix might alter the sound (for example, the unique blues style that grew out of the cultural melting pot of New Orleans, with its Creole and Hispanic influences).

The variety of instruments and instrumental techniques available to the players has a major influence on the development of different blues styles, in addition of course to the individual ingenuities of the artists, producers and bandleaders involved. The influences of other developing musical styles tend to have an irreversible effect on the genres that surround them; in its global spread since its early days in localized pockets of America, the blues has absorbed aspects of other musical styles, while continuing to have a heavy influence on other genres such as rock music. However, whether from Chicago, Texas or London; whether jump, R&B or rock, the raw power of blues music remains constant.

It was in Mississippi bars such as this one that the blues began to take shape.

BLUE OASIS

Work Songs

Jazz, blues, spirituals and gospel music, were rooted in the work songs of black labourers of the South. As Chet Williamson wrote 'These were songs and chants that kept a people moving and advancing through dreadful oppression. These are the voices of those who harvested the fields, drove the mules, launched the boats, and hammered the rails.'

Based on the compelling rhythms, sliding-pitch intonation and overlapping call-and-response traditions of West African music, which persevered in North America during the time of slavery, these work songs resounded in the South during the reconstruction years following the Civil War, which ended in 1865. Whether sung by slaves and, later, sharecroppers picking cotton or husking corn, workers laying track on the railroad line, prisoners on the chain gang breaking rocks and draining swamps or coal miners with pickaxes, work songs were structured in a very similar way to West African percussion ensembles.

In a typical drum ensemble of Ghana, the leader/drummer would give signals or motifs to the rest of the group, which would then respond in overlapping call-and-response fashion. The leader, in effect, poses a question and the group offers an answer (the overlap occurring where the call is still in the air when the response begins, or the call begins again before the response is done). Responsorial singing follows this same procedure, with the leader often improvising above a rhythmic pulse by varying the timing, pitch, attack or decay of words at the beginning or end of a phrase. The leader might also toy with the phrasing by employing rhythmic displacement or a slight altering of the phrases in relation to the underlying beat.

'These long, mournful, antiphonal songs accompanied the work on cotton plantations, under the driver's lash.'

Tony Palmer, *All You Need Is Love: The Story Of Popular Music*

Work songs, often secular and usually relating to the slaves' predicament, helped the slaves in the cotton fields to pick in rhythm and also served to lift their spirits, relieving the pain and boredom of their labour.

A Fount of Creativity and Personal Expression

In most work songs, the rhythm was tied into the pattern of the work itself – the swinging back and down and the blow of a sledgehammer or pickaxe, the hoisting of ropes on a block and tackle – while the lead chanter acted as a coach, directing the teamwork until the job was done.

Each new line was often punctuated by a grunt as the axe or hammer found its mark:

'Dis ole hammer – hunh!
Ring like silver – hunh!
Shine like gold, baby – hunh!
Shine like gold – hunh!'

Field hollers, work songs and the cries of street vendors advertising their wares all incorporated imaginative vocal sounds and various pitch-altering decorations of a note, including the use of 'blue notes'. A good example of this can be heard on an Alan Lomax recording from 1959 of 'Louisiana', sung by prisoner Henry Ratcliff, who was serving time at the Mississippi State Penitentiary at Parchman Farm. Other examples from Lomax's recording include 'Stewball', sung by Ed Lewis leading a group of prisoners at the Lambert State Penitentiary in Mississippi, and 'Berta Berta', sung by Leroy Miller leading a hoeing group at Parchman Farm. Another well-known field holler is 'Mama Lucy', sung by Leroy Gary and recorded by Lomax in 1959, also at Parchman Farm.

Key Artists

Sid Hemphill
Ervin Webb
Ed Young
Ed Lewis
Fred McDowell

The work song was fluid and organic and never repeated exactly the same way twice. This idea of an endless fount of creativity and personal expression within a simple, finite structure, through the use of vocal slurs, falsetto leaps and patches of melisma, is an inherently African device also readily apparent in the blues idiom.

Alan Lomax made these recordings in 1959, when the African-American music of the century's early years was still alive in the South. The collection includes field hollers, Delta blues, spirituals and prison recordings.

Southern Journey
61 Highway
Mississippi
Delta Country Blues,
Spirituals, Work Songs &
Dance Music
Volume 3
The Alan Lomax Collection
Clarksdale
Marks
Batesville
Oxford
University
Lexington
Durant
Kosciusko
Rolling Fork
Pickens
Carthage

Delta or Country Blues

It was in the rich cotton–producing Delta stretching from Mississippi to Tennessee that black labourers working the plantations gave ferment to an earthy style of music born out of African songs, chants, spirituals and gospel tunes that had been handed down for generations. They called it the blues.

The man usually recognized as the first star of Delta country blues is Charley Patton. An acoustic guitarist of impressive facility with a hoarse, impassioned singing style, Patton was a house-rocking entertainer who played plantation dances and juke joints throughout the Mississippi Delta during the early 1920s. Combined with a high-energy performance style, the strong rhythmic pulse of his music was so galvanizing that he held emotional sway over audiences everywhere he played. Legend has it that workers would often leave crops unattended to listen to him play guitar.

Patton's Prototype

When he finally documented his entertaining tunes in the studio (beginning with 'Pony Blues', for the Paramount label, in 1929), his records could be heard on phonographs throughout the South. And while he did not invent the form (nor was he the first Delta bluesman to record), Patton was the genre's most popular attraction: a genuine celebrity whose appetite for food, liquor and women were legendary, and who travelled from one engagement to the next with a flashy, expensive-looking guitar fitted with a custom-made strap and case. In essence, he was the prototypical rock star. When Patton died in 1934, he left behind a total of only 60 recorded tracks but his legacy was a colorful one, thoroughly addressed in 2001's Grammy-winning seven-CD box set, *Screamin' And Hollerin' The Blues: The Worlds Of Charley Patton*, on the Revenant label.

'Blues actually is around you every day. Downheartedness and hardship. You express it through your song.'
Arthur Lee Williams

Blind Willie Johnson was hugely influential to Delta bluesmen Son House and Fred McDowell, who both covered the great man's originals.

The Major Innovators

By the late 1920s, at the time of Patton's first recordings, other Mississippi bluesmen were also making their mark on records, including Patton contemporaries such as Tommy Johnson and Son House.

While Johnson emulated Patton's powerful, rough-hewn vocal delivery and showboating style – playing the guitar behind his neck and the like – he lacked the ambition that drove Patton to the pinnacle of stardom in the late 1920s. Instead, Johnson spent most of the 1920s drinking, gambling and womanizing, until his slow descent into alcoholism started to take its toll. Canned Heat, the popular, California-based boogie-blues band of the 1960s, took its name from the title of a Johnson song about drinking Sterno-denatured alcohol used for artificial heat.

Another major innovator of the Delta blues style, Eddie James 'Son' House brought an extraordinary degree of emotional power to his singing and slide guitar playing on his first recordings in the early 1930s for the Paramount label. A main source of inspiration for both Robert Johnson and Muddy Waters, Son (unlike his contemporary Charley Patton) lived long enough to experience his own rediscovery during the folk blues revival of the mid-1960s. A one-time Baptist preacher, House imbued his blues with an almost demonic intensity on recordings such as 'My Black Mama', 'Preachin' The Blues' and 'Walkin' Blues'. His 1965 recording of 'Death Letter' (cut while in his 60s for the Columbia label) is one of the most anguished and emotionally stunning laments in the Delta blues oeuvre and has been covered in dramatic fashion by a diverse list of artists such as David Johansen, Cassandra Wilson, Diamanda Galas, James Blood Ulmer, Derek Trucks and the White Stripes. In 1965, he played Carnegie Hall in New York and subsequently became an attraction on the folk blues coffeehouse network, where he was rightly hailed as the greatest living Delta singer still actively performing.

Key Artists

Charley Patton
Tommy Johnson
Son House
Robert Johnson
Skip James

After the death of his blues partner Willie Brown, Son House gave up the guitar. It wasn't until 1965 that he played and recorded once more.

Effecting a Generation

Perhaps the most celebrated and mythic figure in Delta blues was Robert Johnson, a guitarist of dazzling technique who could simultaneously juggle independent rhythms and pianistic-type lines by employing the unique finger-style approach he developed.

Legend has it that one night Johnson met the Devil at the crossroads and exchanged his everlasting soul for the gift of unparalleled virtuosity on the guitar. Whether that is folklore or not, Johnson's incredible skills as both a player and a profoundly blue singer soon became apparent to all around the Delta, including elders and inspirations such as Son House, who marvelled at his talent. An itinerant performer, Johnson had a wandering nature that took him well beyond the Delta to places like St. Louis, Chicago, Detroit and New York. His only recordings were made between 1936 and 1937.

Though Johnson died on 16 August 1938 at the age of 27, his approach to playing guitar and singing had a profound effect on a generation of blues musicians, including Jimmy Reed, Elmore James, Hound Dog Taylor and hundreds of others. His most famous songs, such as 'Sweet Home Chicago', 'Crossroads' and 'Love In Vain', have become blues standards, covered endlessly by the likes of the Rolling Stones, Led Zeppelin, Cream, Eric Clapton, Steve Miller and Cassandra Wilson. Other key, early country blues players include Skip James, Bukka White, Mississippi John Hurt, Mississippi Fred McDowell and Robert Johnson partners and disciples Robert Lockwood Jr. (Johnson's step-son and taught by the master himself) and Johnny Shines.

In recent years, renewed interest in Delta or country blues has been triggered by the spirited work of guitarists/singer-songwriters like Corey Harris, Keb' Mo', Guy Davis, Eric Bibb and Alvin Youngblood Hart, who have blended in touches of Delta-style acoustic blues along with their more contemporary pop-oriented offerings on record and in concert appearances all over the world. Present-day exponents of an edgier, electrified version of the raw, uncut Delta blues sound include Mississippi-based guitarists-singers R.L. Burnside, Big Jack Johnson, Paul 'Wine' Jones, Roosevelt 'Booba' Barnes and James 'Super Chikan' Johnson.

Key Tracks

'Sweet Home Chicago' Robert Johnson
'Crossroads' Robert Johnson
'Love In Vain' Robert Johnson
'Illinois Blues' Skip James
'Shake 'Em On Down' Bukka White

Out of all the Delta bluesmen, Robert Johnson probably had the most direct impact on the generations that followed. His intricate guitar work and use of unusual tunings have frustrated budding guitarists for decades.

Louisiana Blues

New Orleans is widely acknowledged as the birthplace of jazz, but it also produced its own indigenous brand of blues, which borrowed from Texas and Kansas City while also making use of cajun and Afro-Caribbean rhythm patterns.

A mix of croaking and yodeling, floating over the top of the music in an independent time scheme, Professor Longhair's singular vocals added to his idiosyncratic charm. Influenced by New Orleans barrelhouse pianists Tuts Washington, Kid Stormy Weather and Sullivan Rock, Longhair developed his unique conception and made his recording debut in 1949 with the anthemic 'Mardi Gras In New Orleans', for the Dallas-based Star Talent label. In typically enigmatic fashion, he named his band the Shuffling Hungarians and scored a hit in 1950 for the Mercury label with 'Bald Head', which combined his rolling piano with some good-time bounce and hilarious lyrics.

'Black or white, local or out-of-town, they all had Longhair's music in common, just that mambo-rhumba boogie thing.'

Allen Toussaint

In 1953, Longhair recorded another New Orleans anthem, 'Tipitina', for the Atlantic label, and in 1959 he revived his 'Mardi Gras In New Orleans' (retitled 'Go To The Mardi Gras') for the regional Ron imprint. After fading from the scene in the 1960s, his performance at the first New Orleans Jazz & Heritage Festival in 1971 ignited a comeback, leading to a slew of recordings and international festival appearances. His last recording, the triumphant Crawfish Fiesta (Alligator Records), was released after his death on 30 January 1980. Longhair's irrepressible piano style was carried on by such Crescent City disciples as James Booker, Allen Toussaint, Fats Domino, Dr. John (Mac Rebennack) and Henry Butler.

Roy Byrd (aka Professor Longhair) started out as a street musician in the 1930s. He went on to influence countless musicians with catchy songs like 'Mardi Gras In New Orleans', which features his trademark whistling.

Good-Time Bounce

An accompanist to Longhair during his comeback years, Snooks Eaglin distinguished himself as a guitarist who could cover any style of music convincingly. Blind since birth, he developed a dazzling finger-style approach, which allowed him to shift easily from Delta-style blues to flamenco, to gospel, R&B, rock, surf guitar or jazz.

His earliest recordings, for the Folkways label in 1958, present him in an acoustic folk blues setting, accompanied only by harmonica and washboard. His early 1960s sides for the Imperial label show him excelling at New Orleans R&B, while his output for the Black Top label from the late 1980s onward highlight his blistering, rock-tinged guitar work in funky, New Orleans-style settings. He remains a top attraction in the Crescent City, at both the Jazz & Heritage Festival and showcase venues such as Tipitina's.

Another significant figure on the New Orleans blues scene was Eddie Jones (a.k.a Guitar Slim). Hailing from the Delta, he turned up in New Orleans at the age of 24, heavily influenced by Texas guitarist Clarence 'Gatemouth' Brown. His 1951 debut on the Imperial label featured the eerily distorted, nasty-toned guitar work and gospel-drenched vocals that would become his trademark. In 1954, his swampy, gospel-tinged track 'The Things I Used To Do', cut in New Orleans for the Specialty label, topped the R&B charts for 14 weeks and influenced a generation of young players, including the guitarist-songwriter Earl King. After recording throughout the 1950s for the Savoy, Specialty and Ace labels, King scored his biggest hits in the 1960s with Imperial, including 1960's rock-flavored 'Come On' (later covered by Jimi Hendrix), 1961's funky 'Trick Bag' and 1962's 'Always A First Time'.

Key Artists

Professor Longhair
Earl King
Guitar Slim
Lightnin' Slim
Champion Jack Dupree

King also wrote for Fats Domino, Professor Longhair and Lee Dorsey during the 1960s. Following a lull in the 1970s, his career was revived in the 1980s through a series of first-rate releases for the Black Top label. He remains a top attraction in the Big Easy, thrilling fans with his scintillating showmanship, as well as his irresistible blend of high-energy jump blues and second-line rhythms.

Blind finger-picker Snooks Eaglin was Professor Longhair's favourite guitarist and can be heard on many 'Fess tracks, as well as on Sugar Boy Crawford's rocking Mardi Gras anthem 'Jock-A-Mo'.

Snooks Eaglin
COUNTRY BOY IN NEW ORLEANS
With Lucious Bridges And
Percy Randolph
ARHOOLIE
CD348
OVER
60
MINUTES OF
CLASSIC
BLUES

Swamp and Gospel

A swampy side of the blues can be heard in the music of Baton Rouge artists such as harmonica aces Slim Harpo and Lazy Lester, as well as guitarists Silas Hogan and Lightnin' Slim, the latter scoring a national hit in 1959 with 'Rooster Blues'.

The Baton Rouge style was characterized by reverb-laden production, laid-back beats, relaxed vocals, snakey guitar riffs and raw, wailing harmonica. That tradition was continued by the harmonica player Raful Neal in the 1970s, and is being continued today by his son, the talented harmonica player/guitarist/songwriter Kenny Neal.

Accordion player Clifton Chenier melded traditional French Cajun dance music with R&B, rock'n'roll and the blues, originating the southwestern Louisiana hybrid known as zydeco. He made his first recordings in 1955, for the Los Angeles-based Specialty label. By the mid- 1970s, Chenier's Red Hot Louisiana Band was an international touring act. He recorded regularly throughout the 1980s for the blues/folk revival label Arhoolie, winning a Grammy in 1982 for the album *I'm Here!* and maintained a relentless touring schedule on the international festival circuit until his death in 1987. Chenier's zydeco heirs include such blues-drenched accordionists and bandleaders as his son C.J. Chenier, Boozoo Chavis, Buckwheat Zydeco and Rockin' Dopsie.

Key Tracks

'Rooster Blues' Lightnin' Slim
'Come On' Earl King
'I Love The Life I live' Slim Harpo
'I'm A Lover Not A Fighter' Lazy Lester
'The Things I Used To Do' Guitar Slim

Zedeco legend Clifton Chenier, who successfully melded blues elements into his hybrid sound.

petosa

Texas Blues

Although Texas has a rich legacy of acoustic country blues artists, its primary contribution to the blues was electric. An inordinate number of dazzling electric guitarists hailed from the Lone Star state, including T-Bone Walker, Clarence 'Gatemouth' Brown, Albert Collins, Lightnin' Hopkins, Freddie King and scores of hotshot six-stringers still on the scene.

Often accompanied by flamboyant showmanship, the Texas electric-guitar style has always been overtly aggressive and rhythmically driving. As Billy Gibbons, of the Texas blues rock band ZZ Top, put it: 'The Texas sound could be described as heavier than light and bluesier than anything else.... And the flamboyancy of most Texans, which is now an established fact throughout the world, has created the flashiness that goes right along with the technical skills of most musicians'.

'In East Texas ... guitar accompanied blues tended to be rhythmically diffuse, with guitarists like Blind Lemon Jefferson playing elaborate, melodic flourishes to answer their vocal lines.'

Robert Palmer

Aggressive Showmanship

That flamboyance was perhaps best exemplified by the archetypal blues showman Aaron Thibeaux (T-Bone) Walker. Although Walker made his mark in Los Angeles in the late 1930s, before spearheading the west coast blues movement, his roots were in Texas. Born on 28 May, 1910 in Linden, Texas, the young T-Bone learned all the stringed instruments but gravitated toward guitar. As a teenager, he often served as 'lead boy' for the Texas acoustic blues master Blind Lemon Jefferson, while the older, sightless man walked the Dallas streets playing for tips.

Walker later worked in touring carnivals and medicine shows with Ida Cox and Bessie Smith, sharing the bill with stars such as Bill 'Bojangles' Robinson and Cab Calloway, who had a major impact on T-Bone's concept of showmanship. He formed his own group in 1928 and recorded his first single for Columbia a year later, billed as Oak Cliff T-Bone. At the height of his popularity in the late-1940s, Walker exuded star quality. His audacious stage act – doing splits while playing his newly amplified Gibson electric guitar behind his head, with his teeth or under his leg – made him the Jimi Hendrix of his day.

Sam 'Lightnin'' Hopkins, a Texas country bluesman of the highest calibre.

Stinging Intensity

Clarence 'Gatemouth' Brown's big break came in the mid-1940s, when he filled in for an ailing T-Bone at the Bronze Peacock Lounge in Houston's Fifth Ward and thrilled the audience with his crowd-pleasing boogie-woogie and blistering finger-picked riffs. He was leading his own 25-piece band by 1947, and in 1949, scored a hit with 'My Time Is Expensive' on the Peacock label.

His next hit, 'Okie Dokie Stomp', came in 1951. In the mid-1960s, Brown served as musical director for the house band on The!!!Beat, a groundbreaking syndicated blues and R&B television show (a black alternative to American Bandstand), broadcast out of Dallas and hosted by the influential WLAC radio DJ Bill 'Hoss' Allen. Right up until his death in 2005 Gatemouth continued to pay tribute to his two biggest influences, jump blues master Louis Jordan and fellow Texan T-Bone Walker, while also blending in bits of country, Cajun and swinging, Count Basie-styled small band arrangements.

Albert Collins emulated both T-Bone's patented licks and his flamboyant stage presence. While his stinging intensity earned him the nickname 'Master of the Telecaster', Collins also engaged the audience by jumping off the stage and strolling through the house with a 46 m (150 ft) guitar cord. His first hit came in 1962 with the million-selling 'Frosty'. He cut his classic sides for the Imperial label from 1968 to 1970. Collins had signed to the Alligator label by 1977, while the late 1980s saw him releasing a string of well-received recordings, including the Grammy-winning *Showdown!*, a 1987 collaboration with the guitarists Robert Cray and his fellow Texan Johnny Copeland.

Key Artists

Clarence 'Gatemouth' Brown
Albert Collins
Freddie King
Blind Lemon Jefferson
T-Bone Walker

Two other Texas guitar slingers of note are Houston's Johnny 'Guitar' Watson and Gilmer's Freddie King. A flamboyant showman and nasty-toned picker in the T-Bone Walker tradition, Watson recorded throughout the 1950s before hitting it big in 1961 with his 'Gangster Of Love'. He reinvented himself as a raunchy disco-funkster in the 1970s, scoring hits with popular numbers such as 'A Real Mother For Ya' and 'Superman Lover'. Freddie King, nicknamed 'The Texas Cannonball' for his dynamic stage presence and intense attack on his Gibson guitar, made a great impact on a generation of players with his electrified output from the 1960s and early 1970s.

Clarence 'Gatemouth' Brown was an extremely versatile musician; he played a wide variety of instruments and his compositions embraced a range of musical styles.

Boogie-Woogie

A rollicking, fast piano style characterized by repetitive eighth-note bass figures in the left hand, meshed with sharp, bluesy single-note runs in the right hand, boogie-woogie was an infectious form that had an immediate appeal to dancers.

While the left hand remained tied to the task of covering driving basslines in a kind of 'automatic pilot' approach through chord changes (repeating continuous eighth-note bass figures in each different harmony), the right hand was liberated to explore, express and create with bluesy impunity.

Although the boogie-woogie fad swept the nation in the late 1930s, its roots go back much further. Jelly Roll Morton and W. C. Handy recalled hearing boogie-woogie-style piano in the American South during the first decade of the twentieth century. By the 1920s, boogie-woogie pianists were making their mark in saloons, juke joints, honky-tonks and at rent parties throughout both the South and North, where their powerfully rhythmic attack could cut through the din of a good time.

'They played a rolling rhythm in the left hand so that they could reach for a drink or a sandwich with the right hand.'

Donald Clark, *The Rise and Fall of Popular Music*

A Powerfully Rhythmic Attack

One of the pioneers of this raucous, rapid-fire, eight-to-the-bar piano style was Jimmy Yancey. Born in 1894 in Chicago, he worked in vaudeville as a singer and tap dancer – starting at the age of six – before taking up the piano in 1915. Although he did not make a recording until 1939, his most famous student, Meade 'Lux' Lewis, would become one of the first to document the boogie-woogie piano style on record with his 1927 'Honky Tonk Train Blues', a masterpiece of intricate cross-rhythms that highlights Lewis's remarkable independence between hands. That same year, Pine Top Smith garnered widespread attention with his catchy 'Pine Top's Boogie-Woogie', in which the pianist shouts instructions to dancers over the top of his rolling keyboard work. The hit tune, covered by several artists – including Bing Crosby with the Lionel Hampton Orchestra – also featured the rhythmic 'breaks' that were an essential part of early ragtime.

Meade 'Lux' Lewis, whose performance at 1938's Spirituals To Swing concert helped kick-start the boogie-woogie craze.

From Spirituals to Swing

In 1938, a single event helped bring boogie-woogie to wider public exposure. Jazz impresario John Hammond, a producer and talent scout who had a keen interest in boogie-woogie piano, arranged to have Meade 'Lux' Lewis and fellow boogie-woogie pianists Albert Ammons and Pete Johnson appear on the bill of his From Spirituals To Swing concert, held at Carnegie Hall on 23 December 1938.

The gala event (which also featured Count Basie's Orchestra, gospel singer-guitarist Sister Rosetta Tharpe, blues shouters Jimmy Rushing and Big Joe Turner, blues harmonica ace Sonny Terry, soprano sax genius Sidney Bechet and his New Orleans Feet Warmers and the Kansas City Six featuring tenor saxophonist Lester Young on the bill) not only helped launch the boogie-woogie boom but also led directly to the formation of Blue Note Records by the German immigrant Alfred Lion.

As Michael Cuscuna wrote in *The Blue Note Years* (Rizzoli): 'Lion attended the legendary From Spirituals To Swing concert at Carnegie Hall. He was so moved by the pulsating, dazzling boogie-woogie artistry of pianists Albert Ammons, Meade 'Lux' Lewis and Pete Johnson that he scraped up enough money for one day's rental on a studio. Exactly two weeks later on January 6, 1939, he recorded Ammons and Lewis. By that evening, Alfred Lion found himself in the record business – Blue Note Records was born'.

Key Artists

Meade 'Lux' Lewis
Albert Ammons
Pete Johnson
Pine Top Smith
Jimmy Yancey

Lion pressed 50 copies each of two 78rpm singles, one by Ammons, the other by Lewis. There followed other sessions with the two boogie-woogie pianists, including an innovative 1941 session with Lewis on celeste, Charlie Christian on guitar, Edmond Hall on clarinet and Israel Crosby on bass. Ammons recorded in the 1940s with the blues singer Sippie Wallace and in 1949 he cut a session with his son, the great tenor saxophonist Gene Ammons, before passing away later that year. Lewis continued playing after the boogie-woogie craze died down, relocating to Los Angeles and recording until 1962. Pete Johnson, the third member of the Big Three of boogie-woogie (the others being Albert Ammons and Meade 'Lux' Lewis), forged a musical rapport with blues shouter Big Joe Turner, releasing popular recordings such as 'Roll 'Em Pete' and 'Cafe Society Rag'. He moved to Buffalo in 1950 and, subsequently, drifted into obscurity.

John Hammond kick-started the careers of the key boogie-woogie players as well as discovering Bessie Smith, Billie Holiday, Bob Dylan, and Robert Johnson.

Down-Home Double Entendre and Humour

Born the year Meade 'Lux' Lewis cut his first tracks, Amos Milburn was a jovial boogie-woogie disciple who picked up the torch and ran with it. The Houston-born pianist pounded out some of the most explosive boogie grooves of the post-war era, beginning in 1946 on the Los Angeles-based Aladdin label.

His first hits included the driving, countrified boogie of 'Down The Road Apiece' (covered in 1960 by Chuck Berry and in 1965 by the Rolling Stones). Milburn excelled at good-natured, upbeat romps about booze and partying, imbued with a vibrant sense of humour and double entendre, as well as vivid, down-home imagery in his lyrics. He scored successive Top 10 R&B hits with 1948's 'Chicken Shack Boogie', 1949's 'Roomin' House Boogie', 1950's 'Bad, Bad Whiskey' and 1953's 'One Scotch, One Bourbon, One Beer'.

Key Tracks

'Pine Top's Boogie-Woogie' Pine Top Smith
'Roomin' House Boogie' Amos Milburn
'Honky Tonk Train Blues' Meade 'Lux' Lewis
'Roll 'Em, Pete' Pete Johnson
'Café Society Rag' Pete Johnson

Milburn's frantic piano-pumping style would have a profound effect on seminal rock'n'rollers such as Floyd Dixon, Fats Domino, Little Richard and Jerry Lee Lewis in the early 1950s. That boogie-woogie piano lineage continues today with explosive players such as Marcia Ball, Billy C. Wirtz and Mitch Woods.

Amos Milburn (piano) & his Chicken Shackers, as the group called themselves after the runaway success of their hit 'Chicken Shack Boogie'.

Pw

Chicago Blues

Chicago blues is a raw, rough-and-tumble music, defined by slashing, Delta-rooted electric slide guitars, raunchy-toned harmonicas overblown into handheld microphones to the point of distortion, uptempo shuffle drummers, insistently walking bass players and declamatory, soulful vocalists who imbued the tunes with Southern gospel fervour.

It became a universally recognized sound by the 1960s, fuelling the British blues movement in the early part of the decade (spearheaded by Alex Korner, Cyril Davies, John Mayall and the Rolling Stones) and the American blues boom of the late 1960s (spearheaded by blues rock pioneers such as Paul Butterfield, Michael Bloomfield, Elvin Bishop and Johnny Winter, and bands such as the Blues Project and Canned Heat).

'Muddy Waters, Howlin' Wolf and Elmore James were already seeming "old", but their dynamism, their fierce shouting ... expressed the swelling anger of the younger blacks.'

Paul Oliver

Urban and Amplified

Just as a generation of New Orleans jazz musicians had migrated from the source of the music to Chicago in the 1920s, a generation of Mississippi bluesmen migrated from the fertile Mississippi Delta region to Chicago in the 1940s. Mississippians such as Sunnyland Slim, Bukka White, Robert Nighthawk, Arthur 'Big Boy' Crudup, Muddy Waters, Otis Spann, Otis Rush, Homesick James, Johnny Young, Eddie Taylor, Jimmy Reed and Hound Dog Taylor were among the Delta blues musicians who came north to the Windy City, where they helped forge an urban, amplified take on the Delta sound. A second wave, including Howlin' Wolf, Hubert Sumlin, Elmore James, Sonny Boy Williamson II, Buddy Guy, Pinetop Perkins, Big Walter 'Shakey' Horton, James Cotton, Magic Sam, Magic Slim, David Honeyboy Edwards and Carey Bell, followed that same path north in the early 1950s, contributing to the post-war Chicago blues explosion.

Howlin' Wolf's primitive style of blues did not at first go down as well as the more sophisticated recordings of his contemporaries. The Rolling Stones helped to popularize his music.

Old-School Sounds

By the 1960s, Chicago's south side was a bustling hub of blues activity. Bands led by Muddy Waters, James Cotton, Otis Rush, Homesick James, J.B. Hutto, Otis Spann, Junior Wells and Howlin' Wolf performed regularly at south side nightclubs such as Peppers Lounge, Turner's Blue Lounge, Theresa's, the J&C Lounge and Curley's.

A significant recording from 1965 documented this vital scene and helped spread the word about lesser-known Chicago blues artists to a much wider audience. Produced by Samuel Charters for the Vanguard label, the three-volume *Chicago/The Blues/Today!* became the Rosetta Stone for many young blues initiates. As Eric Clapton recalled: 'It was a very important slice of history which helped me to understand the nature of modern blues music.'

The acknowledged father of the Chicago blues scene was McKinley Morganfield (aka Muddy Waters). A product of the fertile Mississippi Delta, he grew up in Clarksdale on Stovall's plantation, where he emulated the passionate slide-guitar stylings of Delta patriarch Son House. In 1941, the musicologist Alan Lomax made important field recordings of Waters at Stovall's under the auspices of the Library of Congress, documenting for all time the intensity and unfettered expression of the Mississippi Delta bluesman. Two years later, Waters moved to Chicago, where he sharpened his slide-guitar skills. He took up with the pianist Sunnyland Slim, who played a large role in launching Muddy's career by inviting him to provide guitar accompaniment for his 1947 Aristocrat session. That same day in the studio, Waters cut his own first recordings for Aristocrat. A year later, he had his first national hit with the 78 'I Can't Be Satisfied' backed with 'I Feel Like Going Home'.

Key Artists

Muddy Waters
Hound Dog Taylor
Howlin' Wolf
Elmore James
James Cotton

Muddy Waters was first recorded by Alan Lomax on a Mississippi plantation before heading to Chicago in the 1940s and hitting the big time with songs like Willie Dixon's 'Hoochie Coochie Man'.

A Thriving Blues Centre

Muddy Waters enjoyed a string of chart-toppers throughout the 1950s, backed by a tight band of superior musicians that included harmonica ace Little Walter, guitarist Jimmy Rogers and pianist Otis Spann. His supremacy continued through the first half of the 1960s, until the emerging psychedelic rock movement rendered his old-school Chicago sound passé.

After a relatively low profile in the 1970s, Muddy's recording career was resuscitated in the later part of the decade by his disciple Johnny Winter, who produced a triumphant triumvirate of hard-hitting Chicago blues albums announcing the great man's comeback.

Other important players on the Chicago blues scene include Elmore James, the most influential slide guitarist of the post-war period; Little Walter (Marion Walter Jacobs), the king of amplified blues harp and a key man in Muddy Waters' powerful band of the late-1940s and 1950s; harmonica ace Junior Wells, who replaced Little Walter in Waters' band and later formed a potent partnership with the guitarist Buddy Guy; and Howlin' Wolf (aka Chester Arthur Burnett), who migrated to Chicago from Mississippi in 1953 and would be challenging Muddy Waters' blues supremacy by 1958.

Key Tracks

'I Can't Be Satisfied' Muddy Waters
'I Feel Like Going Home' Muddy Waters
'Dust My Broom' Elmore James
'Juke' Little Walter
'Little By Little' Junior Wells

No summary of Chicago blues can be written without mentioning the ubiquitous session bassist-producer and Chess Records songwriter Willie Dixon, who penned numerous hits for Muddy Waters, Howlin' Wolf, Little Walter, Bo Diddley and Koko Taylor among others. His most famous tunes, including 'Hoochie Coochie Man', 'Evil', 'My Babe', 'Wang Dang Doodle' and 'Spoonful', are staples of the blues repertoire, having been covered countless times by rock and blues bands.

Chicago remains a thriving blues centre, boasting several vibrant nightclubs on the city's south and west sides, as well as two important blues labels in Alligator Records and Delmark. The city also hosts an annual, free summer blues festival in Grant Park, which draws fans from around the world.

Former boxer Willie Dixon was a man of many talents: he was a singer, musician, composer, producer, arranger, manager and promoter. As a composer, he was able to turn a simple blues into a catchy, memorable tune.

Piedmont or East Coast Blues

While the mississippi delta gave birth to guitar–based acoustic blues, in the area known as the Piedmont region – which stretches along the Atlantic seaboard from Virginia to Florida – a wide range of blues styles flourished, from the backwoods sound of the Appalachian foothills of Virginia to the more urbane sound of big cities such as Atlanta.

The characteristic that these varying Piedmont styles have in common, distinguishing them from the Delta blues style, is an emphasis on a sophisticated, syncopated kind of rhythm playing, with a complex fingerstyle technique that closely emulated a pianistic or ragtime approach on the guitar.

Some of the earliest and most famous practitioners of the Piedmont style include three virtuosic sightless players: Blind Blake (whose signature ragtime guitar piece 'Diddie Wah Diddie' was covered nearly 50 years later by Leon Redbone), Blind Boy Fuller (famed for 'Step It Up And Go' and 'Rag Mama Rag') and the formidable 12-string dazzler Blind Willie McTell (whose 'Broke Down Engine' was covered in the 1960s by blues guitar star Johnny Winter and whose 'Statesboro Blues' is still being performed as a blues-rock anthem to this day by the Allman Brothers Band). Other Piedmont pioneers included Curley Weaver and Robert 'Barbecue Bob' Hicks, both of whom recorded in the late 1920s.

'… Emphasis on good execution, rhythmically free-flowing, lighter in texture … it had a distinct flavour which mingled with that of the hillbilly and mountain singers of the white rural tradition.'

Paul Oliver

One of the pioneers of the Piedmont style and one of the greatest blues guitarists of all time, Blind Blake.

Cordially Yours
Blind Blake

A Uniquely American Artist

In the late-1950s, a folk revival swept college campuses from coast to coast, helping to revive the careers of many Piedmont bluesmen. Pink Anderson, John Jackson, Etta Baker and the duo of harmonica ace Sonny Terry and guitarist Brownie McGhee were rediscovered and soon performing on college campuses and in coffeehouses.

Budding folk artists such as Bob Dylan, Taj Mahal, Joan Baez and Bonnie Raitt championed the cause of Rev. Gary Davis, while Ry Cooder, David Bromberg and Jorma Kaukonen studied with him.

Also a blind artist and strictly self-taught on guitar, Davis developed remarkably quickly and, by his twenties, had an advanced technique that was unmatched in the blues field. Davis recorded for the first time in the early 1930s and became an ordained minister in 1937. An appearance at the 1958 Newport Folk Festival helped bring greater attention to Davis, leading to his becoming one of the most popular figures of the folk and blues revival scenes. Some of his signature tunes include 'Cocaine Blues', 'Samson And Delilah', 'Twelve Gates To The City' and 'Lovin' Spoonful'.

One of the most outstanding exponents of the Piedmont style today is the Washington DC based duo of guitarist John Cephas and harmonica player Phil Wiggins.

Key Artists

Blind Blake
Johnny Winter
Blind Willie McTell
Sonny Terry
Brownie McGhee

Rev. Gary Davis's playing style derived from the southeastern Piedmont region.

Jump Blues

Infectiously swinging, full of good humour and hugely popular for its time, the jump blues movement of the pre- and-post-Second World War years was a precursor to the birth of both R&B and rock'n'roll.

Kansas City was an incubator for jump blues in the late 1930s, via the infectious, rolling rhythms of Walter Page's Blue Devils and the Bennie Moten and Count Basie bands. But in the years following America's involvement in the Second World War, Los Angeles became a major breeding ground for a west coast branch of this new sound, characterized by shuffling uptempo rhythms, raucously upbeat spirits, honking tenor saxophones and swaggering vocalists who shouted about partying, drinking and good times. It was there, in the clubs that lined Central Avenue in Los Angeles, that a bevy of saxophonists dubbed 'honkers' for their piercing, squealy tones and frantic showmanship helped to define the scene. Among them were Big Jay McNeely, Chuck Higgins and Joe Houston, all players influenced by Illinois Jacquet's rambunctious tenor soloing on Lionel Hampton's huge 1942 hit, 'Flying Home'.

'Louis Jordan was a great musician and, in my opinion, he was way ahead of his time.'

B.B. King

Setting the Pattern

The undisputed heavyweight champion of the jump blues movement was Louis Jordan, who with his Tympany Five came to personify the spirit of the times with his theme song 'Let The Good Times Roll'. From 1941 to 1952, Jordan reigned as the 'King of Jukeboxes', with a string of catchy, uptempo boogie-woogie influenced hits like 'Caldonia', 'Choo Choo Ch'Boogie', 'Ain't Nobody Here But Us Chickens', 'Five Guys Named Mo' and 'Saturday Night Fish Fry'. Jordan's infectious rhythms, aggressive alto sax playing and dynamic stage presence set the pattern for jump blues.

The jump king Louis Jordan (centre) with his band. Jordan helped bring about the musical transition from big band swing and early R&B to the rock'n'roll sound of artists like Little Richard.

LOUIS JORDAN
"T6"

Pioneer Spirit

Many of the most popular west coast performers who followed in the wake of Jordan's success based themselves in Los Angeles during the 1940s but originally hailed from Texas.

Chief among them were pianist-singer Charles Brown, whose ultra-mellow style made a big impact in 1945 with 'Driftin' Blues' and again in 1947 with the Yuletide classic 'Merry Christmas Baby' (both cut with Johnny Moore's Three Blazers) and the pioneering electric guitarist T-Bone Walker, whose inherent soulfulness and jazzy dexterity on the instrument would influence generations of bluesmen from B.B. King, Lowell Fulson and Pee Wee Crayton to proto-rocker Chuck Berry and blues rock pioneers like Duane Allman, Johnny Winter and Eric Clapton.

Walker arrived in Los Angeles in 1934 and by 1939 was singing in Les Hite's popular Cotton Club Orchestra. After striking out on his own in 1941, he signed with Capitol Records and cut 'Mean Old World' backed with 'I Got A Break Baby' for the fledgling label. The momentum of his recording career was halted by the American Federation of Musicians' recording band which lasted from 1942 to 1944.

Key Artists

Louis Jordan
Charles Brown
T-Bone Walker
Pee Wee Crayton
The Liggins Brothers

After spending two years in Chicago, Walker returned to Los Angeles in 1946 and signed with Black & White Records. His third session for the label, the anthemic 'Call It Stormy Monday', became an immediate and huge hit in 1947, leading to a string of other successful recordings like 'T-Bone Shuffle' and 'West Side Baby'. Walker's success directly inspired guitarist Pee Wee Crayton, another transplanted Texan who relocated to Los Angeles, signed with the Bihari brothers in 1948 and hit big with 'Blues After Hours'.

T-Bone Walker's electric lead guitar play and singing set a precedent for future musicians.

West Coast Talents

Drummer/singer Roy Milton was another successful bandleader on the west coast blues scene who followed both Jordan's and Walker's example with his Solid Senders, a lively jump blues small combo. Milton's steady backbeat and infectious, Jo Jones-styled ebullience behind the kit provided the kinetic pulse behind such mid-1940s hits as 'R.M. Blues', 'Milton's Boogie' and 'Hop, Skip, Jump'.

By late 1947, at the peak of the west coast blues boom, Roy Milton & his Solid Senders became the number two jump blues band in the land, second only to Louis Jordan & his Tympany Five. Camille Howard, an outstanding boogie-woogie pianist, was the group's secret weapon and was heavily featured in the band throughout the Specialty label years, which ended in 1954.

Key Tracks

'Let The Good Times Roll' Louis Jordan
'Call It Stormy Monday' T-Bone Walker
'Driftin' Blues' Charles Brown
'The Honeydripper' Joe Liggins
'Drunk' Jimmy Liggins

Two other key figures on the west coast blues scene were brothers Joe and Jimmy Liggins. In 1945, pianist-bandleader Joe Liggins had a two-million-seller hit with 'The Honeydripper'. After joining Specialty in 1950, he hit big again with 'Pink Champagne', which became his signature song and was promptly covered by both Tommy Dorsey and Lionel Hampton. Jimmy's younger and more frantic brother Joe jumped into the recording business himself after signing with Specialty in 1947, and scored a hit the following year with 'Cadillac Boogie'. After leaving Specialty in 1953, he cut some sessions for Aladdin that anticipated the coming rock'n'roll movement, including the rousing novelty number 'I Ain't Drunk' (later covered by Albert Collins). Joe's wild stage presence and manic delivery also had a direct and lasting impact on rock'n'rollers like Little Richard, Chuck Berry, and Elvis Presley.

Another key figure on the west coast blues scene was bandleader, producer and talent scout Johnny Otis. By 1947, with the decline of the big bands, Otis downsized his larger ensemble to a septet, patterning his new band after the wildly successful examples of Louis Jordan & his Tympany Five and Roy Milton & his Solid Senders. In 1958 he scored a hit with 'Willie And The Hand Jive' and in 1972 formed the Blues Spectrum label to document many of the living jump blues legends of the day like Big Joe Turner, Roy Milton, Roy Brown and Pee Wee Crayton.

Texan guitarist Albert Collins, who successfully covered Joe Liggin's hit 'I Ain't Drunk'.

British Blues

British blues was born when British musicians attempted to emulate Mississippi and Chicago bluesmen during the 1960s. Led by Eric Clapton and the Rolling Stones, these musicians copied the styles of Big Bill Broonzy, Muddy Waters, Howlin' Wolf and B.B. King, and, aided by powerful amplifiers, developed a sound of their own.

In the early 1950s, the first American blues musician to appear in England was Big Bill Broonzy. Although he was a popular, Chicago-style bluesman, his UK performances consisted of acoustic folk blues and protest songs. It was Muddy Waters' visit to the country in 1958 that really sparked off the beginning of the British blues movement. Muddy played with an electric, solid-body Fender guitar, backed by Chris Barber's English blues group featuring guitarist Alexis Korner and blues harpist Cyril Davies. They played at a volume that shocked folk purists, but delighted a growing younger audience.

'I spent most of my teens and early twenties studying the blues – the geography of it and the chronology of it, as well as how to play it.'

Eric Clapton

Inspiration for a New Generation

After Muddy's tour, Korner and Davies pursued their musical ambitions even more passionately and formed Blues Incorporated, the first of the British blues bands. By 1962, the group had a regular slot at London's Marquee Club and a recording contract with Decca. Blues Incorporated inspired a younger generation of musicians, who then formed the three most influential British blues bands: John Mayall's Bluesbreakers featuring Eric Clapton, the Rolling Stones and the original Fleetwood Mac, with Peter Green. Clapton was a phenomenon with the Bluesbreakers – he turned his amp up to gig volume for recordings and obtained a more modern electric sound that influenced the likes of Jimi Hendrix and also Jimmy Page, who went on to form Led Zeppelin.

Alexis Korner was the main man behind the 1960s British blues scene.

Levin

Sex, Drugs and Rock'n'Roll

The Rolling Stones were perceived to be the definitive British blues band. They made a stream of hit records during the mid-1960s, including a chart-topping version of Willie Dixon's 'Little Red Rooster' (1964). They also covered songs by Muddy Waters and Howlin' Wolf, even insisting that Howlin' was a featured guest at a special US appearance. Their legendary 'sex, drugs and rock'n'roll' lifestyle contrasted sharply with the Beatles' squeaky-clean image during the 1960s.

By 1966, British blues was in full flight: the legendary John Mayall's Bluesbreakers With Eric Clapton album was released that year; bands such as Fleetwood Mac, the Yardbirds (with Jeff Beck) and Ten Years After (with Alvin Lee) were forming, and the Animals started to develop their inimitable brand of blues pop.

By the end of the decade, the British blues movement was carried back across to the United States, where it was reabsorbed by larger audiences than the original Chicago and Mississippi bluesmen had enjoyed. The success of the British blues bands also encouraged early American blues rock bands such as the Allman Brothers and ZZ Top, who had already developed their own unique styles.

Key Artists

The Rolling Stones
Eric Clapton
The Yardbirds
John Mayall's Bluesbreakers
Ten Years After

Although British blues is now seen by many as an early step in the conversion of blues into rock and heavy metal, it was a distinct style in its own right. Even today, musicians such as John Mayall, Eric Clapton and Aynsley Lister are waving the British blues flag.

The Rolling Stones were inspired by the likes of Muddy Waters, Howlin' Wolf and Jimmy Reed. They started out playing covers of blues songs, which were largely unknown to British audiences at the time.

Rhythm & Blues

Rhythm & blues (R&B) music evolved out of jump blues rhythms during the late-1940s, but it also had riffs and lyrics that were beginning to point more towards the emergence of rock'n'roll. Using sparser instrumentation than jump blues, R&B was based upon traditional blues chord changes played over a steady backbeat.

R&B placed more emphasis on the singer and the song than on the band's instrumentalists. Although it branched out into rock'n'roll during the 1950s, and soul during the 1960s, it always retained its own following, and R&B artists continue to draw large audiences all over the world.

As rock'n'roll continued to emerge, R&B branched out into further distinct styles, including doo wop, electric blues and New Orleans. Each of these exerted its influence on other R&B forms, as well as popular music in general.

'I was born with music inside me. That's the only explanation I know of.'
Ray Charles

The First Lady of R&B

During the late 1940s and early 1950s, a number of great singers began to emerge from the R&B scene. Ruth Brown was perhaps the first of these. Initially inspired by jazz singers such as Sarah Vaughan, Billie Holiday and Dinah Washington, Ruth developed her own expressive tone and was recommended to the bosses of a fledgling Atlantic Records in 1948. After she was promptly signed up, they produced a string of R&B classics, including 'So Long' (1949), 'Teardrops From My Eyes' (1950), 'I'll Wait For You' (1951), '(Mama) He Treats Your Daughter Mean' (1953) and 'Mambo Baby' (1954). She became well known as 'Miss Rhythm', appeared on the TV program *Showtime At The Apollo* with Miles Davis and Thelonious Monk, and proved to be a big influence on subsequent female R&B singers.

Jazz and blues singer Billie Holiday, whose distinctive voice was filled with emotion, passion and tragedy, was a key inspiration to Ruth Brown.

Legendary R&B Singers

Ray Charles was another hugely influential figure in the 1950s R&B movement, and one of the forefathers of soul music. Born Ray Charles Robinson in Albany, Georgia, on 23 September 1930, and blind since the age of seven, he studied composition and learned to play a number of musical instruments at the St. Augustine School for the Deaf and the Blind in Florida.

He drew from gospel and Southern blues music to develop a unique singing and songwriting style, which encouraged Atlantic Records to sign him up in 1953. Charles and Atlantic hit the jackpot: 'I Got A Woman' was a number two R&B hit in 1955, and Charles followed it with a string of other chart-toppers, combining his unmistakably soulful vocal delivery with R&B rhythms. Ray influenced countless R&B singers and became one of the first soul superstars in the 1960s. He later worked with many popular artists, including Aretha Franklin and Michael Jackson.

Another important name in early R&B music is Clyde McPhatter. Originally a gospel singer with the Mount Lebanon Singers in New York, Clyde switched over to R&B when he joined the Dominoes in 1950. They signed to Syd Nathan's King label and recorded 'Sixty Minute Man' (1951), the biggest R&B hit of the year and, according to some, the earliest identifiable example of a rock'n'roll song. He quit the Dominoes in early 1953 and formed his own band, the Drifters, the same year. They recorded 'Money Honey' (1954) and several other big R&B hits for Atlantic Records during the mid-1950s and McPhatter's extremely versatile tenor voice proved capable of handling both sensitive ballads and raucous rock'n'roll. He left the band for a solo career and released several other hits during the late-1950s, but he had less success in the following decade and, undeservedly, faded into obscurity. Other notable R&B singers from the 1950s included Jackie Wilson and James Brown, who both became soul superstars during the 1960s.

Key Artists

Ray Charles
Ruth Brown
Clyde McPhatter
Johnny 'Guitar' Watson
Bo Diddley

Clyde McPhatter's compelling vocals combined blues and gospel influences, and his stunning, emotionally charged tenor voice served as a forerunner to the 1960s and 1970s soul sounds.

R&B Guitar Icons

Other R&B artists, such as Bo Diddley and Johnny 'Guitar' Watson, were associated with their instruments as much as their singing. Diddley developed an unorthodox, 'hambone' rhythm guitar style, which he played on a trademark rectangular guitar. Perhaps his most famous hit was the two-sided 'Bo Diddley'/'I'm A Man' (1955), which he recorded for Chess records.

Watson grew up listening to bluesmen T-Bone Walker and Clarence 'Gatemouth' Brown and developed a biting, high-treble guitar tone, which he used to strong effect on albums such as *Gangster Of Love* (1958) and *Johnny Guitar Watson* (1963). An eccentric performer, he was reputed to have played the guitar standing upside-down, using a 46 m (150 ft) cord so he could get on top of the auditorium with his instrument. 'Those things Jimi Hendrix was doing; I started that shit!' he said to a music journalist.

Key Tracks

'Mess Around' Ray Charles
'Georgia On My Mind' Ray Charles
'Teardrops From My Eyes' Ruth Brown
'A Real Mother For Ya' Johnny 'Guitar' Watson
'Love Has Joined Us Together' Clyde McPhatter

Although R&B branched off into a number of different music styles between the 1950s and 1970s, countless blues and soul stars have released R&B hits over the past 40 years. Recent R&B revival artists, such as Big Boy Bloater & his Southside Stompers, continue to ensure that the genre is very much alive.

Two of the finest rhythm guitar players in rock – Bo Diddley and Keith Richards.

KINMAN
turbo · 5 speed

Blues Rock

Blues rock grew out of the British blues movement that started during the late-1950s, which was in turn developed in the 1960s. The Brits used more powerful amplification than their American counterparts, resulting in a harder, more imposing sound. Jimi Hendrix, Led Zeppelin and other artists developed this into a riff-oriented rock style.

Among the earliest blues rock bands were Cream, the Paul Butterfield Blues Band and Canned Heat. Cream were formed when Ginger Baker, drummer with the Graham Bond Organisation, decided to start his own band with guitarist Eric Clapton and bassist Jack Bruce. 'Things were going badly with Graham', Baker told music journalist Chris Welch, 'so I decided to get my own thing together. I was unaware that Eric had such a huge following. I just dug his playing, so I went to a Bluesbreakers gig in Oxford. In the interval Eric asked if I'd play a number with them, and it really took off! So I told him I was getting a band together and was wondering if he'd be interested. He said that he was and recommended Jack as the bass player.'

'I had a Les Paul before Eric but I didn't have a Marshall. And when Eric got all of that together he was a delight to listen to. He really understood the blues.'

Jimmy Page

As all three band members were well known around the British blues circuit when they formed, each with a reputation for being a virtuoso on his respective instrument, Cream was, effectively, the first 'supergroup'. They were louder and more riff-oriented than previous blues-influenced bands, and their style incorporated extended solos – a regular feature for subsequent blues rockers. Despite only lasting for three years, Cream's first three albums, *Fresh Cream* (1966), *Disraeli Gears* (1967) and *Wheels Of Fire* (1967), are widely accepted as both blues rock classics and milestones in the birth of rock music. Influential American bands had also developed blues rock styles by the late 1960s: the Paul Butterfield Blues Band, with Mike Bloomfield and Elvin Bishop on guitars, and Canned Heat, a white blues band formed by singer Bob 'The Bear' Hite and harmonica player Alan 'Blind Owl' Wilson, were the most notable of these.

The brilliant Cream fused blues and rock.

A Dazzling Showman

Another key figure in the transition from blues to rock was the legendary Jimi Hendrix. Born Johnny Allen Hendrix in Seattle on 27 November 1942, he later changed his name to James (Jimi) Marshall Hendrix.

Influenced by legendary bluesmen such as Robert Johnson and B. B. King as a schoolboy, he taught himself to play guitar before working with musicians such as Little Richard in the early 1960s. His break came when Chas Chandler, the bassist with the Animals, heard him play in New York's Greenwich Village. Chas persuaded him to move over to London, where the Jimi Hendrix Experience was formed, with Jimi on guitar, Noel Redding on bass and Mitch Mitchell on drums.

Key Artists

Jimi Hendrix
Cream
Led Zeppelin
Canned Heat
The Rolling Stones

Jimi was a dazzling showman, playing the guitar behind his head and with his teeth, but it was his extraordinary soloing and mastery of controlled feedback that set a new standard in electric blues lead guitar playing. His best albums, *Are You Experienced?* (1967), *Axis: Bold As Love* (1968) and *Electric Ladyland* (1968), demonstrate that something seriously interesting was happening to the blues by the late-1960s. Although he tragically died in 1970, Jimi was to influence countless blues and rock players for many years to come.

Jimi Hendrix helped to popularize the use of feedback and wah-wah, as well as widening the rock palette by his use of unusual intervals (e.g. the diminished fifths in the 'Purple Haze' intro) and chords (the so-called 'Hendrix chord' of E7#9, also used in 'Purple Haze').

Broadening Out

By the end of the 1960s, blues rock began to diversify into heavy metal in the UK and southern blues rock in the US. Led Zeppelin was, perhaps, the first band to be described as heavy metal, but the group's blues roots are apparent in all of its recordings, including the hugely popular *Led Zeppelin II* (1969) and *Led Zeppelin IV* (1971) albums.

The band's guitarist, Jimmy Page, grew up listening to blues and rock'n'roll recordings, but one of his biggest influences was hearing Eric Clapton's Gibson Les Paul guitar through a cranked-up Marshall amp at a Bluesbreakers gig. 'I had a Les Paul before Eric but I didn't have a Marshall,' Page recalled. 'And when Eric got all of that together he was a delight to listen to. He really understood the blues.'

Meanwhile, in the States, the Allman Brothers Band was fusing electric blues with country and folk elements, to form what is now known as 'southern rock'. Albums such as *The Allman Brothers Band* (1969), *Idlewild South* (1970) and *Live At The Fillmore East* (1971) paved the way for a whole family of southern rock bands, including Lynyrd Skynyrd and Black Oak Arkansas. ZZ Top, a trio from Texas, also emerged out of the blues rock scene. Led by the bearded Billy Gibbons (guitar, vocals) and Dusty Hill (bass, vocals), the trio developed their own style of boogie-style blues rock, which became hugely popular in the 1970s and 1980s.

Key Tracks

'Start Me Up' The Rolling Stones
'Voodoo Child' Jimi Hendrix
'Dreams' The Allman Brothers Band
'Sunshine Of Your Love' Cream
'On The Road Again' Canned Heat

Meanwhile, over in the UK, the group Free inspired generations of British blues rockers with major hits like 'All Right Now' (1970) and 'Wishing Well' (1973). Many other notable blues rock artists have since appeared on both sides of the Atlantic, including Bernard Allison, Bonnie Raitt, Walter Trout, Dave Hole and Ronnie Earl.

Led Zeppelin star Jimmy Page initially refused to join his first band, the Yardbirds, thinking he would make more money as a session musician.

Modern Electric Blues

Although the first generations of electric bluesmen played louder and more flamboyantly than their acoustic forefathers, their music was still traditional in its delivery and structure. The British blues players who emulated them during the 1960s were also fairly traditional in their approach to the genre.

Jimi Hendrix opened things up a bit more when he first appeared on the scene in 1967, but the musicians he in turn influenced tended to lean towards the rock side of the musical spectrum. Another group of electric bluesmen also began to emerge during the late-1960s and early 1970s – guitar players such as Roy Buchanan and Johnny Winter, who had taken on board the new sounds of rock but were steeped in the traditions of the blues.

Blues Got them Early

The son of a Pentecostal preacher, Roy Buchanan grew up in California and, as a teenager, joined Dale Hawkins' band in 1958. After a stint as a session player in the 1960s, he decided to try his luck as a solo artist with *Roy Buchanan* (1972), an accomplished album highlighting his distinctive, treble-sounding Fender Telecaster tone. He was asked to join the Rolling Stones after Brian Jones died but, surprisingly, he turned the offer down. His career, like that of many other blues musicians, was plagued by booze and drug problems, and, after a number of unsuccessful suicide attempts, he hung himself in a police cell in 1988.

'Stevie Ray Vaughan is the best friend I've ever had, the best guitarist I ever heard and the best person anyone will ever want to know.'

Buddy Guy

Johnny Winter, an albino bluesman who grew up in Texas, also began playing and singing the blues early in life; he cut his first record at the age of 15, and produced a demonstration disc known as *The Progressive Blues Experiment* in 1968. An excellent review in *Rolling Stone* magazine led to lucrative management and recording deals. His first proper album, *Johnny Winter* (1969), established his standing as an outstanding performer with an exceptionally dexterous guitar style and paved the way for more than 20 further, critically acclaimed Winter blues albums.

Outstanding guitarist Johnny Winter has released many critically acclaimed blues albums over the course of his career.

Blues Fusions

Robben Ford is another great blues artist who emerged during the early 1970s. He also showed a mastery of jazz, unlike most blues guitar players, and his music developed into a compelling blend of the two styles.

Inspired by Eric Clapton and Mike Bloomfield, Robben learned blues guitar during the 1960s and performed with Charlie Musselwhite in 1970. He also toured and recorded with George Harrison and Joni Mitchell in the mid-1970s and with Miles Davis in the 1980s. *His Talk To Your Daughter* album (1988) was nominated for a Grammy, while later, *Robben Ford And The Blue Line* (1992) won considerable acclaim for its original, earthy approach to the blues. Robben's soloing is more sophisticated than that of most other blues players and his chord progressions are often laced with rich jazz harmonies.

Another musician who effortlessly fused jazz with the blues is the Connecticut-born John Scofield. Although John spent many of his early years studying the work of jazz and fusion players such as Jim Hall and John McLaughlin, his *Still Warm* (1986) and *Blue Matter* (1987) albums are full of original, angular blues-style licks.

Key Artists

Robben Ford
John Scofield
Robert Cray
Stevie Ray Vaughan
Roy Buchanan

The two blues giants of the 1980s were undoubtedly Robert Cray, from Georgia, and Stevie Ray Vaughan, from Texas. Cray formed his first band in 1974, but did not really hit the big time until his *Bad Influence* album was released to critical and commercial acclaim in 1983. A mainstream fusion of blues, soul and rock, his style was particularly popular throughout the 1980s, introducing a wider pop audience to the blues. He was invited to play with Eric Clapton during the ex-Bluesbreaker's famous series of concerts at London's Albert Hall in 1989.

Robben Ford started out as a saxophonist and it was his love for this instrument – and its masters, such as John Coltrane and Wayne Shorter – that helped to shape his unique jazz-tinged blues guitar sound.

A Recent Legend

Stevie Ray Vaughan was heavily influenced by his older brother, Jimmie Vaughan (of the Fabulous Thunderbirds), as well as by Albert King and Jimi Hendrix. He played in various local bands in Austin, Texas before forming Double Trouble (named after an Otis Rush song), with bassist Tommy Shannon and drummer Chris 'Whipper' Layton.

In 1982 the ensemble played at the Montreux Jazz Festival, where Vaughan's stunning, high-energy blues style was noted by David Bowie, who poached him for his *Let's Dance* album (1983). The same year, Double Trouble also recorded *Texas Flood* with the legendary blues producer John Hammond, to critical and commercial acclaim. The second Double Trouble album, the Hendrix-influenced *Couldn't Stand The Weather* (1984), was an even bigger success – it went platinum.

Vaughan battled with alcohol and drug problems during the mid-1980s, and was admitted to a rehabilitation centre in Georgia, but he straightened out to make the Grammy-winning *In Step* (1989). Tragically, he died in a helicopter accident in 1990, after playing at an Eric Clapton concert in Milwaukee. As with Hendrix, Vaughan's reputation has grown since his death, with recent guitar magazine reader polls indicating that he is one of the most popular blues artists of all time.

Key Tracks

'Pride And Joy' Stevie Ray Vaughan and Double Trouble
'Couldn't Stand The Weather' Stevie Ray Vaughan and Double Trouble
'Talk To Your Daughter' Robben Ford
'Born Under A Bad Sign' Robben Ford
'Phone Booth' Robert Cray

Thanks to players such as Vaughan and Ford, modern electric blues evolved during the 1980s and 1990s and, like every current musical style, continues to do so. Players including Walter Trout, Susan Tedeschi, Dave Hole, Tinsley Ellis and Bernard Allison continue to delight audiences.

Stevie Ray Vaughan's amazing guitar technique and understanding of the blues won him two W. C. Handy National Blues Awards in 1984: Entertainer of the Year and Blues Instrumentalist of the Year. He was the first white person to win either award.

INFLUENCES OF THE BLUES

Albert King famously sang 'If you don't dig the blues, you got a hole in your soul' and the wide-ranging influence that the blues had on so many popular music styles across the globe would suggest that most people do find blues music accessible, easy to connect with and, put simply, a pleasure to listen to.

This section explores a number of musical styles that have developed either in parallel with, in relation to, or as a direct result of blues music. Blues and jazz came from similar African-American roots, and indeed in the early years were closely related – many early jazz tracks are blues songs – but the two styles gradually moved in different directions as the twentieth century progressed. Gospel music was yet another African-American-based music style that grew from its beginnings in the cotton fields, and had many crossover performers such as Sister Rosetta Tharpe.

Country music is often referred to as the 'white man's blues', and shares many characteristics. One of country music's earliest stars, Jimmie Rodgers, blended blues with hillbilly, earning the moniker 'the Blue Yodeler', while honky tonk artists such as Hank Williams wrote and performed their own blues songs that have established their own place in the repertoire. Similarly, there are crossovers between folk music and the blues – blues music is in a sense a type of folk music. Artists such as Leadbelly, Woody Guthrie and Mississippi John Hurt could legitimately be labelled as either blues or folk singers, and Bob Dylan's folk-based music shows a strong blues influence.

Blues music formed the basis of much of the pop music of the 1950s in both the US and UK, including rock'n'roll, doo wop and skiffle, and also went on to underlie the rock music of the 1960s, 1970s and beyond. The list goes on, and goes some way to showing that the humble 12-bar blues has perhaps contributed more to modern music than any other musical genre.

Woody Guthrie's refusal to profit from any of his music during his lifetime did not prevent him from reaching legendary status after his death.

Ragtime

A forerunner of jazz, ragtime was derived from brass-band music and European folk melodies, African-American banjo music and spirituals, minstrel songs, military marches and European light classics.

The 'raggy' style, or ragged-time feeling, of this jaunty, propulsive, toe-tapping piano music refers to its inherent syncopation, where loud right-hand accents fall between the strong beats of the left-hand rather than on top of them. One noted practitioner, the pianist Eubie Blake (composer of the 1920s hit song 'I'm Just Wild About Harry'), summed it up simply: 'Ragtime is syncopation and improvising and accents'.

While this highly syncopated style involved only limited improvisation and lacked a jazz-swing feel, it directly informed the work of the early jazz giant Jelly Roll Morton and served as a precursor to the Harlem stride piano movement of the 1920s, pioneered by James P. Johnson, Willie 'The Lion' Smith and Fats Waller. Ragtime could be heard as early as the 1880s in camps of workers building the great railroads across the American continent, as well as in travelling minstrel shows and vaudeville shows. By 1892, the composer Charles Ives had come across it in his hometown of Danbury, Connecticut. At the Chicago World's Fair that same year, many people heard ragtime for the first time. By 1896, the first pieces labelled 'ragtime' were published. The following year, some 20 rags were published. By 1899, 120 rags were issued in New Orleans.

'Scorned by the Establishment as ephemeral at best, trashy at worst, ragtime was the fountainhead of every rhythmic and stylistic upheaval that has followed in a century of ever-evolving American popular music.'

Max Morath

As piano rolls and sheet music appeared at the turn of he century, a ragtime fad swept the nation. Hordes of young people shocked their parents by kicking up their heels to this infectious new music, which was described alternately by critics and newspaper columnists as 'syncopation gone mad' and 'the product of our decadent art culture'.

Thomas 'Fats' Waller, along with his one-time piano tutor James P. Johnson, pioneered the stride piano style that grew out of ragtime. Stride (originally called 'shout') shared the basic structure of ragtime but was rhythmically looser.

The Ragtime King

Although Scott Joplin became the figurehead for this burgeoning new American music movement, there were several ragtime piano players who preceded him, including Walter Gould (known as One Leg Shadow), Tom Turpin, James Scott and One-Leg Willie Joseph, along with other ivory-tinkling 'professors' who plied their trade in brothels, gambling joints, saloons and private clubs.

Following the phenomenal success of Joplin's 'Maple Leaf Rag', which sold 75,000 copies of sheet music in 1899 for the publisher John Stark and 500,000 copies within 10 years, he was dubbed 'King of Ragtime Writers' and presided over ragtime's reign as the main popular musical style of the US for nearly 20 years.

The son of a former slave, born in Texarkana, a town in the northeast corner of Texas, on 24 November 1868, Joplin was a piano prodigy with a musical education financed by his mother's work as a domestic servant. With aspirations to become a classical concert pianist, he played at the Chicago World's Fair in 1892 and later enrolled at the George R. Smith College for Negroes in Sedalia, Missouri (where he would write 'Maple Leaf Rag'). In 1901, Joplin moved to St. Louis to begin working with Stark, where he began to expand his writing from ragtime tunes to full-length pieces such as ballets and operas. The first of these, *A Guest Of Honor*, emerged in 1903.

Key Artists

Scott Joplin
Tom Turpin
James Scott
Joseph Lamb
Eubie Blake

Rather than being improvised, Joplin's music was as formally composed and carefully worked out as any of Frédéric Chopin's études. And while he easily enchanted the masses with catchy numbers such as 'Maple Leaf Rag' and 'The Entertainer' (an infectious quality that Irving Berlin strived to emulate in 1911 with his 'Alexander's Ragtime Band'), Joplin longed to be taken seriously as a composer. He saw himself as a black American counterpart to Chopin or Strauss, a composer of new music for a new century.

The sheet music for 'Maple Leaf Rag' by Scott Joplin.

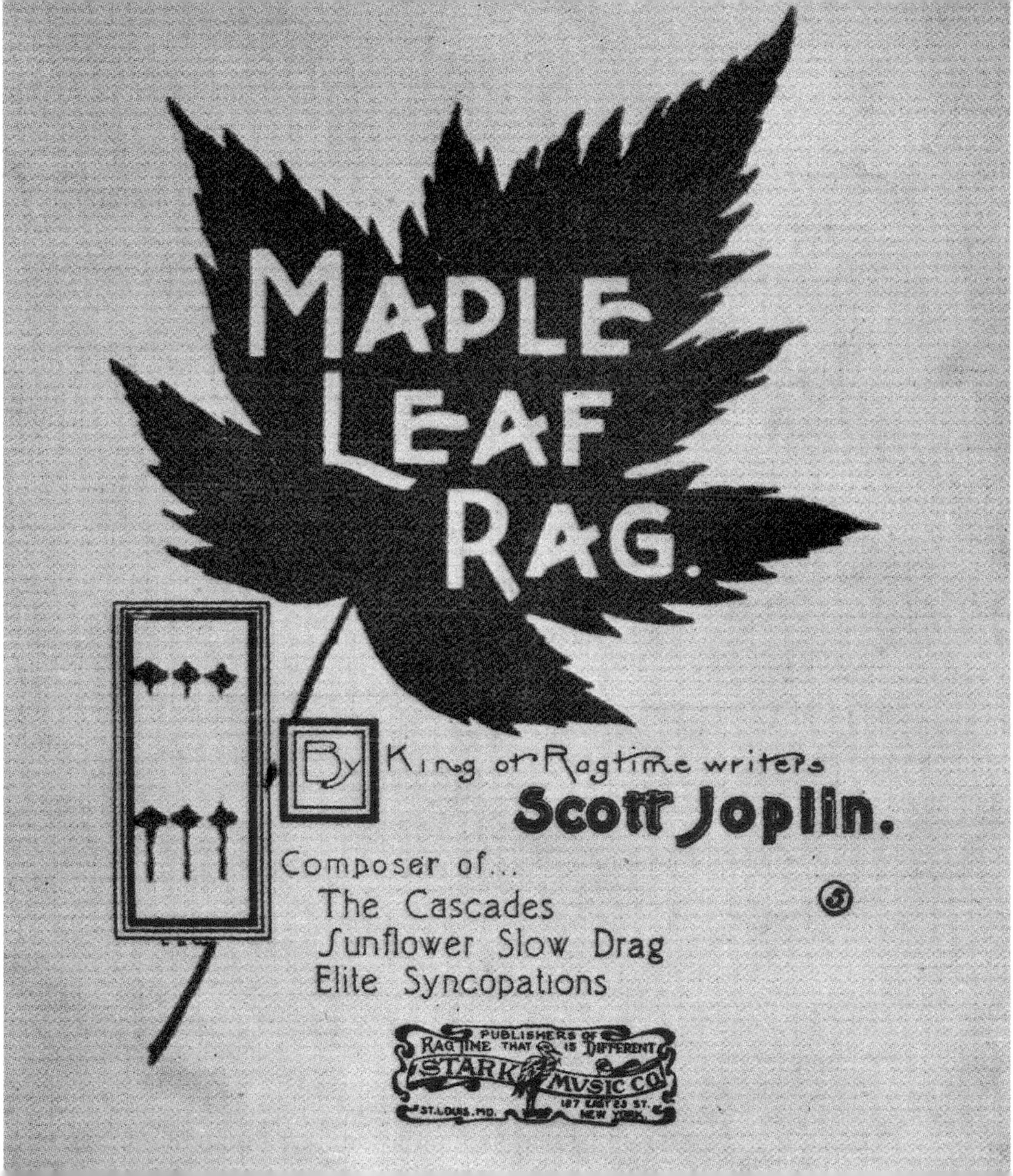
MAPLE LEAF RAG.
By King of Ragtime writers
Scott Joplin.
Composer of...
The Cascades
Sunflower Slow Drag
Elite Syncopations
PUBLISHERS OF
RAG TIME THAT IS DIFFERENT
STARK MUSIC CO.
ST. LOUIS, MO.
NEW YORK.

Ragtime Revival

Scott Joplin's death in 1917, just before the end of the First World War, effectively marked the beginning of the end of ragtime's supremacy in America. And although Zez Confrey had some success in the early 1920s with tunes such as 'Kitten On The Keys' and 'Dizzy Fingers', by the second decade of the twentieth century, attention had shifted dramatically to the new phenomenon of 'hot music' or 'jazz'.

By 1930, ragtime was largely extinct. The legacy of the early ragtime pioneers lived on only through sheet music and piano rolls of their compositions: there were no recordings. In fact, the year Joplin died was the same year in which the Original Dixieland Jazz Band made the first jazz recording.

More than half a century after Joplin's death, this rollicking, syncopated music enjoyed a revival in the early 1970s, sparked by three significant events. In 1971, the musicologist and pianist Joshua Rifkin recorded an album of Joplin's pieces for Nonesuch, which caught on with critics and the public alike. The following year, Joplin's 1915 ragtime opera, Treemonisha, was resurrected and staged at Atlanta's Memorial Arts Center. Then, in 1973, the pianist-composer Marvin Hamlisch used Joplin's 'The Entertainer' as the main theme for the Hollywood blockbuster *The Sting*, starring Paul Newman and Robert Redford. That Academy Award-winning film made Joplin a household name, helping to rigger renewed interest in his jaunty and sophisticated music.

Key Tracks

'Maple Leaf Rag' Scott Joplin
'The Entertainer' Scott Joplin
'I'm Just Wild About Harry' Eubie Blake
'Harlem Rag' Tom Turpin
'Frog Legs Rag' James Scott

Treemonisha was again staged by the Houston Grand Opera in May 1975 and brought to Broadway that October, contributing to Joplin being posthumously awarded a special Pulitzer Prize in 1976 for his contribution to American music. Joplin's legacy has been kept alive through the 1980s and 1990s by ragtime piano interpreters such as Terry Waldo, Butch Thompson, Dick Hyman and Marcus Roberts, as well as by prominent jazz instrumentalists such as Anthony Braxton, Archie Shepp, Ran Blake, Ron Miles, Bill Frisell and Wynton and Branford Marsalis. Original composers in the ragtime style, such as Mississippi's David Thomas Roberts and Chicago's Reginald Robinson, have helped to keep this nearly extinct music alive on the concert and recording scene over the past 10 years.

Scott Joplin wisely secured a royalty contract on 'Maple Leaf Rag', one of his most successful compositions. He received one cent for each copy sold, which, although hardly a princely sum, provided him with a steady income.

New Orleans Jazz

Conditions were ripe for jazz to evolve in New Orleans at the turn of the twentieth century. A thriving port of immigration, where Africans and Creoles lived side by side with Italians, Germans, Irish, French, Mexicans and Cubans, New Orleans' unprecedented ethnic diversity allowed for a free and easy mingling of musical ideas between cultures.

Other factors contributed to the coalescing of jazz as a cultural expression unique to New Orleans. The call-and-response tradition of West African music was retained in many Baptist churches of the South, particularly in New Orleans, while concepts of polyrhythm and improvisation within group participation (qualities inherent in African drumming ensembles) were kept alive in the Crescent City at Congo Square, an authorized venue where slaves would gather to recreate their drumming and dancing traditions. These African drumming concepts, and indeed the very notion of percussiveness as musical expression, would seep into the cultural consciousness of New Orleans.

'Arguably the happiest of all music is New Orleans jazz. The sound of several horns all improvising together on fairly simple chord changes with definite roles for each instrument but a large amount of freedom cannot help but sound consistently joyful.'

Scott Yanow

Let the Good Times Roll

The foundation for a new hybrid music was set by a combination of the African notion of rhythm that swings, or has a propulsive motion, with the European classical influences brought into the mix by ragtime and sophisticated Creole musicians. Add a thriving brass band tradition, which developed in the late-nineteenth century from the plentiful supply of cheap brass band instruments left behind after the Civil War, blend in rhythmic and melodic elements from Cuba, the West Indies and the Caribbean, and factor in the slightly decadent and pervasive 'party time' atmosphere of the City That Care Forgot (typified by the pageantry of Mardi Gras, as well as the city's unofficial motto, 'Laissez les bons temps rouler' or 'Let the good times roll'), and you have a potent recipe for jazz.

Canal Street, New Orleans, c. 1900, as jazz music was developing.

The Cornet Kings

Out of New Orleans' rich cultural gumbo came Charles 'Buddy' Bolden, the first bona fide jazz star of the twentieth century. A cornetist of unparalleled power, Bolden's innovative approach took the essence of ragtime and put a looser, hotter, bluesier spin on it, grabbing dancers in the process.

By 1895, Bolden was leading his own group in residence at New Orleans' Globe Theater, where he held court as 'King' Bolden. By 1901, his popularity spread from playing dancehalls scattered throughout the city and in outlying communities, including Preservation Hall, the Tin Roof Café and Funky Butt Hall. In 1903, he began to fade from the scene, plagued by spells of dementia and drunkenness, until he was ommitted to the East Louisiana State Mental Hospital on 5 June 1907: the first jazz casualty.

Succeeding Bolden as the cornet king of New Orleans was Freddie Keppard, who, in 1906, led the Olympia Orchestra. Legend has it that Keppard, leery of having other cornet players 'steal his stuff', turned down an offer from the Victor Talking Machine Company to become the first New Orleans musician to record. Another prominent cornetist was Joe Oliver, who began playing in local dance bands and with the Onward Brass Band in 1907. By 1917, he became the star cornetist in a popular band led by the trombonist Edward 'Kid' Ory. An early master of mutes, Oliver pioneered the 'wah-wah' and other vocal effects on his horn, which would later become a signature of the Ellington trumpeter Bubber Miley. When Oliver went north to Chicago in February 1919, Ory hired the 18-year-old Louis Armstrong as his replacement on cornet.

Key Artists

Buddy Bolden
Sidney Bechet
Jelly Roll Morton
King Oliver
Original Dixieland Jazz Band

Oliver's contemporary on the New Orleans scene was the Creole clarinettist Sidney Bechet. A child prodigy, Bechet held his own with Freddie Keppard's band at the age of 10. He left school at 16 and began working with various bands, thrilling audiences and players alike with his forceful attack, soaring passion and unusually fast vibrato. Bechet relocated to Chicago in 1918 and, a year later, became one of the first Americans to spread jazz to Europe as a member of the travelling Southern Syncopated Orchestra. It was while he was in London that he ran across the instrument with which he would eventually make jazz history: the soprano saxophone.

King Oliver's Creole Jazz Band made some of the most important jazz recordings of the 1920s. The band, including such greats as Louis Armstrong, Johnny Dodds and King Oliver himself, took group improvisation to new heights.

The Jazz Age

A key figure in New Orleans jazz was the pianist, composer, entertainer and raconteur Jelly Roll Morton. A natural extrovert who bragged that he had invented jazz, Morton began embellishing on ragtime, blues and light classics while performing at the 'sporting houses' of the Storyville red-light district as early as 1902.

By 1907, he began touring in vaudeville shows throughout the Gulf Coast and the Midwest. He settled in Chicago in 1914, then relocated to the West Coast from 1917 to 1922. He had composed numerous works by that time, including his classic 'King Porter Stomp' and 'Winin' Boy Blues', but remained unrecorded until 1923.

A plethora of jazz musicians were active in New Orleans during the first decade of the twentieth century, but the first jazz recording was not made until 1917. That honour went not to pioneers such as Keppard, Ory, Oliver, Bechet or Morton (all of whom went unrecorded until after they had left New Orleans), but to a group of five young, white New Orleans musicians calling themselves the Original Dixieland Jazz Band. Led by Sicilian-American cornetist Nick LaRocca, the ODJB assembled in the Victor studio in New York City on 26 February 1917 to record 'Livery Stable Blues'. A lively novelty number that featured passages where the instruments imitated barnyard animals, it immediately caught on with the public. Following the extraordinary success of their recording debut (it would eventually sell 1.5 million copies), the ODJB toured British variety theatres, where they audaciously billed themselves as 'The Creators of Jazz'. The ODJB later introduced such Dixieland standards as 'Margie', 'Indiana' and 'Tiger Rag', spawning a number of copy bands and sparking a craze that quickly swept America, as well as setting the stage for what the writer F. Scott Fitzgerald characterized as 'The Jazz Age' of the 1920s.

Key Tracks

'King Porter Stomp' Jelly Roll Morton
'Winin' Boy Blues' Jelly Roll Morton
'Savoy Blues' Kid Ory
'Livery Stable Blues' Original Dixieland Jazz Band
'Indiana' Original Dixieland Jazz Band

Pianist, composer and bandleader Jelly Roll Morton advocated the 'Spanish tinge' element in jazz music.

Chicago Jazz

Jazz was the by-product of cultures coming together in New Orleans at the turn of the twentieth century. the music, along with some of its greatest practitioners, moved north by 1917. That year Storyville, the red-light district, was forced to close and jazz musicians headed north to Chicago, where jazz matured into a fine art form.

Chicago held the promise of a new life for the Southern black population, which migrated from the fields of the cotton industry to the blast furnaces and factories of big Northern cities. A centrally located, active transportation hub that provided easy access to Los Angeles and New York, Chicago was an attractive destination for working jazz musicians, many of whom worked in the gangster-owned speakeasies created by the Volstead Act of 1919 (outlawing the manufacture and sale of alcohol in the US).

Blow the Way You Feel

While the North Side of Chicago had its famous clubs – the Green Mill, College Inn, Blackhawk, Kelly's Stables and Friar's Inn – the hottest jazz bands of the early 1920s could, primarily, be found on a nine-block stretch of State Street on the city's predominantly black south side, known as 'The Stroll'. There, jazz lovers could choose between the Pekin Inn, Dreamland Café, Plantation Café, Elite Café and Sunset Café. Among the patrons who frequented The Stroll was a group of jazz-hungry, white teenage students who attended Chicago's Austin High School – cornetist Jimmy McPartland, tenor saxophonist Bud Freeman, drummer Dave Tough and reedman Frank Teschemacher. Along with developing young players, such as guitarist Eddie Condon, pianist Joe Sullivan, cornetists Muggsy Spanier and Leon 'Bix' Beiderbecke, clarinetist Benny Goodman and drummer Gene Krupa, this next generation of jazz musicians originated the 'Chicago style', building on the rhythmic innovations of the New Orleans pioneers while injecting a frenetic intensity and reckless spirit that reflected the city itself.

'Armstrong plays with such bravura and rhythmic intensity that when you listen to it you hear the future. At that moment you know that something is in the works and it's never going to be contained.'

Gary Giddins, critic, 2000

Jazz cornet genius Bix Beiderbecke, who took Chicago by storm.

Hypnosis at First Hearing

The Austin Gang and other architects of the extrovert Chicago style were fans of the Original Dixieland Jazz Band, but they quickly fell under the spell of another white group from New Orleans, playing in Chicago in 1920 under the name of the New Orleans Rhythm Kings.

They made their recording debut in 1922, and a year later teamed up in the studio with Jelly Roll Morton for one of the first-ever integrated sessions. Another focal point for the Austin Gang's adulation was the dazzling cornet virtuoso Louis Armstrong, who came to town in 1922 to join his mentor King Oliver in the ranks of the Creole Jazz Band. With its two-cornet frontline, underscored by an intuitive call-and-response chemistry between its leader and 22-year-old star, the impact of King Oliver's Creole Jazz Band on young audiences was devastating. As guitarist Eddie Condon recalled in his memoirs, *We Called It Music: A Generation of Jazz* (Henry Holt): 'It was hypnosis at first hearing. Armstrong seemed able to hear what Oliver was improvising and reproduce it himself at the same time. Then the two wove around each other like suspicious women talking about the same man.'
In the early part of 1923, Oliver's pace-setting group went into a rickety studio in Richmond, Indiana, and cut its first historic recording ('Chimes Blues') for the small but influential Gennett label.

Key Artists

King Oliver's Creole Jazz Band
Louis Armstrong
Jimmy McPartland
Joe Sullivan
New Orleans Rhythm Kings

Armstrong left Chicago in 1924 to join Fletcher Henderson's band in New York. The following year, he returned to Chicago to lead a band organized by his new wife, Lil (Hardin) Armstrong, at the Dreamland Café. Soon afterward, he began doubling with Erskine Tate's Vendome Theater Orchestra, where he was the featured hot soloist. Then, on 12 November 1925, he went into the Okeh studios in Chicago to make the first of a series of five dozen tracks recorded between 1925 and 1928, which have come to be known as the Hot Fives and Hot Sevens sessions. With these revolutionary recordings, Armstrong single-handedly shifted the focus from jazz as an ensemble music to a soloist's art form. As noted critic Gary Giddins put it, 'It's the moment when jazz becomes an art form. With these pivotal recordings, he virtually codifies what jazz is going to be for the next half century'. By 1929, Armstrong shifted his home base from Chicago to New York, where jazz was poised for its next evolution.

Featuring ex-members of King Oliver's band, Louis Armstrong's Hot Five recordings may represent the greatest jazz of all time. Pictured from left to right are Armstrong, Johnny St. Cyr and Johnny Dodds.

Gospel

The first African slaves arrived in America in 1619 and brought their music with them. From then until the Civil War of 1861–65, the music both fascinated and frightened the white slave owners who would flock to see the black people celebrating their weekly 'day off' in New Orleans's Congo Square.

At the same time, slave owners suppressed the drumming that they saw as a possible means of communication between tribal groups who might rebel. During this period, the evangelical aspect of western religion led to efforts to Christianize these heathen 'children'.

Throughout the nineteenth century the emphasis was placed heavily on the supposed sinful unworthiness of congregations. However, a reaction to this brought about the more moderate movement instigated in the 1870s by Dwight Lyman Moody, who abandoned the hell-and-damnation approach in favour of compassion and redemption. A stream of white religious songwriters appeared, too, headed by Moody and his associate Sankey, and including P.P. Bliss, D.W. Whittle and Henry Date. Influential to both these and to later black composers was the work of the eighteenth-century English hymnist Isaac Watts.

'Every tone was a testimony against slavery, and a prayer to God for deliverance from chains.'

Frederick Douglass, *My Bondage and My Freedom*

In both black and white traditions, although more so in the case of the black songwriters, congregations would be largely illiterate, leading to the practice of 'lining out' songs – a technique whereby the leader sang each line so that the flock could sing it after him. This left room for the development of innovative, overlapping answers, and was the basis of the call-and-response style so prominent in gospel song.

A gospel choir.

Music and Progression

In the wake of the Civil War and emancipation, America's black population was faced with the problem of integrating itself into the white mainstream society, instigating a process that culminated in the Civil Rights Movement of the 1960s.

Education was a major issue, but many newly founded black academic institutions found it a struggle to remain afloat during the economic upheavals of the 1870s. In an attempt to generate money to support Nashville's Fisk University, the choirmaster and treasurer George Leonard White, aided by his black protégé, the singer and pianist Ella Sheppard, assembled the formally trained Fisk Jubilee Singers and took them on a fund-raising tour of North America. The success of this ploy led to other such institutions forming their own travelling choirs. None, however, approached the stature of the Fisk group, who also toured Europe to wide acclaim.

Simultaneously, in more humble venues, liberated and increasingly urbanized black singers were adapting the popular style of four-part harmony group singing known as the 'barbershop quartet' to their own ends, working a unique musical alchemy upon it with their rhythmic approach and loosening up its hitherto tight format. Their initial undertakings in this idiom were probably interpretations of popular secular songs, but they soon expanded their repertoire to include new arrangements of much-loved hymns. These were the roots of music that was to accompany the progress of black America throughout the upheavals of the twentieth century, developing through 'jubilee', 'quartet' and other styles into the sounds heard in black churches today.

Key Artists

Sister Rosetta Tharpe
Dwight Lyman Moody
P.P. Bliss
Ella Sheppard
Mahalia Jackson

Sister Rosetta Tharpe, who recorded blues as well as gospel material.

Early & Old-Time Country

There is no distinct boundary line between the early and old-time country era, when the music was still relatively unshaped by the American mainstream, and the modern age, when country music's popularity and ubiquity have made it very much a part of the mass culture.

But it was in the 1920s, due to the emerging radio and recording industries, that the US's varied regional and ethnic rural, grassroots musical forms began to find popularity beyond the isolated regions that spawned them. By the 1940s and early 1950s, as the commercial country radio and record industries gathered force, the music's connections to its grassroots origins became a bit more tenuous, and the old-time era was beginning to come to an end.

Blue Yodellers

Though many successful and noteworthy artists preceded him, Meridian, Mississippi-born Jimmie Rodgers is most often hailed as the 'father of modern country music' and one of its earliest national stars. Though Rodgers died of tuberculosis in 1933 aged 35, his ubiquitous influence was unrivaled until the emergence of Hank Williams in the late 1940s. Even 70 years after his death, his impact can still be heard in the music of latter-day stars such as Merle Haggard, Lefty Frizzell, George Jones, Gene Autry, Hank Snow and Ernest Tubb. With his warm, laconic, seemingly effortless vocal style (which included a thrilling falsetto and yodel), Rodgers brought to the country table a strong feel for black blues. Some of his classic recordings sold hundreds of thousands of copies – huge numbers for the time – and their sales were bolstered by his many live appearances on radio and in the vaudeville and tent shows that were popular throughout the southern US in the 1920s and early 1930s.

'The songs were different than the norm. They had more of an individual nature and an elevated conscience ... I was drawn to their power.'

Bob Dylan on Jimmie Rodgers

Jimmie Rodgers, the 'Singing Brakeman', links early country music to the Delta blues with his black-sounding vocals, down-home yodelling and Mississippi-style guitar technique.

The Singing Brakeman.

Family Values

The Carter Family, often hailed as the 'first family of country music', came from Virginia. Like Rodgers before them, they were first captured on disk by pioneering record executive Ralph Peer in Bristol, Tennessee in 1927.

While Jimmie Rodgers' music was edgy and adventurous for its time, the Carter Family made music that was soothing, acoustic and heavily steeped in mountain traditions. Timeless recordings like 'Keep On The Sunny Side', 'Wildwood Flower' and 'Will The Circle Be Unbroken' (a Tin Pan Alley tune that they rustically reinterpreted) often spoke of the comfort of home, hearth and the old ways. With these songs and others the Carter Family explored a wide variety of genres, including blues, gospel, traditional ballads and nineteenth-century parlour songs.

This emphasis on the family tradition continued from the 1930s to the 1950s, when there was a rise of various influential sibling harmony ensembles like the Delmore Brothers, the Blue Sky Boys and Charlie & Bill Monroe. Familial vocal harmonies were further popularized by the Bailes Brothers from West Virginia, the Allen Brothers, the Dixon Brothers and Johnnie (Edwards) & Jack (Anglin – Johnnie's brother-in-law).

Key Artists

Jimmie Rodgers
The Carter Family
J.E. Mainer's Mountaineers
Gid Tanner & his Skillet Lickers
Roy Acuff

Showtime at the Grand Ole Opry

From the time it first went on the air, the *Grand Ole Opry* on Radio WSM in Nashville was a springboard for dozens of country music's most important artists – Roy Acuff, Hank Williams and Loretta Lynn not the least among them. One of the earliest figures to find fame via the *Opry* was Tennessee-born Uncle Dave Macon. Macon started out as a banjoist and comedian on the vaudeville circuit before appearing on the *Opry*'s first formal broadcast in 1925. He was an accomplished banjo player and an effervescent showman and raconteur, with a vast repertoire of songs, including many of the rural ballads he'd learned as a child. Yet Macon was also amazingly adept at tailoring down-home adaptations of the pop hits he'd learned on the vaudeville stage as well as spinning out vivid originals like 'Farm Relief' and 'From Earth To Heaven'.

Maybelle Carter (left) was a talented guitarist and had her own unique style, in which she played chords on the upper strings as an accompaniment, while simultaneously picking out the melody on the lower strings.

Music from the Mountains

J.E. Mainer's Mountaineers, from North Carolina, were foremost among the numerous guitar-fiddle-banjo Appalachian string bands that were popular in the 1930s. J.E.'s brother Wade left the Mountaineers in 1936 and formed his own band, the Sons of the Mountaineers. Wade Mainer's band, driven by its leader's innovative two-finger banjo style, foresaw the bluegrass music style, which would rise out of the string band tradition in the mid- and late 1940s.

Another archetypal and influential string band was Gid Tanner & his Skillet Lickers. Tanner (real name James Gideon) was a chicken farmer from Dracula, Georgia and a gifted singer, showman and old-time fiddler. In 1924, he began recording for Columbia and performing as a duo with blind singer-guitarist Riley Puckett. A couple of years later they were joined by two other popular musicians: fiddler Clayton McMichen and five-string banjo player Fate Norris. The Skillet Lickers brought an extroverted, often comic bent to a repertoire that included everything from old-time mountain ballads and humorous skits to popular Tin Pan Alley tunes of the day.

It was during the 1930s that Roy Acuff, the roughhewn, diminutive son of an East Tennessee preacher/lawyer, made his sensational debut on the *Grand Ole Opry*. Acuff sang in a bold, emotional, high-keening style. Many of his signature hits from the 1940s – 'Great Speckled Bird', 'Night Train To Memphis' and 'Fire Ball Mail' – intimated his direct links to the East Tennessee mountain ballad singers and string bands that he istened to as a youngster. Acuff would remain a dominant figure in country music well into the 1950s and 'the grand old man of the *Opry*' until shortly before his death in 1992.

Key Tracks

'Blue Yodel' Jimmie Rodgers
'Will The Circle Be Unbroken' The Carter Family
'Farm Relief' Uncle Dave Macon
'Fire Ball Mail' Roy Acuff
'Tramp On The Streets' Molly O'Day

One of the first women to enter country's front ranks was Kentuckian Molly O'Day. O'Day was in many ways rooted in the same Appalachian mountain styles as Roy Acuff. She possessed a clear, booming voice that imbued with earnestness and earthy conviction everything she sang, whether tearjerkers like 'The Drunken Driver', gospel standards like 'Tramp On The Street' or her early covers of Hank Williams originals like 'Six More Miles'.

The Ryman Auditorium, home to the Grand Ole Opry *from 1943–74 and the place where many country stars rose to fame.*

ALLRIGHT
AUTO PARK
WSM
GRAND
OLE
OPRY
OPRY TOURS

Western Swing

Western swing is an innovative, free-wheeling yet complex instrumental amalgam drawn from blues, jazz and Dixieland syncopations and harmonies. Central to the style is an emphasis on instrumental solos, often involving the transposition of jazz-style horn parts to fiddle, guitar and steel guitar.

It is indicative of western swing's sophistication that Bob Wills' Texas Playboys, the definitive western swing band, included at various times a Dixieland drummer (Smokey Dacus), a jazz piano player (Al Stricklin) and a jazz-flavoured guitarist (Eldon Shamblin). Wills' innovations with his long-time band the Texas Playboys were crucial to the mergence of this hybrid music that merged horns and the free-wheeling, improvisatory spirit of jazz big bands with country fiddle music and elements of honky tonk instrumentation like the electric guitar, steel guitar and twin fiddles.

Rivaling Wills' influence in establishing and propagating early western swing was his fellow Texan and one-time band mate, Milton Brown – the two played together briefly in the early 1930s as part of a trio called the Aladdin Laddies, and later the Light Crust Doughboys. Brown and his band the Musical Brownies were, until Brown's untimely death in a car accident in 1936, pioneers of a number of the genre's essential ingredients, including New Orleans jazz rhythms, twin fiddles playing in harmony, slap-bass fiddle playing and some of the earliest uses of electrified instruments in country music. Brown, just as importantly, brought a smooth and rhythmic vocal style to western swing that drew more heavily from jazz masters like Jack Teagarden and Cab Calloway than from country sources. He also recorded and popularized songs like 'Right Or Wrong' and 'Corrine Corrina' that still endure as western swing standards. Unfortunately, without Brown, the Brownies' innovations ceased and the band's popularity quickly waned.

'When dancers spotted the Texas Playboys at one end of Cain's dancehall outside Tulsa, what they saw was a traditional country string band. What they heard, however, was a new kind of jazz band.'

Charles Townsend

Trombonist Jack Teagarden, who revolutionized the instrument's status within jazz music.

Doughboys and Playboys

Bob Wills' career began modestly in 1929 when a trio he'd formed landed a spot on a Fort Worth, Texas radio station. In the early 1930s, as he moved on to larger radio stations and his budget increased, Wills added additional players (including Milton Brown) to his band, which was called at various times the Aladdin Laddies and the Light Crust Doughboys.

In Tulsa, Oklahoma in 1934 the name Texas Playboys finally stuck for good. By then Wills had further expanded his instrumental line-up to include two fiddles, two guitars and a bass, piano and banjo. Four years later, he had boosted the band to 14 members, including a third fiddle, two saxophones and a trumpet player.

By 1935, after more personnel shuffles, Wills assembled what some consider to be the most talented line-up of Playboys. Players included vocalist Tommy Duncan, banjo player Johnnie Lee Wills, bass player Son Lansford, trumpeter Everett Stover, saxophonist Zeb McNally, guitarist Herman Arnspiger, trombonist Art Haines, fiddler Jesse Ashlock, steel guitarist Leon McAuliffe, guitarist Sleepy Johnson, drummer Smokey Dacus, piano player Al Stricklin and Wills himself, also on fiddle. In the next few years, Wills enlarged his already substantial band still more, adding an entire six-man horn ection and innovative guitarist Eldon Shamblin. He soon was recording some of the songs that have endured as western swing's universal standards, including 'Time Changes Everything', 'San Antonio Rose' and 'Take Me Back To Tulsa'.

Key Artists

Bob Wills & the Texas Playboys
Milton Brown & his Musical Brownies
Tommy Duncan & the Western All-Stars
Merle Haggard
Ray Benson & Asleep At The Wheel

Wills' popularity continued unabated throughout most of the 1940s and the personnel shifts continued. In the late 1940s, he added the brilliant Texas fiddler Johnny Gimble to the Playboys' line-up and employed his younger brother Billy Jack Wills as his vocalist after Tommy Duncan – western swing's most celebrated singer, who sang lead on many of Wills' landmark recordings – left in 1948 to form his own band, the Western All-Stars. Wills also gradually reduced his once-expansive horn section to a single trumpet. During these years he added yet another enduring hit, 'Faded Love', to his celebrated repertoire.

Bob Wills (right of centre) shows jazz and blues influences in his music, which he absorbed from working and playing with the cotton-field slaves. He once travelled 50 miles on horseback to see Bessie Smith perform.

Western Swing's the Thing

As Wills' popularity had begun to spread in the 1930s, the Texas Playboys became the inspiration for a number of other talented western swing bands. Many of these were led by former Texas Playboys like Leon McAuliffe, Jesse Ashlock and Wills' brothers Lee and Billy Jack.

The western swing sound even spread as far afield as Kentucky, where a band called the Prairie Ramblers picked up on it. Adding Patsy Montana, a talented Arkansas singer, to their line-up, they became popular members of Chicago's *National Barndance* radio show during the 1930s and 1940s. However, practically all these bands, as well as notables like Cliff Bruner's Texas Wanderers and Jimmie Revard & his Oklahoma Playboys, borrowed heavily from Wills' arrangements and repertoire and never quite escaped his long shadow. By the mid-1950s, Wills' star was on the wane, as was his health, and the golden age of western swing had largely run its course. The western swing king was sidelined forever in 1969 by a debilitating stroke and died in 1975 following a series of strokes.

Bob Wills is Still the King

Even decades after its 1930s and 1940s heyday, western swing in general and Wills' repertoire and Texas-style big-band sound in particular, have been revisited time and again by contemporary country stars like Merle Haggard and George Strait, as well as celebrated honky tonkers like Ray Price, Red Steagall and, most notably, Texan Hank Thompson. A real milestone in western swing revivalism came in 1970 when Merle Haggard, a lifelong admirer of Wills, reassembled many of the original Texas Playboys and recorded a magnificent album-length salute to Wills called *A Tribute To The Best Damn Fiddle Player In The World*.

Key Tracks

'Ida Red' Bob Wills & the Texas Playboys
'Swinging Doors' Merle Haggard
'Taking Off' Milton Brown & his Musical Brownies
'The Wild Side Of Life' Hank Thompson

Oddly enough, western swing also got a fresh hearing in the 1970s and 1980s through the music of several eclectic, youthful hippy-era bands. The most enduring of these neo-western swingers is Asleep At The Wheel, a band headed by Texas singer Ray Benson. Through thick and thin, Benson and the Wheel are still going strong as the most vital contemporary purveyors of this intricate yet robust and eminently danceable music.

Perhaps one reason why Merle Haggard's songs are so compelling is the fact that he really did live in the way they describe. Raised in a converted boxcar and living a chequered life of gambling and crime, Haggard was the genuine article.

GEORGE
Dickel
MERLE

Bluegrass

Unlike practically any other strain of indigenous American music, bluegrass can be traced back to a particular time and a particular group of men: Kentucky-born mandolin player/bandleader Bill Monroe and a select handful of musicians he gathered in his band, the Bluegrass Boys.

Monroe and the celebrated 1940s vintage line-up of the Bluegrass Boys first transformed traditional acoustic guitar-fiddle-bass-fiddle country stringband music into something fresh, exciting and revolutionary in its innovation. They did this by kicking it into a higher gear and giving it a driving, syncopated beat along with close, high-pitched lead and harmony vocals on favourites like 'Uncle Pen', 'Muleskinner Blues' and 'Blue Moon Of Kentucky'. Monroe also elevated the mandolin from a rhythmic to a fully fledged lead instrument. Earl Scruggs essentially did the same with the five-string banjo.

'I think Bill Monroe's importance to American music is as important as someone like Robert Johnson was to blues, or Louis Armstrong. He was so influential; I think he's probably the only musician that had a whole style of music named after his band.'

Ricky Scaggs

The music that Monroe and a handful of his talented contemporaries forged more than half a century ago has not only endured, but has also enjoyed renewed popularity in recent decades. In fact, one of the most acclaimed and best-selling country albums of the new millennium, despite getting practically no airplay on country stations, is the soundtrack from the 2000 feature film *O Brother, Where Art Thou?* A quirky, dark comedy directed by the Coen Brothers, *O Brother* transferred a Homeric epic to a rural 1930s setting. Its rich soundtrack featured vintage bluegrass by veterans such as Ralph Stanley, as well as old-time country and gospel music by an imaginative line-up of popular and obscure musicians, and contemporary newgrass and alt. country figures like Alison Krauss and Gillian Welch. The soundtrack sold several million copies, won five Grammy Awards and sparked yet another revival in rural musical Americana.

Bill Monroe, creator and undisputed king of the bluegrass sound. Monroe's plaintive, wailing vocals, combined with the dense textures and frenetic playing of his band, took country music in a new and exciting direction.

The Grass is Always Bluer

It was the stellar 1945–48 line-up of Bill Monroe's Bluegrass Boys – Earl Scruggs on five-string banjo and vocals, Lester Flatt on guitar and vocals, Chubby Wise on fiddle, Cedric Rainwater and Monroe himself on mandolin – that deserves the lion's share of credit for forging this intricate, high-energy musical hybrid from its more traditional antecedents. To this day the seminal mid- and late 1940s Bluegrass Boys recordings serve as the template, and the Holy Grail, of the traditional bluegrass sound.

Tennessee-born Flatt and North Carolina-born Scruggs, a pair of former textile mill workers, left the Bluegrass Boys in 1948 and formed their own band, the Foggy Mountain Boys. This new ensemble would play nearly as central a role as Monroe and the Bluegrass Boys in further defining the bluegrass spirit and style. With his intricate three-finger banjo style, Scruggs elevated the banjo from a traditional rhythmic role to a lead instrument as crucial to bluegrass's soul as Monroe's kinetic mandolin style. The Foggy Mountain Boys also imbued their bluegrass sound with smoother lead vocals while adding a second guitar and speeding the rhythm up even more, with an emphasis on Scruggs's intricate breakneck speed banjo playing. In 1955 Flatt & Scruggs added the dobro (resonator guitar) of Josh Graves to the Foggy Mountain Boys. It was Graves' expertise that has since established the dobro's mournful presence as a central ingredient in bluegrass. Until they went their separate ways in 1966, Flatt & Scruggs did much to popularize bluegrass with non-country audiences with favourites like 'Foggy Mountain Breakdown', 'Roll In My Sweet Baby's Arms' and 'Old Salty Dog Blues'.

Key Artists

Bill Monroe & the Bluegrass Boys
Lester Flatt & Earl Scruggs
Carter & Ralph Stanley
Jim & Jesse McReynolds
Don Reno & Red Smiley

Monroe's innovations on the *Grand Ole Opry*, both with Flatt & Scruggs and after their departure from the Bluegrass Boys, did not go unnoticed in the heartlands where the *Grand Ole Opry's* powerful 50,000-watt AM signal boomed far and wide on Saturday nights. It had a particularly important impact on a pair of young Virginia musicians, Ralph and Carter Stanley. The Stanley Brothers, who were steeped in the harmony-driven old-time music traditions of their native state, began covering songs by Monroe and the Bluegrass Boys and incorporating the new bluegrass sound into their own distinct mountain style on classic recordings like 'Molly And Tenbrooks'.

Earl Scruggs and Lester Flatt perform at the Grand Ole Opry *with the other Foggy Mountain Boys. Flatt & Scruggs' popularity was furthered by the popular 1960s TV show* The Beverly Hillbillies, *which featured music by the duo, as well as cameo appearances.*

WSM's
GRAND
OLE
OPRY

O Brother

The Stanley Brothers soon became one of bluegrass's most popular bands and they remained in the front ranks until Carter Stanley's death in 1966. After that, Ralph, who until then had pretty much worked in older brother Carter's shadow, assumed the role of lead singer and bandleader of the Clinch Mountain Boys and has since enjoyed great musical longevity.

Virginians Jim and Jesse McReynolds rose to bluegrass's front ranks in the 1960s on the strength of Jim's brilliant tenor and Jesse's imaginative transposition of the syncopated 'cross-picking' banjo technique to the mandolin. Jim & Jesse, much like the Stanley Brothers, were anchored in the traditional mountain stringband sound early in their career, but by 1964, when they became members of the *Grand Ole Opry*, they were expanding bluegrass's parameters by masterfully weaving mainstream country elements into their repertoire and sometimes even using electrified instruments.

In the 1960s, the Osborne Brothers from Hyden, Kentucky, also found success on country radio (which by and large had shied away from playing bluegrass, which it deemed too strident and old-timey for its listeners). The Osbornes adventurously augmented their individualized bluegrass sound with typically non-bluegrass instrumentation like steel guitars, drums and pianos. Mac Wiseman, a lead vocalist and rhythm guitarist with Monroe's Bluegrass Boys, also achieved popularity with country audiences by occasionally refashioning pop songs of the day like 'Love Letters In The Sand' into bluegrass odes. Other ensembles, like the great, innovative banjo-guitar-vocal duet team Don Reno and Red Smiley and fiddler Kenny Baker, would enrich and expand upon bluegrass's traditional roots throughout the 1960s and 1970s.

Key Tracks

'Foggy Mountain Breakdown' Lester Flatt & Earl Scruggs
'Muleskinner Blues' Bill Monroe & the Bluegrass Boys
'I'm Using My Bible For A Roadmap' Don Reno & Red Smiley
'The Ballad Of Jed Clampett' Foggy Mountain Boys
'Molly And Tenbrooks' Carter & Ralph Stanley

After Carter's death, Ralph formed The Clinch Mountain Boys. Cry From The Cross *remained true to the bluegrass style.*

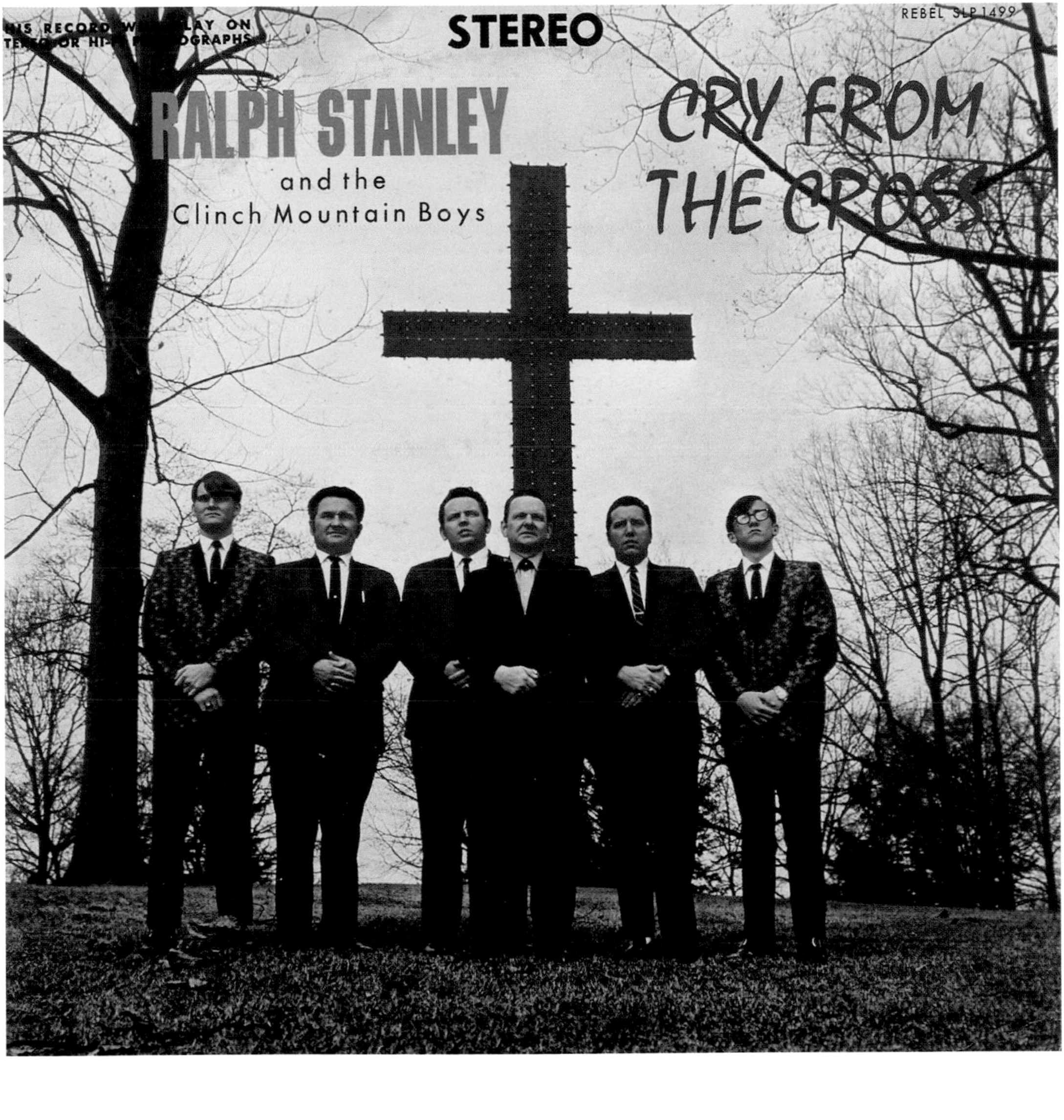
STEREO
REBEL SLP 1499
RALPH STANLEY
and the
Clinch Mountain Boys
CRY FROM
THE CROSS

Honky Tonk

At least until the 1930s and 1940s the dominant themes in country music were a celebration of bedrock rural values like family, faith, fidelity and the redeeming powers of true love and honest labour. The music served to offer listeners comfort, reassurance and a soothing sense of place and identity.

But as America's national zeitgeist began to reflect dramatic social shifts like the industrial-age migration from country to city, country music, especially in the unsettled, temporary, Second World War-era oil field, factory and shipyard settlements of Texas and the great American Southwest, underwent a similar transformation. The rise of honky tonk music was a manifestation of that social upheaval. It is strident, electrified and utterly worldly music that drew its very name from the rough-hewn saloons and dancehalls, known as 'honky tonks', in grungy working-class cities.

Honky tonk's emphasis on electrification and heavier percussion was also a departure from largely acoustic-based traditional country music. It was both a reflection of a faster-paced life as well as a practical means of being heard over the late-night din in an oil-field or factory-town barroom. The first major star to arise in the genre was Texas-born Ernest Tubb, whose illustrious recording career stretched from 1936 until 1982. A gruff-voiced yet plaintive singer, Tubb started out in the 1930s as an earnest disciple of Jimmie Rodgers, but he found his own laconic voice with earthy honky tonk anthems like 'Walking The Floor Over You', 'Wasting My Life Away' and 'Warm Red Wine'. Tubb further widened honky tonk's audience in the early 1940s when he became a member of Nashville's *Grand Ole Opry*.

'We gotta play music that'll make them goddamn beer bottles bounce on the table.'

Moon Mullican

But few if any artists would transfigure country music, and define honky tonk for decades to come in the way that Alabama-born Hank Williams did, beginning in the late 1940s. Williams' timeless originals ('Cold, Cold Heart', 'Jambalaya', 'Your Cheatin' Heart', etc.) and his stark, lonesome and evocative singing style both personified and transcended honky tonk's earthbound parameters. His original compositions, in the half-century since his death in 1953, have been recorded hundreds of times by everyone from George Jones and Patsy Cline to Tony Bennett and Cassandra Wilson.

Hank Williams, the leading exponent of the honky tonk style and one of the most influential musicians of the twentieth century.

Humpty-Dumpty and Honky Tonk Angels

Nearly as influential as Hank Williams as a honky tonk vocalist was Corsicana, Texas-born Lefty Frizzell. Like Tubb before him, Frizzell was heavily steeped in the Jimmie Rodgers legacy. Yet by the early 1950s, when he had an almost unprecedented flurry of hits like 'If You've Got The Money I've Got The Time' and 'Mom And Dad's Waltz', Frizzell had developed his own vividly original and emotional clenched-teeth, slip-note, vowel-bending vocal style.

His vocal influence lingers vividly today in the voices of more recent honky tonk and country stars like George Jones, George Strait, Randy Travis and Merle Haggard. Although Haggard's vocal mannerisms are heavily rooted in the Lefty Frizzell style and as an artist he has been a major proponent of honky tonk since the late 1960s, his amazing versatility and stylistic range transcend any one particular strain of country music.

Another major player who has enjoyed great longevity in the field is Texan Hank Thompson, who had parallel importance as a proponent of western swing and scored hits with 'Humpty Dumpty Heart' (1948) and 'The Wild Side Of Life' (1952). Kitty Wells, the demure, retiring wife of singer Johnny Wright (of Johnny & Jack) unwittingly became one of the first and only honky tonk queens when 'It Wasn't God Who Made Honky Tonk Angels', her answer song to Hank Thompson's 'Wild Side Of Life', became a surprise number one radio and jukebox hit in 1952.

Key Artists

Al Dexter
Ernest Tubb
Hank Williams
Lefty Frizzell
George Jones

Though best known for lighter 1960s and 1970s Nashville sound crossover-style hits like 'Danny Boy' and 'For The Good Times', Texan Ray Price began his recording career in the 1950s with pivotal hits like 'Crazy Arms' and 'City Lights'. The intense rhythmic brand of honky tonk that Price introduced with these recordings has been so widely emulated that it has since become known as the 'Ray Price Beat'.

The definitive honky tonk singer, Lefty Frizzell.

Legacy of the Honky Tonk Blues

The man whose music has became as synonymous with 1960s–90s honky tonk as Lefty Frizzell's and Hank Williams' names were to the 1950s is East Texas native George Jones.

An early devotee of Frizzell, Williams and *Grand Ole Opry* star Roy Acuff, Jones, by the late 1950s, had subsumed these worthy vocal influences into his own uncannily powerful and subtle octave-swooping baritone that plumbs the depths of emotional profundity and clenched-teeth sorrow like no one before.

Also like Williams and Frizzell before him, Jones, throughout his half-century recording career, has emerged as a tortured, ambivalent soul whose despair and confusion often echo hauntingly in his music. As such, his hit, beer-stained lamentations like 'He Stopped Loving Her Today' and 'Bartender's Blues' and his unabashed celebrations of the wild side like 'Tennessee Whiskey' and 'White Lightning' have come to embody honky tonk for many country fans.

The honky tonk influence has persisted over the decades, even through the more mellow eras of the Nashville sound and the urban cowboys. Today it's clearly heard in the music of contemporary stars like Alan Jackson (chart-topping hits like 1991's 'Don't Rock The Jukebox' and 1992's 'She's Got The Rhythm (And I've Got The Blues)') and Dwight Yoakam (his brilliant 1986 cover of Johnny Horton's 'Honky Tonk Man' and his 1988 hit duet with Buck Owens, 'Streets Of Bakersfield') whose vocal styles have been profoundly inspired by an earlier generation of practitioners like Hank Williams, Merle Haggard, Lefty Frizzell and George Jones.

Key Tracks

'Your Cheatin' Heart' Hank Williams
'Blue Christmas' Ernest Tubb
'Saginaw, Michigan' Lefty Frizzell
'The Wild Side Of Life' Hank Thompson
'Crazy Arms' Ray Prince

George Jones has an expansive, soulful, clench-toothed baritone style all his own that repeatedly earned him critical raves as the greatest country singer ever.

Rock'n'Roll

Although he did not coin the term 'rock'n'roll' – which was an African-American slang term for sex – New York disk jockey Alan Freed did popularize it when he attached it to a teen-oriented form of music that evolved from a fusion of rockabilly, R&B and, to a lesser extent, gospel and boogie-woogie.

In its early forms, rock'n'roll was often so similar to R&B (known as 'race music' until *Billboard* journalist Jerry Wexler provided it with a more appropriate name) in terms of structure and feel that it is not easy to discern which of the categories certain records fell into or even to ascertain what was, in fact, the first true rock'n'roll record.

Jackie Brenston's 1951 classic, 'Rocket 88', which he cut as a member of Ike Turner and the Kings of Rhythm, is one of the most popular choices in this regard, but there are many, many other contenders, ranging from 1948 recordings such as Wynonie Harris's 'Good Rockin' Tonight' and Wild Bill Moore's 'We're Gonna Rock, We're Gonna Roll' to Jimmy Preston's 'Rock The Joint' in 1949 and Muddy Waters' 'Rollin' And Tumblin'' in 1950. Waters' assertion that 'the blues had a baby and they called it rock'n'roll' was only part of the story; other musical genres also played a major role in the evolutionary process.

'Let's face it – rock'n'roll is bigger than all of us.'

Alan Freed

Jackie Brenston, whose 1951 recording of 'Rocket 88' is claimed as the first rock'n'roll record.

Shaking the World

'Rocket 88' was produced by the legendary Sam Phillips a year before he formed Sun Records, the small independent label which, along with his tiny Memphis Recording Service studio, soon became synonymous with the birth of rock'n'roll.

Phillips worked with local country acts while searching for a white artist who could bring black music to the masses by conveying the true feel and passion of the blues. As it turned out, that artist was Elvis Presley, who, through a process of trial and error, under guidance from Phillips, and in collaboration with guitarist Scotty Moore and bass player Bill Black, utilized his innate talent, steeped in country, gospel and the blues, to contrive a hybrid sound that would shake the world. In 13 months at Sun, from July 1954 to August 1955, Presley released five singles, each of which featured an R&B standard on one side and a souped-up country track on the other. While the latter category helped to define rockabilly, the former held the key to rock'n'roll. When white Southerners heard the first of these R&B cuts, Elvis's feverish, yearning cover of Arthur 'Big Boy' Crudup's 'That's All Right (Mama)', many of them assumed they were listening to a black singer; by the time of the second, a heavily suggestive version of 'Good Rockin' Tonight', they knew not only that he was white, but that it was time to lock up their daughters.

Key Artists

Chuck Berry
Buddy Holly
Jerry Lee Lewis
Little Richard
Elvis Presley

After Elvis's contract was sold to the huge RCA corporation in late 1955, he recorded the seminal 'Heartbreak Hotel', a sombre, haunting single that not only sustained its predecessors' blues feel and levels of sexual insinuation, but also gained him worldwide recognition. With its blues-laced piano, strident guitar solos and depressive, self-pitying lyrics, 'Heartbreak Hotel' served as a call to arms for disgruntled teenagers; from then on, Presley, whose youthful good looks and Brando-like sexuality stood in sharp and favourable contrast to the pudgy, kiss-curled visage of Bill Haley, pressed home his advantage with a series of blistering rock'n'roll recordings. 'Blue Suede Shoes', 'Hound Dog' and 'Jailhouse Rock' were just a few of the many classic tracks he laid down during a four-year period (along with the songs for the movie *King Creole*, which awkwardly merged rock with Dixieland jazz), yet while they epitomized the genre, some also smacked of manufactured pop rather than heartfelt R&B.

Being considered threatening and corruptive by the authorities only further ensured Elvis Presley's iconic status. In fact, despite his risqué onstage moves, Presley was really a sweet, home-loving boy.

Energy and Attitude

Another Sam Phillips discovery was Jerry Lee Lewis, 'The Killer' from Ferriday, Louisiana, whose arrogant, aggressive performances quickly established him as one of rock'n'roll's most inspirational figures during its halcyon period.

Melding country and R&B with frenetic, boogie-style piano, Lewis turned out songs that would get the whole joint jumping: 'Whole Lotta Shakin'', 'Great Balls Of Fire', 'Breathless' and 'High School Confidential'. If Elvis Presley was rock'n'roll's greatest sex symbol, Jerry Lee Lewis was certainly its wildest white performer.

Nevertheless, whereas Lewis belted out his songs' lyrics with manic intensity, and Presley traversed the musical boundaries to sound alternately raucous, gospel-tinged, crooner-like, countrified and bluesy, neither man could match Little Richard, another classic voice of rock'n'roll, for raw, throat-grating, lightning-quick delivery.

Richard's exhaustingly energetic singing, punctuated with falsetto shrieks and breathless asides, perfectly matched his flamboyant appearance and short-changed no one, least of all the kids for whom 'awop-bop-a-loo-bop-a-lop-bam-boom' had complete meaning. Gibberish or not, it was a language they could instantly identify with, for it somehow encapsulated the energy and attitude prevalent in numbers such as 'Tutti Frutti', 'Long Tall Sally', 'Rip It Up', 'She's Got It', 'Lucille' and 'Good Golly Miss Molly'. What's more, it was a language that most parents could in no way understand, and that had to make it all the more pertinent.

Key Tracks

'Johnny B. Goode' Chuck Berry
'Peggy Sue' Buddy Holly
'Great Balls of Fire' Jerry Lee Lewis
'Tutti Frutti' Little Richard
'Hound Dog' Elvis Presley

'The Killer' performs a storming rendition of the title track in the opening scenes of High School Confidential, *a film that involved a tongue-in-cheek exposé of drug abuse in American schools.*

Fifties Pop Singer/Songwriters

Until the advent of rock'n'roll, pop singers and songwriters were, for the most part, divided into two separate camps. The singers were typically faced with the daunting task of unearthing new hit material, unless, like Frank Sinatra, they were so esteemed that they had the best songwriters in the business lining up to write for them.

All of this began to change in the mid-1950s, however, as pop music commenced its evolution into a do-it-yourself art form in which, as with country and western and the blues, the performance of a song was often less about perfection than about feel.

Rockabilly singer/songwriter Carl Perkins secured his own place in pop history by way of his one major chart hit, 'Blue Suede Shoes', which became a rock'n'roll anthem when it was covered by Elvis Presley in 1956. At around the same time, the R&B field delivered the likes of Little Richard (real name Richard Penniman), an electrifying, gospel-rooted singer/pianist who co-wrote many of his biggest hits, including 'Tutti Frutti', 'Lucille', 'Long Tall Sally', 'She's Got It', 'Keep A Knockin'', 'Slippin' And Slidin'' and 'Jenny, Jenny'; and singer/guitarist Bo Diddley (born Otha Ellas Bates), innovator of the pounding, Latin-tinged rhythm and beat that infused not only self-referential compositions such as 'Bo Diddley' and 'Diddley Daddy', but also numerous classic songs by other artists down the years, such as The Strangeloves' 'I Want Candy', Buddy Holly's 'Not Fade Away', Johnny Otis's 'Willie And The Hand Jive', Shirley And Company's 'Shame, Shame, Shame', George Michael's 'Faith' and U2's 'Desire'.

'A lot of songs I sang to crowds first to watch their reaction, that's how I knew they'd hit.'

Little Richard

The Iowa plane crash in which Buddy Holly died also killed fellow singers J.P. Richardson (aka The Big Bopper) and Ritchie Valens. The tragic event was commemorated in Don McLean's 1972 single 'American Pie'.

Pure Poetry for a New Generation

Perhaps the single most influential singer/songwriter of the era was Chuck Berry, whose driving guitar licks and topical, witty and ingeniously quick-fire, poetic lyrics pretty much defined rock'n'roll.

A native of St. Louis, Missouri, Charles Edward Anderson Berry threw country, R&B and boogie-woogie into the mix when concocting major chart hits such as 'Maybellene', 'Roll Over Beethoven', 'Rock And Roll Music', 'Sweet Little Sixteen', 'Carol' and 'Johnny B. Goode'. The results were pure poetry for a new generation of car-cruising, guitar-strumming, record-playing, dancing and dating teens. As John Lennon once said, 'If you tried to give rock'n'roll another name, you might call it Chuck Berry.'

As attested to by his chart success and influence over 1960s superstars ranging from the Beach Boys and the Beatles to Bob Dylan and the Rolling Stones, Berry had little trouble appealing to white audiences.

Meanwhile, another singer/songwriter who made a more concerted effort in that regard was Sam Cooke, who crossed over from his gospel origins as the lead singer with the Soul Stirrers to lend his sublime voice to self-penned mainstream white pop, flavoured with an assortment of soul, R&B and, on occasion, unadulterated kitsch. In 1957, Cooke enjoyed his first solo American number 1 with 'You Send Me', a romantic ballad complemented by white backing vocalists, and moved even further away from his roots with overtly commercial follow-ups such as 'Everybody Likes To Cha Cha Cha' and 'Only Sixteen' before really hitting his stride during the early part of the ensuing decade.

Key Artists

Chuck Berry
Sam Cooke
Bobby Darin
Jerry Lee Lewis
Neil Sedaka

The ingenious songs of Chuck Berry combined clever and witty lyrics with fast-moving tunes and intricate guitar playing. Onstage, Chuck had a number of popular moves, including the famous 'duck walk'.

Inspiring Tomorrow's Composers

While Sam Cooke stood as a symbol of African-American achievement and prosperity, writing most of his hit material in addition to running his own management and publishing companies alongside an independent record label, several of his white contemporaries were also inspiring the composers of tomorrow by honing their skills as singer/songwriters.

Bobby Darin (born Walden Robert Cassotto) enjoyed his first chart success in 1958 with the co-written novelty number 'Splish Splash', and he built on that the following year by penning the smash hit 'Dream Lover'. At the same time, while 'Words Of Love' was a Buddy Holly solo composition that would later be covered by the Beatles, Holly co-wrote several of his most memorable songs with members of his backing band The Crickets, as well as with producer Norman Petty; among them were 'That'll Be The Day', 'Peggy Sue', 'It's So Easy', 'Well ... All Right', 'Think It Over' and 'True Love Ways'.

Shortly after his death in a plane crash in February 1959, Holly topped the UK charts with the posthumous (and ironically titled) single 'It Doesn't Matter Anymore'. This had been penned by Paul Anka, yet another multi-talented youngster who had enjoyed international success by recording his own material. A native of Ontario, Canada, Anka was only 16 when 'Diana', his 1957 paean to a girl four years his senior, made him an international star, and during the next couple of years he capitalized on this with a string of highly dramatic ballads focusing on teen romance (or the lack thereof), including 'You Are My Destiny', 'Lonely Boy' and 'Put Your Head On My Shoulder'. He also wrote the lyrics to the big Sinatra hit, 'My Way'.

Unlike the veteran Tin Pan Alley composers, Anka was able to connect with teenagers and convey their emotions because he was one himself. This trend would pick up pace during the decades to follow.

Key Tracks

'School Days' Chuck Berry
'Wonderful World' Sam Cooke
'Splish Splash' Bobby Darin
'Whole Lotta Shakin' Goin On' Jerry Lee Lewis
'Happy Birthday Sweet Sixteen' Neil Sedaka

Sam Cooke's magnificent voice made an easy transition from gospel music to mainstream pop.

Rockabilly

A slapped upright bass, twanging lead guitar and acoustic rhythm guitar; a blues structure with country and blues inflections; a strong beat and moderate-to-fast tempo; a wild, yelping, often stuttering vocal style, together with plenty of echo on the recordings are the main ingredients of rockabilly.

The rockabilly style was an eclectic hybrid of R&B, hillbilly music and country-boogie that emerged during the mid-1950s, and again owed much to Sam Phillips and his Sun Records label.

While country-boogie had drawn on jazz boogie-woogie rhythms during the previous decade, and been popularized by acts such as The Delmore Brothers, Webb Pierce, Red Foley and Moon Mullican, the acoustic bass and steel guitar prevalent in the hillbilly sound of Hank Williams exerted just as much influence on the likes of Bill Haley and, a little later on, Carl Perkins.

When Perkins arrived at Sun, he was performing hillbilly honky-tonk infused with the rhythm of black blues music. With Phillips' guidance he then added some R&B touches by way of scatting his vocal phrases and completing them on guitar, resulting in cuts such as 'Gone, Gone, Gone', which appeared on the flip side of his first Sun single, and the seminal self-penned 'Blue Suede Shoes'. Perkins sold two million copies of 'Blue Suede Shoes' before Elvis's cover version was released. A true country boy, Perkins originally wrote the song on a potato sack.

'I can hear rockabilly in the music that they play today ... bluegrass and the cotton-patch blues. They're still coppin' from that today.'

Charlie Feathers

Blind in his left eye since childhood, Bill Haley was self-conscious about his appearance. To draw attention away from his eye Haley wore his hair in a kiss curl, which became his trademark and sparked a kiss curl craze.

A More Commercial Sound

Complemented by Sam Phillips' trademark use of slap-back echo and over-amplification, songs such as 'Gone, Gone, Gone' and 'Blue Suede Shoes' were quintessential rockabilly (or 'hillbilly bop', as they were sometimes described), a style that the producer had largely concocted in collaboration with Elvis Presley. The B-side of Elvis's first single ('That's All Right', issued in July 1954) was a total revamping of Bill Monroe's 1947 bluegrass waltz, 'Blue Moon Of Kentucky'.

Searching for a more commercial sound that might appeal to a widespread audience, Phillips tried to encourage the young singer, as well as guitarist Scotty Moore and bass player Bill Black, to find a comfortable uptempo groove. This began to take shape over the course of several takes – 'Hell, that's fine! That's different!' Phillips can be heard exclaiming at one point on the session tape: 'That's a pop song now, nearly 'bout!' – until what finally emerged was a jumped-up, freewheeling, echo-bathed version, the feel of which was light years away from that of the Monroe original.

The process continued through subsequent Presley recordings such as 'I Don't Care If The Sun Don't Shine', 'Milkcow Blues Boogie' and, most supremely, an electrifying cover of Junior Parker's 'Mystery Train', which borrowed a guitar riff from Parker's earlier 'Love My Baby' to bridge the gap between country and R&B. Still, it was Carl Perkins' 1956 recording of the self-penned 'Blue Suede Shoes' that gained rockabilly worldwide recognition, encouraging major labels such as Capitol, Columbia, Decca, Mercury and RCA to jump on the bandwagon and exploit the genre.

For its part, Sun served as the main rockabilly hub, and although only Presley and Perkins experienced large-scale success in this field, a number of other artists signed to the label did make some notable recordings. Prime among them was Charlie Feathers, who, with Stan Kesler, co-wrote 'I Forgot To Remember To Forget' – which Elvis subsequently recorded – before moving to other labels and recording classics of the genre such as 'Tongue-Tied Jill' and 'Get With It'. At a time when rock'n'roll was breaking big on both sides of the Atlantic, Feathers felt that he never got the record company support he deserved – a view shared by Billy Lee Riley.

Key Artists

Sonny Burgess
Charlie Feathers
Bill Haley
Carl Perkins
Elvis Presley

Carl Perkins, one of rockabilly's finest, sold two million copies of his song 'Blue Suede Shoes' before Elvis's cover version was released. A true country boy, Perkins originally wrote the song on a potato sack.

Limited Chart Success

Billy Lee Riley's more memorable recordings at Sun included 'Rock With Me Baby' and 'Red Hot', but none made the chart inroads he hoped for and expected. A similar fate befell the efforts of, among others, Sonny Burgess, Ray Harris, Hayden Thompson and Warren Smith.

Rockabilly's place in the spotlight was limited and its time was short-lived; its performers came from a very specific background, too. Indeed, because only a handful of the artists were black, Sam Phillips wasn't even comfortable with the genre's name.

'I've always thought 'rock'n'roll' was the best term,' he'd comment more than four decades later, 'because it became all-inclusive of white, black and the whole thing, whereas "rockabilly" tended to just want to lend itself so specifically to white. It also promoted the feeling that maybe we were stealing something from the blacks and wanted to put it in a white form, so I never did like "rockabilly".'

Still, numerous people consider the golden era of rockabilly, which burned out towards the end of the 1950s, to be a shining period in the annals of popular music; a time when often basic instrumentation and primitive recording equipment combined with uninhibited energy to produce rough-edged music that was vital, honest and, to many minds, the purest form of rock'n'roll. It was also a musical form that encapsulated the feelgood party spirit of the mid-1950s: as Carl Perkins once said, 'We shook the devil loose! We bopped those blues!' In the 1970s and 1980s rockabilly enjoyed a revival with bands such as the Stray Cats playing down-home 1950s-style music with a punk-rock edge. There were also purist rockabilly revival bands who followed the original style more closely.

Key Tracks

'Peepin' Eyes' Charlie Feathers
'Rock Around The Clock' Bill Haley
'Blue Suede Shoes' Carl Perkins
'Daddy Sang Bass' Carl Perkins
'I Don't Care If The Sun Don't Shine' Elvis Presley

The Stray Cats, one of the bands who led the rockabilly revival in the 1970s and 1980s.

Doo-Wop

While many hit doo-wop records featured full instrumental accompaniment, the groups themselves had usually started out singing a cappella. It was, in short, a music that required collaborative effort but no instrumental outlay or expertise, to be performed on street corners as a means of escape, public entertainment, personal fulfilment and professional ambition.

Deriving its name from the nonsense backing vocals that often provided its rhythm, R&B-flavoured doo-wop was one of the most popular veins of music to attach itself to rock'n'roll during the second half of the 1950s. The most prominent characteristic of the emotive romantic ballads and jaunty, uptempo, sometimes comical numbers was their interweaving harmonies, whose roots lay not only in gospel but also in black American vocal outfits of the 1940s such as the Mills Brothers and the Ink Spots.

'We sang on the beaches, or on rooftops, or in hallways of tenement buildings. We must have been sensitive artists, even back then, because we always looked for the hallway that had the best sound.'

Dion De Mucci

Arguably, the first doo-wop hit was the Orioles' 'It's Too Soon To Know' in 1948. Thereafter, a number of similar, bird-named groups emerged throughout the early 1950s, including the Cardinals, the Crows, the Larks, the Ravens, the Robins, the Wrens and the Penguins; the latter's 1954 hit, 'Earth Angel (Will You Be Mine)', was latched on to by white kids who could readily identify with lyrics concerning youthful romance. Consequently, a form of music that had initially been aimed at a predominantly adult, African-American audience began to cross over to a multiracial teenage market. In turn, this led to integrated doo-wop groups such as the Impalas and the Del-Vikings – whose 1957 hit 'Come Go With Me' was the first song that the adolescent Paul McCartney ever saw John Lennon perform – as well as all-white outfits such as Dion & the Belmonts, the Mystics and the Skyliners.

Doo-wop usually suggests sweet harmonies and tender ballads, but this was not always the case. This compilation contains a selection of more up-tempo doo-wop songs.

BIM
BAM
BOOM
THE EL DORADOS
THE SPANIELS
THE DU MAURIERS
THE DU-DROPPERS
THE DUKAYS
THE MOONGLOWS
THE DELLS
THE FLAMINGOS
THE THUNDERBIRDS
THE IDEALS
THE "C" NOTES
RE-VELS
THE MONOTONES
THE ORIOLES
THE HARMONAIRES
THE LOVE NOTES
28 Rockin' Doo Wops

The Doo-Wop Bandwagon

Doo-wop had made vast strides within a very short time, and many of the teens who were buying the records were also inspired to form their own a cappella groups.

As singles by the Dominoes and Hank Ballard & the Midnighters made the transition from the R&B charts to the mainstream pop market, and as acts such as the Jewels, the Cadillacs, the Chords, the El Dorados and the Five Satins enjoyed short-lived success, so many of the record companies jumped on the doo-wop bandwagon and hundreds of 'new discoveries' were rushed into studios all over the US. Cities such as Los Angeles and Philadelphia produced a fair number of the acts, but the main hub was New York, where both African-Americans and Italian-Americans with little cash in their pockets, but with melody in their hearts, harmonized on teen-oriented songs that conveyed the innocence of a now long-gone era.

Key Artists

The Coasters
The Penguins
Dion & the Belmonts
Frankie Lymon & the Teenagers
The Platters

Thanks to the exploitative, cut-throat practices of the record industry at that time, many of the relatively small percentage of performers who did manage to have their efforts released still emerged without cash in their pockets. Still, some did profit from their endeavours, and others did enjoy an extended stay in the charts. These included the Clovers, the Moonglows, Little Anthony & the Imperials, and Frankie Lymon & the Teenagers, while the plateau was occupied by the Platters and the Coasters.

Hank Ballard brought a mixture of gospel influences and raunchy R&B to the vocal group that he joined in 1953. Their big hit, 'Work With Me Annie', inspired answer records from various musical spheres.

Crossover Success

One of the most pop-oriented of all the doo-wop groups, the Platters achieved crossover success in several regards, attracting not only a multiracial audience but also a worldwide, multigenerational one courtesy of such smash-hit ballads as 'Only You (And You Alone)' in 1955 and 'The Great Pretender', whose chart success peaked the following year, both composed by manager Buck Ram.

While 'The Great Pretender' made the Platters the first black act of the rock era to top the pop charts, 'Twilight Time' and 'Smoke Gets In Your Eyes' also occupied pole position and helped the group defy the convention of white artists enjoying greater success with covers of R&B songs.

Meanwhile, the other massive doo-wop favourites of the late-1950s were the Coasters, whose wild, comedy-filled songs contrasted sharply with the Platters' plaintive, soul-stirring ballads. Thanks to the input of legendary composer-producers Jerry Leiber and Mike Stoller, as well as manager Lester Sill, the Coasters turned out a string of million-sellers such as 'Young Blood', 'Searchin'', 'Yakety Yak', 'Charlie Brown' and 'Poison Ivy' that, in the case of the first two numbers, capitalized on the vocal and improvisational talents of bass lead Bobby Nunn and lead tenor Carl Gardner. Tenor Leon Hughes and baritone Billy Guy completed the quartet. 'Young Blood' and 'Searchin'' were, in fact, released as a double-A-sided single, but by the time 'Yakety Yak' and 'Charlie Brown' were recorded for Atlantic's new Atco label, the group had relocated from Los Angeles to New York with a revamped line-up. This saw Nunn and Hughes replaced by bass lead Will 'Dub' Jones and tenor Cornell Gunter, with Adolph Jacobs added on guitar, while among the choice session musicians were the likes of saxophone virtuoso King Curtis.

Key Tracks

'Yakety Yak' The Coasters
'Earth Angel (Will You Be Mine)' The Penguins
'Where Or When' Dion & the Belmonts
'Only You (And You Alone)' The Platters

Thanks to the Coasters and their brilliant songwriting/production team, doo-wop was accorded an all-around brassier treatment in the form of strident sax solos and raucous vocal interplay. However, this only fuelled many people's tendency to not take the genre too seriously, and by the end of the decade it had run out of steam.

The winning combination of the Coasters' vocal talents, Leiber & Stoller's humorous lyrics and King Curtis's stonking saxophone solos led to a string of hits that reflected the light-hearted side of doo-wop.

Skiffle

A cheap acoustic guitar, a washboard, some thimbles, a tea chest, a broom handle and a length of string, together, with a modicum of musical talent – these were all that was required for skiffle, an amalgam of American jazz, blues and folk that caught on with Britain's largely cash-strapped teenagers in 1956 and 1957, temporarily challenging the supremacy of rock'n'roll.

Rhythmic and decidedly upbeat, skiffle was a white, Anglicized extension of the black music that, drawing on blues, jazz, rag and traditional country, had originated in America during the late nineteenth century and been performed all over the South during the 1920s and 1930s by what were variously known as skiffle, skuffle, spasm, hamfat, washboard, jook and, most popularly, jug bands.

These makeshift outfits usually consisted of a fiddle, a banjo, a kazoo and, sometimes, a guitar, mandolin and/or harmonica, together with percussive, rhythmic household items such as spoons, tin cans and washboards (upon which thimbled fingers and thumbs would be run up and down). Nevertheless, whereas the bass line was provided by at least one band member blowing into or across the top of a jug, when the 1950s skiffle revival took place in England, said jug was supplanted by a crude imitation of an upright bass in the form of a broom handle poked through a hole in an upturned tea chest, with a cord attached between the two.

'It was a simple way into music because a lot of the songs had just two chords, and the maximum was three.... Everyone was in a skiffle group.'

George Harrison

The 6.5 Special, *launched by the BBC in 1957, featured live music including traditional folk and the latest craze, skiffle. Popular at first, the show went into decline when producer Jack Good defected to rival channel ITV.*

LONNIE DONEGAN
JIM DALE
DICKIE VALENTINE
JOAN REGAN
RUSS HAMILTON
PETULA CLARK
JUST SOME OF THE STARS in
"6·5 SPECIAL"
ANGLO AMALGAMATED FILM DISTRIBUTORS LTD.

A Raw, American-Accented Style

The king of British skiffle – and the only one of the artists to earn international recognition – was Lonnie Donegan, who introduced the music to concert audiences during the early 1950s when he performed his versions of blues, country and folk standards in between sets by Ken Colyer's Jazzmen.

Playing banjo or acoustic guitar while backed by an upright bass and drums, Donegan delivered the vocals in a raw, American-accented style that quickly made him more popular than the star attraction. When Colyer's outfit evolved into Chris Barber's Jazz Band in 1954, Donegan took the lead on what turned out to be a seminal track on the group's debut album, *New Orleans Joys*. Featuring Barber on bass and Beryl Bryden on washboard, Lonnie Donegan's rendition of the old Huddie 'Leadbelly' Ledbetter blues standard, 'Rock Island Line', was released as a single and sold a staggering three million copies, spending 22 weeks on the UK charts, where it peaked at number eight, while also making the American Top 10.

Key Artists

Lonnie Donegan
The Vipers Skiffle Group
The Chas McDevitt Skiffle Group featuring Nancy Whiskey
Johnny Duncan
Tommy Steele

Still, although the sales figures were more than a little impressive, what made 'Rock Island Line' unique in the annals of British pop at that time was the fact that most of the people who bought the record were teenagers. Suddenly, like an oasis in a desert of staid formality, here was a raucous, bluesy, homegrown sound that not only caught the kids' attention but also inspired them to form their own bands in an attempt to duplicate the Lonnie Donegan formula. By the time Donegan's single 'Lost John' climbed to number two on the UK chart in early 1956, there was a full-scale skiffle boom taking place in Britain, with anywhere up to half a million teens forming their own bands while their idol was appearing on stage and nationwide television in America.

Lonnie Donegan, 'The King Of Skiffle', became a more homogeneous UK equivalent to Elvis Presley than Tommy Steele. His first album, The Golden Age of Donegan, *reached number three during a 23-week stay in the music charts.*

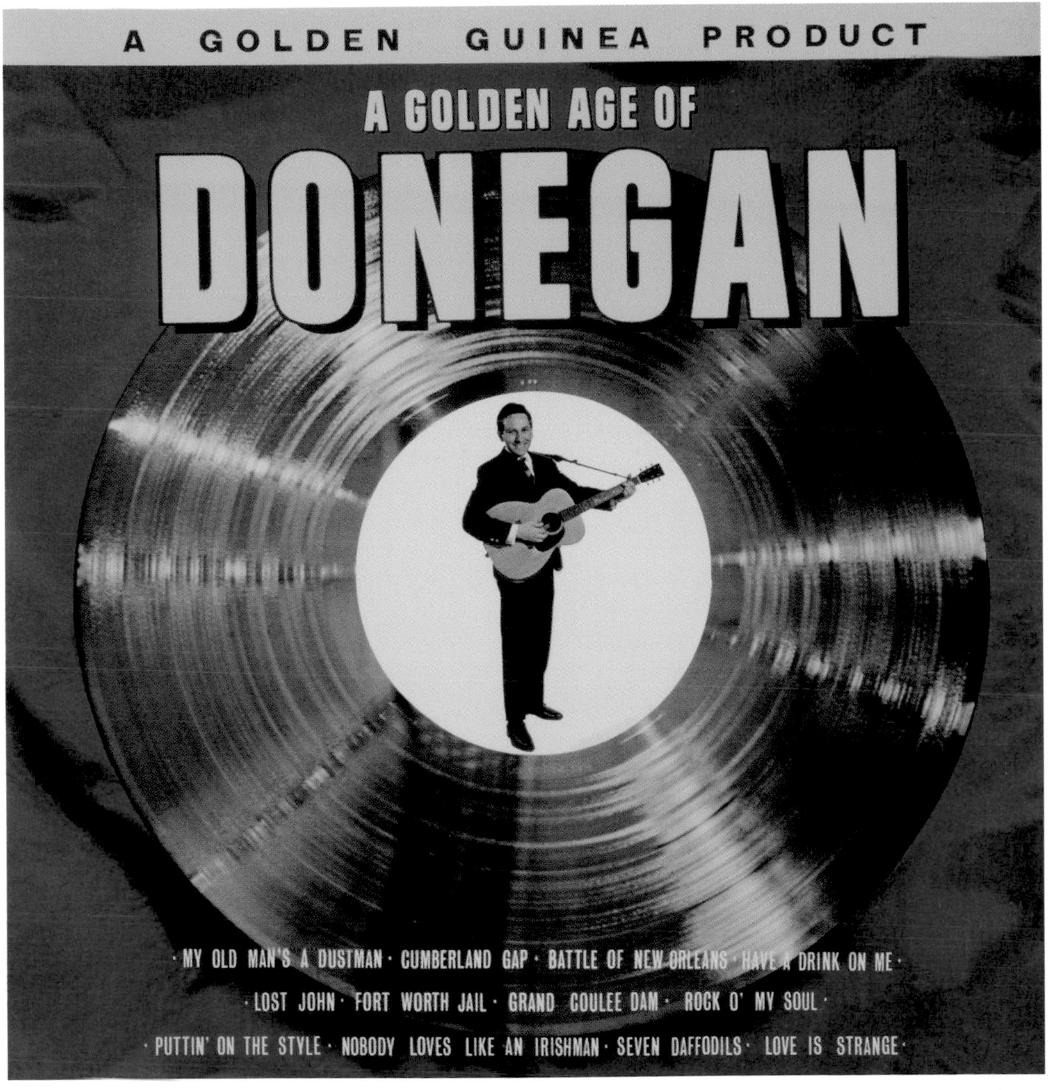
A GOLDEN GUINEA PRODUCT
A GOLDEN AGE OF
DONEGAN
· MY OLD MAN'S A DUSTMAN · CUMBERLAND GAP · BATTLE OF NEW ORLEANS · HAVE A DRINK ON ME ·
· LOST JOHN · FORT WORTH JAIL · GRAND COULEE DAM · ROCK O' MY SOUL ·
· PUTTIN' ON THE STYLE · NOBODY LOVES LIKE AN IRISHMAN · SEVEN DAFFODILS · LOVE IS STRANGE ·

An Enduring Effect

Lonnie Donegan's first album, *Showcase,* sold in the hundreds of thousands, and he continued to make the Top 10 on the British singles chart with tracks such as 'Bring A Little Water Sylvie', 'Don't You Rock Me Daddy-O', 'Cumberland Gap' and 'Putting On The Style'.

Meanwhile, a number of other acts were appearing on the scene. The Vipers Skiffle Group, whose sound was rougher than Donegan's, and more firmly steeped in folk and the blues, also enjoyed a Top 10 hit with 'Don't You Rock Me Daddy-O' (penned by Vipers singer/guitarist Wally Whyton). Courtesy of several subsequent releases, the Vipers were second only to Donegan in terms of their success. That of certain others, however, was altogether more brief: the Chas McDevitt Skiffle Group featuring Nancy Whiskey charted with 'Freight Train', and an American by the name of Johnny Duncan climbed to number two in the UK with 'Last Train To San Fernando'. Even Britain's first true rock'n'roll star, Tommy Steele, started out playing skiffle.

It was, of course, rock'n'roll that, by the end of 1957, put an end to the skiffle boom. However, although its time in the sun was short-lived, skiffle's invaluable contribution to popular music was the enduring effect that it had on a generation of teenagers who would be at the vanguard of the British – and subsequently international – rock scene of the 1960s: the Who, the Hollies, the Kinks, the Moody Blues, the Searchers, Procol Harum.... These and many more all had band members who cut their musical teeth on a skiffle-inspired acoustic guitar, washboard or tea-chest basis. In fact, Lonnie Donegan's 'Putting On The Style' was sitting at the top of the UK chart when an outfit by the name of the Quarry Men performed the song at a church fête in Liverpool on 6 July 1957. The lead vocalist that day was a 16-year-old John Lennon; in the audience to see him for the first time was a 15-year-old Paul McCartney. Skiffle's role doesn't come any bigger than that.

Key Tracks

'Rock Island Line' Lonnie Donegan
'Putting On The Style' Lonnie Donegan
'Don't You Rock Me Daddy-O' The Vipers Skiffle Group
'Freight Train' The Chas McDevitt Skiffle Group featuring Nancy Whiskey
'Last Train To San Fernando' Johnny Duncan

The Vipers grew from the vibrant music scene that converged at the 2I's Coffee Bar in Soho, London, along with countless other performers, including Tommy Steele, Joe Brown, Hank Marvin and Adam Faith.

Soul & R&B

In 1949, two apparently small events took place, which in hindsight were to have monumental significance for popular culture. The first of these saw *Billboard* magazine change the name of its 'Race Records' chart to the more relevant and politically correct 'Rhythm & Blues' chart, reflecting the success of the American dance music of the moment.

Meanwhile, a 19-year-old blind Georgia orphan called Ray Charles Robinson (he dropped the Robinson to avoid confusion with the legendary boxer Sugar Ray Robinson) released his first single 'Confession Blues'. By the mid-1950s, rhythm & blues had mutated into rock'n'roll, the ultimate crossover between black and white popular music, and in the form of R&B would remain the dominant label attached to pop music of Afro-American origin. By 1954, the visionary and eclectic Charles, with his arrangement for bluesman Guitar Slim's 'The Things That I Used To Do' and the irresistible fusion of jazz, blues and gospel on his own 'I Got A Woman' (later covered by Elvis Presley), had invented soul music – rock's spiritual, sensual Afro-American twin.

'It was a slang that would relate to the man on the street, plus it had its own sound: the music on one-and-three, the downbeat, in anticipation.'

James Brown on 'Papa's Got A Brand New Bag' pop, country, jazz, and early rock'n'roll.

Soul is an innovative blend of musical styles: the Baptist hymn and the juke joint dance exhortation, the plantation field holler and the sophisticated jazz standard, the romantic vocal flights of doo-wop and the driving rhythms of small-band R&B, the gospel plea for deliverance and the altogether earthier blues lament. It rose to prominence through the innovations of two further black male pioneers from the Southern states. Mississippi gospel heart-throb Sam Cooke made a controversial move to secular pop in 1956. By 1957 his 'You Send Me' – a heart-melting mix of teen pop and Cooke's alternately tender and roaring gospel vocals – had gone to number one in the US and truly ignited the soul era. He continued to be one of pop's most loved crossover pioneers until his shocking death in 1964, at the hands of a motel manager who claimed she shot the singer in self-defence after he had allegedly raped another woman.

Although undoubtedly a key influence in R&B, Ray Charles has successfully turned his hand to a number of musical styles, including blues, gospel, pop, country, jazz and early rock'n'roll.

Leaps of Artistic Faith

Georgia's James Brown released his first single, 'Please Please Please', in 1956, a record so vocally intense and rhythmically tough that it made a romantic plea to a woman sound like a hysterical scream from the very depths of sexual desperation and despair.

Brown's prolific writing and recording schedule was sent into commercial overdrive by the most extreme live performances of the period, a theatrical and almost militarily precise singing and dancing spectacular that had a profound influence on Mick Jagger, Michael Jackson, Prince and every star since who has combined flamboyant sexual display, bravura dance moves and unstoppable physical energy with playful drama and driving rhythm. A recorded document of that show, 1962's *Live At The Apollo*, along with another Ray Charles innovation, *Modern Sounds In Country And Western Music* from the same year, established soul as an album-selling genre. James Brown, of course, was key in turning soul music into funk and disco, and through his ability to make African-derived rhythm into a complex but universally understood musical language, he had the most profound influence upon hip hop and all subsequent genres of dance music.

Key Artists

Ray Charles
Sam Cooke
James Brown
Marvin Gaye
Stevie Wonder

By late-1963, soul was so dominant in the American singles market that the black chart was abolished, for the first and only time, until early 1965. Over the next 30 years, the original soul impulse was taken in so many different directions that the term is now largely applied only to the 1960s/early 1970s Golden Era. Nevertheless, just as all white rock and pop eventually refers back to the blues, Elvis, the Beatles or Dylan, the black pop we now (rather ironically) call R&B owes its existence to the leaps of artistic faith made by Charles, Cooke and Brown.

James Brown, one of the most exciting performers of his day, had a profound effect on subsequent generations of artists.

Classic Soul

The story of soul's golden age is linked with the story of two American record labels: Berry Gordy's Motown and Jim Stewart & Estelle Axton's Stax. They discovered artists, wrote songs and developed recording and marketing methods that would irrevocably change popular music, and have a profound effect on the perception of race all over the world.

The inexhaustible supply of Motown hits dominated the 1960s, in Europe as well as America. The unmistakable Motown blend of powerful R&B rhythm, highly sophisticated orchestral arrangements and poetic lyricism came to define the language of pop. The peerless parade of charismatic virtuoso gospel-derived vocal groups and solo artists beguiled white fans as much as black, and raised the level of artistry that pop could attain. The likes of Robinson, Diana Ross & the Supremes, Marvin Gaye, the Four Tops, the Temptations and Stevie Wonder fronted hit after hit, rising from pop ingénues to era-defining artists within the ten years of Motown's peak period. Although they may have signed to Motown in 1968, after its peak, the Jackson Five's debut single 'I Want You Back' was the label's fastest-selling record ever, and three of their subsequent five singles reached the number one spot in the US.

Key Artists

Aretha Franklin
Diana Ross & the Supremes
The Temptations
Dionne Warwick
Al Green

The Southern Melting Pot

1960 saw the formation of Stax, a label that, by signing a distribution deal with Atlantic, would see their completely contrasting style of soul cross over to the rapidly growing rock audience. The Stax/Atlantic phenomenon was based upon a complete racial mix: raucous and untamed black gospel-raised vocalists such as the Stax label's Otis Redding, Sam & Dave, and Carla Thomas; plus Atlantic's Aretha Franklin, Ben E. King, Solomon Burke and Wilson Pickett, worked with multi-racial R&B bands Booker T & the MG's (from Memphis) and the Muscle Shoals rhythm section, performing the songs and sounds of racially integrated backroom geniuses. If Stax/Atlantic's true reflection of the young Southerners' rebuffal of segregation was challenging, then the music was incendiary: power-packed testimonies of love, sex, spiritual freedom and political protest matched with horn-driven proto-funk that gave a feeling of earthy, spontaneous, almost live authenticity, and contrasted perfectly with Motown's highly sophisticated studio symphonies.

Otis Redding recorded 'Sittin' On the Dock Of The Bay' just three days before he died in a plane crash near Madison, Wisconsin, in 1967. It was number one for four weeks in 1968.

Political Folk & Protest Songs

The relationship between politics and folk music has always been fuel for lively debate. Some argue that the two should not mix, and that aligning traditional song with politics demeans it. Front-line singers such as Dick Gaughan and Roy Bailey, however, argue that folk songs are inextricably linked with politics, and perform plenty of strident material to prove it.

The modern folk revival, in fact, is indelibly linked with songs of dissent. While the folk music that Shirley Collins talks about is merely an expression of people's daily lives – whether it involves ploughing fields, falling in love or getting drunk – protest song is inextricably tied to modern folk song. Protest music of the 1960s took its cue from Woody Guthrie and his acolytes, who founded the Almanac Singers and People's Songs musical co-operative in the 1940s and devoted themselves to union benefits and workers' groups. Most of Guthrie's best work had a political edge, from his early songs about the plight of the migrants heading west after their lives had been wrecked by dust storms, to championing causes and fighting the corner of the oppressed wherever he found them – as in 'Deportees', a song about a group of nameless refugees killed in a plane crash. Even his most famous song, 'This Land Is Your Land', was conceived as a workers' antidote to Irving Berlin's sentimental patriotic anthem, 'God Bless America'. The folk movement was outraged when Guthrie's edgiest verse was removed from this work, and the song was used as an anthem in Ronald Reagan's presidential election campaign. Bruce Springsteen's later version, though, reclaimed it for the people.

'Never underestimate the power of songs. Martin Luther King wasn't much of a singer but he still made "We shall overcome" sound beautiful.'

Pete Seeger

Guthrie adapted many of his songs from existing country blues, itself a fiery conduit of protest, and became close friends with the great blues star Leadbelly. Leadbelly himself wrote a catalogue of protest songs that have long passed into folk legend, such as 'Midnight Special', 'Scottsboro Boys' and 'Bourgeois Blues', all confronting the realities of racism, poverty and workers' rights.

Woody Guthrie's refusal to profit from any of his music during his lifetime did not prevent him from reaching legendary status after his death.

Social and Political Tirades

In the 1950s, Pete Seeger, one of Woody Guthrie's main cohorts in New York, found himself on the front line of the struggle when, as a communist, he was targeted by Senator Joseph McCarthy's witch-hunt. Seeger was blacklisted – effectively killing the career of his group the Weavers, who had taken the songs of Guthrie and Leadbelly to the top of the US charts.

This was the background from which Bob Dylan, Phil Ochs and others launched their careers in a blaze of blistering social and political tirades. Dylan's 'The Times They Are A-Changin'' was the call to arms for a rebellious new generation, and songs such as his 'Masters Of War', Ochs's 'I Ain't Marching Anymore' and Buffy Sainte-Marie's 'Universal Soldier' became a powerful soundtrack to the anti-Vietnam War campaign. Joan Baez invited audiences at her concerts to burn their draft cards; Peter, Paul & Mary audiences chanted 'Make love not war'; and half the nation bopped along to Country Joe & Fish's brilliantly sardonic singalong anthem 'Fixing To Die Rag'. Folk music, then, played a big role in shaping the anti-war movement that helped force an end to the Vietnam conflict.

Pete Seeger continued to play a key role in protest song and the civil rights movement. His adaptation of the old gospel/work song 'We Shall Overcome' became the anthem of protest marches and human rights campaigns all over the world. At the height of such movements in the US, Seeger sang it while marching shoulder to shoulder with Martin Luther King. In the UK, too, plenty of artists were adapting existing gospel, blues or folk songs to fit their own pet causes, and many fine songwriters emerged to put their spin on protest music. The Scotsman Ian Campbell wrote one of the best of them in 'The Sun Is Burning', a chilling account of a nuclear explosion that was regularly sung on the annual Aldermaston marches for nuclear disarmament. And Ewan MacColl, an influential giant of the British folk revival who was originally noted as a traditional singer, had a long career as a compelling political songwriter, from his telling insights into the lives of working people in the Radio Ballads, to a suite of songs reacting to apartheid and the Sharpeville Massacre in South Africa. Age didn't wither the conviction of MacColl, who, with his wife, Peggy Seeger, continued to write barbed songs of social consciousness all his life.

Key Artists

Woody Guthrie
Pete Seeger
Phil Ochs
Bob Dylan
Bruce Springsteen

By including introspective lyrics, politics and poetry in his songs, Bob Dylan became one of the greatest singer/songwriters of all time.

Taking on the System

Songs of social consciousness had fallen out of fashion by the 1980s, but they enjoyed a renaissance with the emergence of Eric Bogle (whose anti-war epics 'And The Band Played Waltzing Matilda' and 'No Man's Land' were covered widely all over the world) and Billy Bragg.

Articulate Londoner Bragg had a top 10 hit with his personal socialist anthem, 'Between The Wars', inspiring a new generation of singer/songwriters. 'Between The Wars' has since become a standard on a British folk scene rediscovering its social conscience. The right-wing Thatcher administration – and the 1984 miners' strike – focused a lot of minds and re-ignited the art of radical songwriting, with Ewan MacColl, Dick Gaughan and the Oyster Band all penning stirring material.

The most consistently radical of the English singer/songwriters, though, has perhaps been Leon Rosselson, who boasts a long history of writing scathing, topical songs, effectively denouncing the establishment and fearlessly tackling unspoken taboos such as religion, the royal family, business corporations, marriage and ecology. His greatest song of all is 'The World Turned Upside Down', a dramatic and ultimately disturbing account of the Diggers uprising of workers in 1649, which was so brutally put down. It set a benchmark for radical songwriting that few have been able to match, and as the record industry has become more corporate, it has not been conducive to songs of dissent.

One who has taken on the system and won, however, is Ani DiFranco, a singer/songwriter from Buffalo, New York, who, with her daring lyrics, acerbic songs, razor-sharp wit, charismatic personality and outrageous sense of humour, has established a huge live following. DiFranco has gained much respect for her opposition to the commercial record industry, refusing offers from all the major companies to manage herself and release material on her own label, Righteous Babe.

Inspiring songs of struggle have played a central role in the lives of working people for decades. Where there is oppression or injustice, folk music will usually have something to say about it.

Key Tracks

'This Land Is Your Land' Woody Guthrie
'Midnight Special' Woody Guthrie
'Casey Jones (The Union Scab)' Joe Hill
'If I Had A Hammer' Pete Seeger
'The Times They Are A-Changing'' Bob Dylan

With his anti-folk electrified sound and deep lyrics, Billy Bragg's reputation earned him the privilege to record archived Woody Guthrie songs.

The Folk Revival

Mention of the folk revival is generally applied to the late 1950s and early 1960s, when a new generation of enthusiasts earnestly set about exploring the history of folk music and recreating its passionate, social ideals. It was a naturally organic affair generated by the musicians themselves, rather than the academic view of social culture that had been at the heart of previous revivals.

Its American roots began with groups such as the Kingston Trio, the Weavers and the New Christy Minstrels bringing folk, blues and country songs to the masses. Their arrangements may have been trite and sanitized, but the Weavers had massive hits with Woody Guthrie's 'So Long (It's Been Good To Know You)' and Leadbelly's 'Goodnight Irene'. They also opened the commercial door to a roots music that had previously been confined to its rural locality, be it the Appalachian mountains, Mississippi cotton fields or Texas bars. It was enough to inflame the curiosity of a new, young generation of guitarists and singers researching those roots, who were further spurred on by the political implications of the McCarthy witch-hunt and the refusal of Pete Seeger and others to bow to establishment values. Their guru was Oklahoma-born Woody Guthrie, whose own songs vehemently addressed issues close to him, including the human agony caused by the dust storms, or were created at singalongs for his own children.

'Without Woody Guthrie there'd be no Ramblin' Jack Elliot and without Ramblin' Jack Elliot there'd be no Bob Dylan.'

Arlo Guthrie

Woody's legacy was a new generation of acolytes who were inspired by his simple tunes and abrasive lyrics and sought to embody his maverick lifestyle. Most famously, Bob Dylan visited Woody at his bedside and wrote his first song as a tribute to his hero, but a closer embodiment of the Guthrie spirit was represented by his friend, Ramblin' Jack Elliot, who travelled extensively with Woody, aped his voice and attitude and performed many of his songs. Yet Guthrie's legend was best perpetuated by his own son Arlo Guthrie, who went on to achieve a commercial breakthrough that obliterated anything his father had done, with the long, autobiographical singing blues tome 'Alice's Restaurant', which captured the anti-Vietnam War mood of the times so acutely it was made into a film.

Pete Seeger refused to bow to the establishment. His adaptation of the work song 'We Shall Overcome' became an unofficial anthem for civil rights and is still sung by protesters all over the world.

TO SURRENDER

A Lasting Legacy

Woody Guthrie's legacy flowered in Greenwich Village, New York, where a new breed of singer/songwriter with attitude, wordy songs and idealistic values descended to energize a new scene. With his sharp lyrics and revolutionary message, Bob Dylan was the most visible and successful of the new breed of folk star.

There were many others, too, including Dylan's then-partner, Joan Baez. She was a highly rated singer of ballads, stridently political and often to be found on the front line of various anti-war demonstrations and marches. An explosion of singer/songwriters with acoustic guitars followed, with Paul Simon, Joni Mitchell, James Taylor, Phil Ochs, Tom Paxton, Tim Hardin, Gordon Lightfoot, Dave Van Ronk, Judy Collins and Buffy Sainte-Marie among them. Despite their mix of styles and backgrounds, they were all associated with the folk revival.

The growing popularity of the scene also refocused attention on the lesser-known artists providing inspiration – and often material – for the main attraction. The likes of Doc Watson, the Carter Family, Sonny Terry & Brownie McGhee, Muddy Waters and Mississippi John Hurt thus came to prominence, the focus on the latter accelerated by the emergence of British bands such as the Rolling Stones and the Yardbirds, with a rock take on the blues tradition. Odetta, a black folk-blues singer from Alabama who worked early on with Harry Belafonte and Pete Seeger, also achieved an important international breakthrough. A network of clubs, coffeehouses and informal 'hootenannies' emerged, along with famous festivals, such as the Newport Folk Festival in Rhode Island, to give the music a high profile. The revival achieved widespread commercial success for a while, too, with Peter, Paul & Mary playing huge concerts all over the world.

Key Artists

Woody Guthrie
The Weavers
Ramblin' Jack Elliot
Bob Dylan
Joan Baez

With shifts in her folk music to country and pop, Joan Baez remains one of the most influential artists on the folk scene. This image shows a performance in a typical Greenwich Village folk venue in the 1960s; note the artist in the audience, busy sketching Baez.

An Abiding Interest in Folk Blues

The UK folk revival had similar roots, and it occurred at about the same time as that in the US. But it emerged in a very different form. Those Kingston Trio and Weavers hits caught the imagination of young British fans and musicians, too, but interest in the roots of this music manifested itself in an unexpected way.

Lonnie Donegan was playing rhythm guitar with Ken Colyer's jazz band and, as a leftfield concert-filler, started playing primitive American folk blues. After a 1930s term coined to describe bands that played household implements, he gave it the name 'skiffle'. Donegan broke through with 'Rock Island Line' in 1956 and the following year went to number one with 'Cumberland Gap'. This gave licence to young hopefuls to form groups whether or not they had talent, instruments or places to play. Although it did not last, its legacy was an abiding interest in the folk blues songs that had driven it.

While several of them, such as the Ian Campbell Folk Group, homed in on the songs of Dylan and the rest coming across the Atlantic, a network of clubs with different values was also emerging. Ewan MacColl opened one of the first dedicated folk music venues – the Ballad & Blues Club – in London and caused great debate when he declared that musicians would only be permitted to perform music of their own culture at his club. It may have seemed bizarre, but MacColl's aim was to force young British musicians to research their own tradition for material. It was controversial, but it worked, as artists such as the Watersons, Martin Carthy, Shirley Collins, Young Tradition, Anne Briggs and Louis Killen quickly developed into popular performers, playing a rapidly growing network of folk clubs throughout the country.

Key Tracks

'Deportees' Woody Guthrie
'The Manchester Rambler' Ewan MacColl
'Diamonds & Rust' Joan Baez
'Blowin' in the Wind' Bob Dylan

The momentum of those early days of the revival lasted into the 1970s, when other musical forces came into play and folk music splintered into different sub-genres. Folk clubs are not as plentiful now, but the music is still there and it generally wields the same values. That is its own tribute to the work of the folk revival pioneers.

Known as Britain's first musical superstar, Lonnie Donegan's mix of folk, jazz, gospel and blues continues to influence British folk music today.

Rock Music

During the mid-1960s, America's military action in Vietnam was escalating out of control; students around the world were becoming more politically involved, civil rights and feminism were hot issues and the burgeoning youth movement was turning onto the effects of mind-bending drugs. Accordingly, certain strains of popular music melded attitude, experimentation and a social conscience, and the newly defined rock genre was the all-encompassing result.

By the second half of the decade, many record buyers regarded pop as a tame and dated form of escapism for oldies and prepubescent teens. Rock, by comparison, diverted some of its listeners through psychedelic, acid-drenched terrain, yet it also provided a heavy dose of realism, serving as an introspective outlet for a growing number of composer-performers, while expressing the concerns of those who were no longer prepared to look at the world through rose-tinted spectacles.

'Pop music often tells you everything is OK, while rock music tells you that it's not OK, but you can change it.'

Bono

John Lennon and his fellow Beatles led the way among the handful of artists who made a successful transition from pop to rock. These included the Rolling Stones, the Yardbirds and the Who, who had already started out with a more aggressive rock sensibility. Add to them former folkies such as Bob Dylan and the Byrds, as well as emerging west coast acts like the Doors, Jefferson Airplane and the Grateful Dead, and it was clear that rock was the new voice of youth.

As the optimism of the Summer of Love gave way to late-1960s cynicism fueled by civil unrest, bloody anti-war riots and the hippy counterculture, so psychedelic and Eastern-tinged music were superseded by the vocal histrionics of Janis Joplin and Joe Cocker, as well as the blues-based hard rock of bands like Cream and the Jimi Hendrix Experience. Yet even though this was largely touted as music for the mind rather than for the body, it wasn't long before the record companies tried to match the popularity of so-called supergroups like Pink Floyd and Led Zeppelin. This was attempted with what many among the press and public perceived as the formulaic, watered-down product of 'corporate' acts such as Boston, Kansas and Foreigner.

Originally planning to call themselves the New Yardbirds, Led Zeppelin's name came from either Keith Moon or John Entwistle, who commented that the band's new, raw sound would go down like a 'lead zeppelin'.

Pushing for Bigger Sounds

In a world where Alice Cooper and David Bowie were displaying a thespian-like theatricality, innovative psychedelia transmogrified into razzle-dazzle glam rock, people were pushing for bigger sounds onstage and in the studio and concerts were being produced on an increasingly grand scale.

It was evident that, just 20 years after the likes of Elvis Presley, Little Richard and Jerry Lee Lewis had inspired teenagers, outraged parents and revolutionized Western culture, contemporary music had basically lost touch with its original *raison d'être*. No longer all that exciting, liberating or even controversial, it promoted an instrumental virtuosity that was completely at odds with the easy-to-play, do-it-yourself appeal of early rock'n'roll. Then along came punk rock, and for a brief time, the entire scene was treated to the shake-up that it so badly needed.

Between 1976 and 1978, the British punks in particular pumped up the aggression and devil-may-care attitude of their 1950s rock predecessors and quite literally spat in the face of authority and middle-class values. Drawing on often limited musical talents, outfits such as the Sex Pistols and the Clash channelled their anger and their energy into some blistering songs that once again helped to express the frustration and disenchantement of disaffected youth. The music was simply structured rock, and it had an invigorating effect on those who had grown tired of overblown and highly polished material. Nevertheless, almost as soon as the punk movement became an international phenomenon, it started to disintegrate, hijacked by kids from comfortable backgrounds who didn't have a clue about life on the streets.

Key Artists

The Rolling Stones
The Who
The Grateful Dead
Cream
Guns 'n' Roses

Recalling how rock'n'roll had been usurped by parent-friendly pop at the start of the 1960s, the record companies attempted to broaden punk's appeal by associating numerous more mainstream acts with the genre, and the result was a watered-down hybrid that the media dubbed 'new wave'. There were still traces of a surly attitude, and in the case of artists such as Elvis Costello there were clear musical skills, yet the spirit of punk had been laid to rest; for the next few years it would remain submerged while middle-of-the-road hard rockers and exotically-attired 'new romantics' catered to the rapidly emerging MTV generation.

For many, the Clash were the ultimate punk rock band. They lacked the careful management of the Sex Pistols, although it was supporting the Pistols with his previous band that turned singer Joe Strummer on to punk.

the

Reinventing the Wheel

Once easy to categorize, rock music continued to fragment throughout the 1980s and 1990s, with heavy metal splitting off into subgenres ranging from thrash, speed and progressive to black, death and doom.

At the same time, the alternative/indie tag served as a catch-all for a variety of styles, including that whose aesthetic – if not its unmelodic structure – was closest to that of vintage rock'n'roll, and which consequently had the most far-reaching impact on the latter-day rock scene. Merging dissonant early 1970s heavy metal guitars with the hostile attitude, alienated lyrics and in-your-face music of punk, grunge first rose to prominence thanks to bands such as Soundgarden, Mudhoney and Green River, and then reached its apotheosis with the more melodic approach of Nirvana and Pearl Jam during the first half of the 1990s.

Still, history has a well-known habit of repeating itself, and in the case of the most successful rock music this is usually connected to financial considerations. For example thanks to astute marketing and the cooperation of the media, Nirvana's name became synonymous with grunge, and when the band went the way of so many others by joining the mainstream, the genre did likewise, trading in its punk ensibilities for more widespread popularity.

Key Tracks

'Baba O'Riley' The Who
'Touch Of Grey' The Grateful Dead
'Welcome To The Jungle' Guns 'n' Roses
'Bohemian Rhapsody' Queen
'Smoke On The Water' Deep Purple

At the beginning of the twenty-first century, rock music keeps subdividing and reinventing itself, continually absorbing new influences from other musical spheres. Yet partly due to this mutation process, it also lacks freshness and vitality, and in the face of the cultural influence exerted by rap and hip hop, it no longer shapes opinions to the extent that it once did. Whether it can once again become the predominant force remains open to question.

Kurt Cobain, frontman of grunge pioneers Nirvana.

BLUES INSTRUMENTS

Leaving aside the human voice, which of course plays an intricate part in the music's emotional power, the blues is based around the diverse tone colours and versatility of one instrument – the guitar.

Early blues musicians such as Charley Patton used the acoustic guitar almost as an extension of their own voices, and often simultaneously utilized the instrument for percussive effect by slapping the strings and tapping the body of the instrument. The use of slides created a moaning sound that heightened the emotional flavour of the music, and bending the strings added further colour. As the post-war era beckoned, electric guitars began to infiltrate the blues scene, offering a whole new range of sounds, techniques and effects to blues musicians.

The piano has also been a significant instrument in the development of the blues, especially in the more urban areas where an upright piano provided the basic entertainment in the majority of bars, clubs and party venues. The development of boogie-woogie from ragtime piano styles crossed the blues with jazz influences, and took piano blues into new directions.

Other common instruments used in blues music include the harmonica, whose wailing tones punctuate many a blues recording, often in dialogue with the vocalist or other instruments; the drums and bass guitar that form the essential rhythm section of most bands; and the Hammond organ, which added an extra layer and many a catchy riff to a number of significant blues records in the 1960s and 1970s.

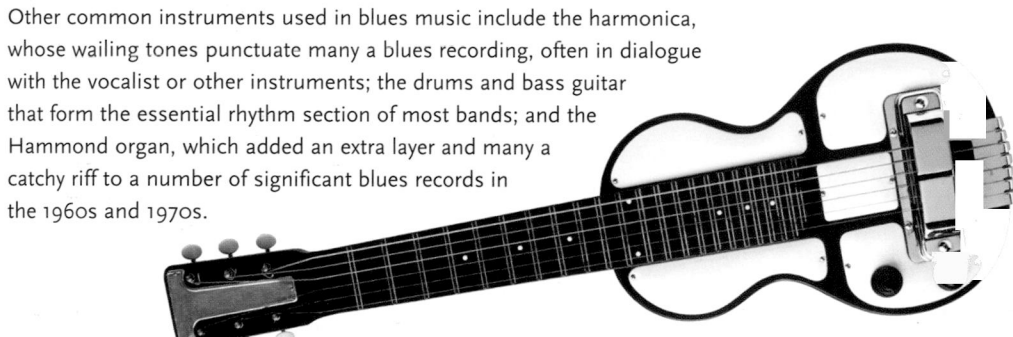

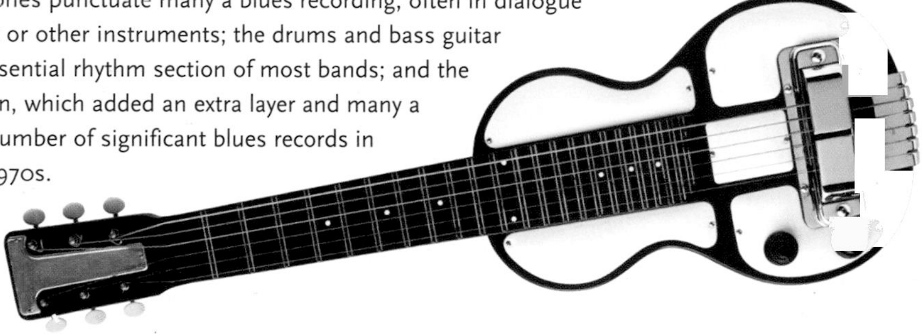

Right: The inimitable Howlin' Wolf, owner of one of the most distinctive voices in the blues, blows a solo on the harmonica.

Acoustic Guitar

Throughout its history, the guitar has – perhaps more than any other instrument – managed to bridge the gap between the often disconnected worlds of classical, folk and popular music. Its roots go back to Babylonian times, when reliefs reveal a plucked, guitar-like instrument; by the 1500s it was prevalent in Spain, and is still sometimes called the Spanish guitar.

Medieval versions – such as the lute – often had smaller bodies and sometimes sported rounded backs and paired strings; the 12-string guitar still exists (its ringing tone can be heard on the Byrds' 'Mr Tambourine Man'). Guitars at this time were used to accompany dancing and singing and to play simple tunes, and were generally played by strumming, although there was no standard technique regarding whether to strike the strings with the nail or not.

The work of Spanish instrument maker Antonio de Torres Jurado was central to the development of the modern guitar. He set a standard length for the vibrating strings, increased the instrument's overall dimensions, used 19 frets, altered the construction of the soundbox and set the standard string tuning of E-A-D-G-B-E. These alterations were so successful that Torres's model became the standard to which every other maker aspired – and which is known today as the classical guitar.

Key Players

Big Bill Broonzy
Blind Lemon Jefferson
Leadbelly
Robert Johnson
Charley Patton

The acoustic guitar remained relatively unchanged until the twentieth century, when additions included steel strings (as opposed to traditional gut strings) for greater attack in dance-band settings, where it took over from the banjo. This marked the beginning of the guitar's rise to a major role in popular music, leading directly to the development of the semi-acoustic and fully electric versions. The standardized modern acoustic guitar has a flat back and sound board with a pronounced curved 'waist' to the body.

Above: Martin Dreadnought guitars are popular among folk musicians as their large, wide bodies make them particularly suited to expressive, acoustic performances. Right: Ex-convict Leadbelly was notable for his virtuosity on the 12-string guitar.

Electric Guitar

An electric guitar usually has a solid wooden body with no acoustic resonance. All the sound is created by the vibration of strings being translated into electrical signals by pickups and then amplified.

The modern electric guitar has its origins in the Hawaiian or steel guitar, particularly popular in the 1920s and 1930s. These instruments were the first examples of guitars that depended on electrical amplification rather than the properties of acoustic resonance.

Three names are particularly associated with the development of the electric guitar – Rickenbacker, Fender and Gibson Les Paul. Adolphe Richenbacher (later changed to Rickenbacker) worked making components for the Dopera Brothers' National Resonator Guitars. Together with George Beauchamp and Paul Barth, he formed the Electro String Company and, in the 1930s, began building Hawaiian-style guitars using their newly developed magnetic-pickup system.

Fender Strat

In the late 1940s, electrician and amplifier-maker Leo Fender designed the Broadcaster guitar. After a dispute with the company Gretsch over the name 'Broadcaster', the guitar was re-christened the Telecaster. In 1954, Fender introduced an instrument that was to become the most famous, and most copied, electric guitar of all time – the Stratocaster, or 'Strat'.

Key Players

John Lee Hooker
Jimi Hendrix
B.B. King
Stevie Ray Vaughan
T-Bone Walker

Gibson Les Paul

The Gibson Company's response to the huge popularity of Fender guitars was to seek out the service of jazz guitarist and inventor Les Paul. Paul had built his so-called 'log' guitar out of a simple, solid block of wood with an attached neck in the early 1940s. His association with Gibson was to produce another iconic instrument – the Gibson Les Paul of 1952.

Above: The electric guitar has had an impact on all styles of popular music. Right: Electric guitar legend Jimi Hendrix, whose love of the blues is evident in the blues-tinged rock music he produced.

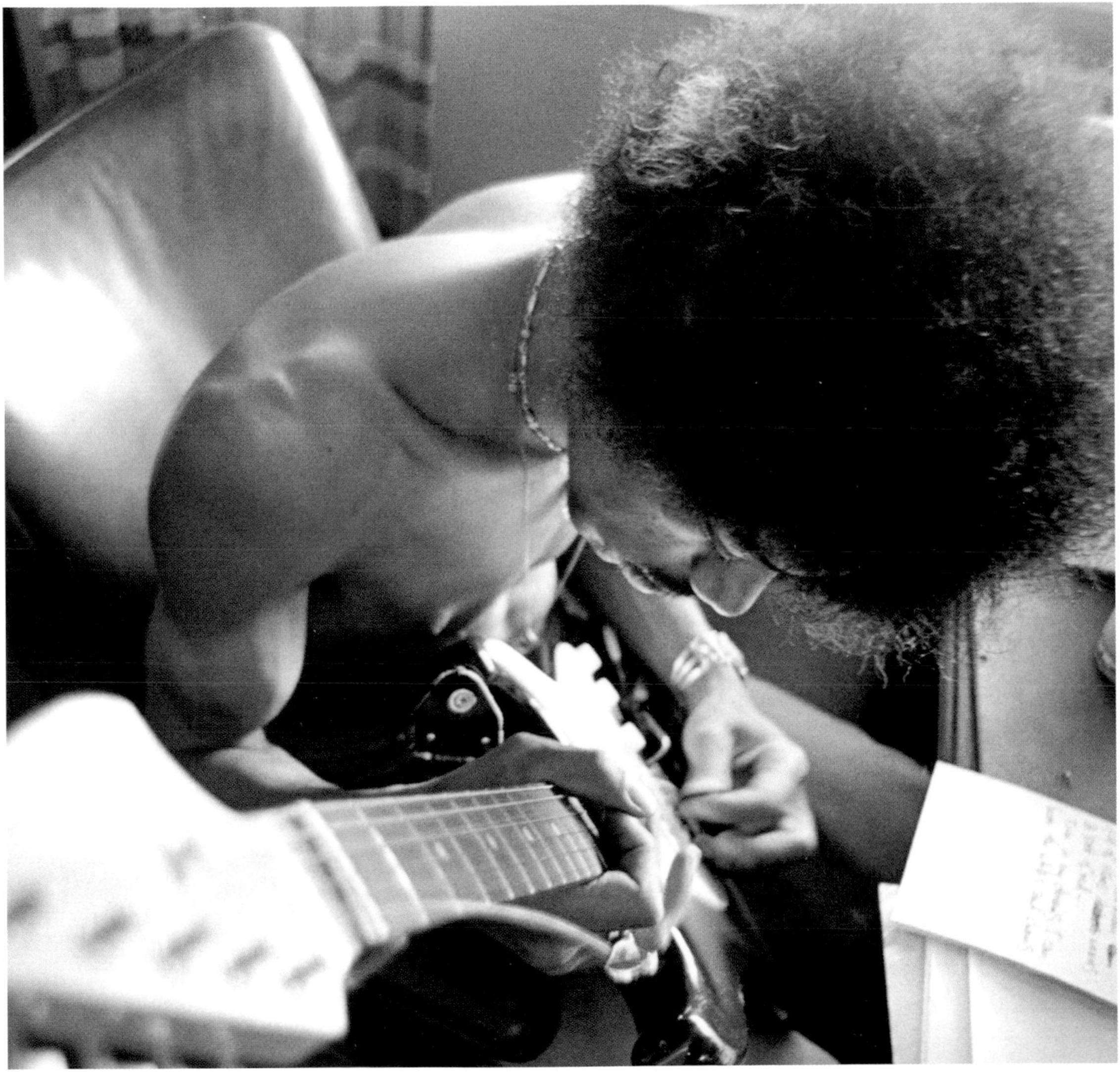

Electric Bass Guitar

The electric bass is similar in both appearance and operation to the electric guitar, but is actually a descendent of the upright acoustic double bass. The double bass had long been an integral part of the jazz rhythm section, but the increasing need to compete with amplified instruments – not to mention the transportation problems caused by its sheer bulk – made players and manufacturers seek amplified alternatives.

Electric Bass Fiddle

The earliest-known example of a solid-body electric bass dates back to 1935 in the form of an upright instrument designed by musician and amplifier-maker Paul H. Tutmarc, for the Audiovox Manufacturing Company of Seattle. The same company later developed a bass instrument played across the body, like a guitar. The Model #736 Electric Bass Fiddle, as it was known, was also innovative in that, unlike the double bass, it was fretted, enabling less secure players to achieve precise intonation.

This idea was also incorporated into the first mass-produced electric bass, the Fender Precision Bass of 1951. The instrument evolved into a design that has remained relatively unchanged since 1957. A similar classic instrument was the Fender Jazz Bass of 1960.

Bass Models

The electric bass has a slight larger body and longer neck than an electric guitar and usually has four strings – tuned in fourths, E, A, D and G. Variants include different numbers of strings – often adding a fifth, tuned to B or A below the bottom E string – and fretless models. The fretless design has a characteristic mellow tone and facilitates the technique of sliding between notes. The bass is usually plucked with the thumb or a plectrum but players, such as Mark King of Level 42, have pioneered percussive 'slap bass' styles.

Key Players

Jerome Arnold
Jack Bruce
Chas Chandler
John Paul Jones
Norman Pingrey

Above: A solid-body electric bass guitar. Right: Influential bassist John Entwistle (left) of The Who.

Steel & Resonator Guitars

During the 1830s, Mexican cattle-herders introduced the guitar to Hawaiians, who quickly incorporated it into their own music-making, typically tuning all the strings to the notes of a major triad. Joseph Kekuku is credited with developing a technique of using a comb to slide up and down the neck to create *glissandi*. Clearly this was difficult to achieve holding the guitar in a conventional manner, so instead it was laid across the lap.

Lap Steel Guitar

As the Hawaiian style of playing increased in popularity, the guitars were increasingly made in rectangular form and the comb was replaced with a steel rod. When they began to be commercially manufactured in the 1930s they acquired the name 'lap steel guitar'.

Since the playing style of the lap steel limits the performer to a few keys, players began using instruments with more than one neck in order to increase the number of pitches available without having to retune. Having multiple sets of strings soon became cumbersome, however, and makers in the 1940s began fitting pedals that would simultaneously alter the tunings of a complete set of strings.

Pedal Steel Guitar

The pedal steel guitar, as it came to be known, had two necks as standard, with eight sets of pedals and 10 strings on each neck, though as many as 12 or 14 is not uncommon. One neck is normally tuned to a chord of E9 (a combination of the notes E–G#–B–D–F#) and the other to a chord of C6 (a combination of C–E–G–A). Both the lap steel and the pedal steel are fretless guitars; the strings are stopped using a metal bar known as the 'steel' which, like Kekuku's comb, is used to slide up and down them, creating *glissandi*.

Key Players

Blind Boy Fuller
Son House
Tampa Red
Peetie Wheatstraw
Bukka White

Above: A lap steel guitar. Centre: A pedal steel guitar. Far Right: This National Style O guitar has a brass alloy body and cone resonator.

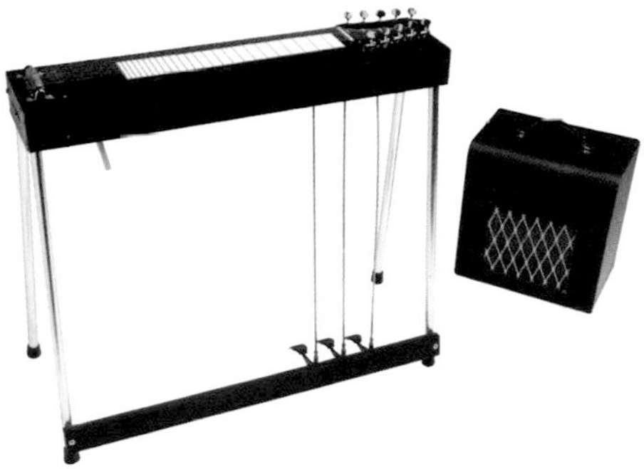

Four legs normally support the guitar with the performer sitting on a stool. The right foot will be used to control the volume while the left leg controls the pedals using both the foot and the knee to move the pedals. The strings are plucked using finger and thumb picks – metal picks that are worn like thimbles.

Resonator Guitar

The early twentieth century also saw the development of the resonator guitar. This technology used metal discs that acted in a similar way to the skin on a banjo, amplifying the soundwaves generated by the strings. The resonator guitars were somewhat louder than their wooden siblings.

The Arrival of the Dobro

In the 1920s, a refinement to the resonator guitar was designed in the United States by the Slovak instrument maker John Dopyera and his brothers. They used three spun aluminium cones as their amplification system. The new design became known as the dobro guitar, partly based on the brothers' name and partly because 'dobro' means 'good' in Slovak. It has the characteristic guitar shape with a large, decorated aluminium disc where the sound hole would normally be.

The Dobro was developed in the same period as the electric guitar; the latter's greater efficiency and lower cost meant it overtook the former in popularity. Nevertheless, the Dobro's characteristic sound became an important component of both the bluegrass and blues traditions, and remains in use today.

Banjo

The banjo is a plucked stringed instrument with a circular body and fretted neck. Its roots lie in the French and British colonies of Africa, where instruments made from a hollowed-out gourd covered with animal skin, bamboo neck and catgut strings were popular. Particularly associated with celebrations and dancing, these instruments went by various names including banza and banjer. Similar instruments also existed in South Africa which were possibly adaptations of the cavaquinho.

The Travelling Banjo

The journey from Africa to America was made during the slave trade. There are paintings from South Carolina in the late 1700s showing slaves dancing to the music of gourd banjos. The transition from the gourd-body to the instrument we know today is generally believed to have been due to the innovations of Joel Walker Sweeney (1810–60) in the 1830s. Some doubt has been cast on the extent of his role in the banjo's modernization, but he certainly had a strong influence.

Sweeney's use of the banjo was in his minstrel group the Sweeney Minstrels, a band who blackened their faces as a comedy gimmick. This rapidly caught on and by the 1850s the banjo and its minstrel musicians were popular throughout the southern states of America. During the American Civil War (1860–65), minstrel shows were a popular entertainment among soldiers, who took back home with them their appreciation of the banjo.

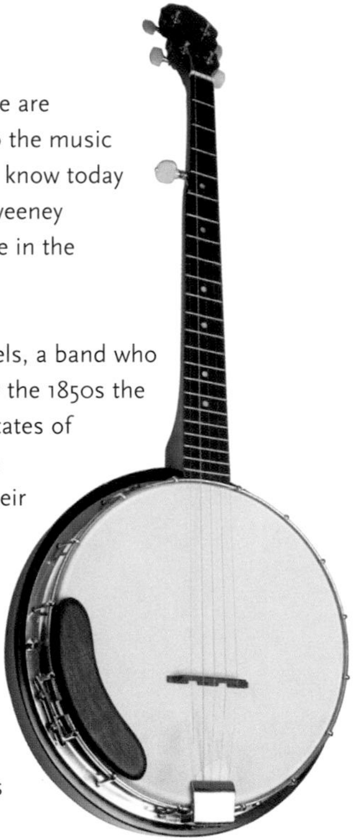

Key Players

Dock Boggs
Gus Cannon
Leadbelly
Johnny St Cyr
Taj Mahal

Playing Styles

The banjo's big break came with the growth of parlour music. This association lifted the instrument from its links with the lower classes and brought it to almost universal attention. By this time, two distinct styles of playing had developed. The traditional, or stroke, style is today known as 'clawhammer' or 'frailing', in which the

The earliest banjos were unfretted, like the African instruments that inspired them.

player strikes the string using a downward motion of the finger and making contact with the upper portion of the nail. In contrast, the 'fingerpicking' style is more akin to guitar technique, using the underside of the nail and the finger in an upward motion.

Use in Ragtime

The banjo's staccato sound made it ideally suited to the ragtime style that developed around the turn of the century. The jagged, syncopated character of ragtime increased the banjo's appeal and by the 1920s it had begun to play a part in the birth of jazz, appearing in the Dixieland bands of New Orleans. Surprisingly, the banjo was also used in blues, where its role was much more like that of a guitar.

Ragtime used the banjo mainly as a rhythm instrument, working together with the drum section, and its qualities as a solo voice were increasingly overlooked. It soon began to give way to the guitar, and the electric guitar in particular. The 1940s, however, saw a revival in the banjo's fortunes with the development of bluegrass in southern USA. A combination of dance and religious music, bluegrass showed off the best of the banjo's attributes: strong rhythm, clear articulation and agility.

Few names other than Sweeney's have endured from the banjo's early history, but the bluegrass style has made many more recent players household names, most notably the American performer Earl Scruggs. The banjo has regained some ground in jazz, but it remains less well regarded in art-music circles. Its occasional appearances have been in the lighter side of the repertoire, in works such as Kurt Weill's (1900–50) *Mahogany* (1927).

Drum Kit

The drum kit is a collection of drums and cymbals played in all styles of rock, pop, jazz and blues. It is also widely used in urban music across the world, such as Afrobeat and reggae.

Drum-Kit Construction

A typical drum kit comprises a bass drum and hi-hat cymbal played with foot pedals, a snare drum, two or three tom toms and suspended cymbals. The drummer sits on a stool. A right-handed player will play the bass drum with the right foot, the hi-hat pedal with the left foot, and will place the snare drum immediately in front of them between the knees, with the tom toms arranged from left to right in descending order of pitch. The suspended crash cymbal is placed by the hi-hat and the suspended ride cymbals are placed over the tom toms.

Drums

The drums are constructed like the orchestral snare drum and bass drum. The bass (or kick) drum (45–60 cm/18–24 in diameter and 35–45 cm/14–18 in deep) is placed on the floor with the playing head vertical. The pedal is clamped to the hoop of the drum. It has a chain or spring action and bounces back after being struck. The outer head of the drum may be decorated with a logo, and the cavity of the drum is often filled with absorbent material to deaden the sound. Two tom toms are mounted on a stand on the bass drum, and the largest tom toms, or floor toms, stand on the floor on legs. The tom toms are unpitched (20–45 cm/8–18 in diameter, 18–40 cm/7–16 in long), and are usually tuned to sound lower than the snare drum.

Key Players

John Bonham
Jack Casady
Sam Lay
Jim McCarty
Charlie Watts

Hi-Hat

The hi-hat cymbal comprises two matched cymbals (30–35 cm/12–14 in diameter) on a stand operated by a foot pedal. The lower cymbal is stationary and lies facing upwards. It is not normally struck with the stick. The upper cymbal faces downwards and is clamped to the stand so that it moves as the foot pedal is depressed. The upper cymbal can be played in a closed or open position, notated + and o respectively, making a short or a sustained sizzling sound as the two cymbals vibrate against each other. A typical jazz or swing rhythm exploits this feature of the cymbal.

The modern drum kit was not established until the 1950s.

Other Cymbals

Rhythms are played on the ride or bounce cymbal (45–52 cm/18–21 in diameter), which is designed to have a clean articulation and a dry timbre. Crash cymbals (20–40 cm/8–16 in diameter) are used for single crashes in solos and drum fills, and are built to have a more brilliant ringing sound with a pleasing mix of overtones. Drummers often customize their kits to include extra drums and cymbals. These might include: the Chinese or *pang* cymbal (35–40 cm/14–16 in diameter), which has an upturned rim and imitates a Chinese gong; the splash cymbal (15 cm/6 in diameter); and the sizzle cymbal. In the late 1970s and 1980s, drummers of stadium-rock bands like Asia, Kiss, Queen and Styx used very large drum kits that might include 25 to 30 items, among them two bass drums, two hi-hats, extra tom toms, bongos and roto-toms (tuneable tom toms with no shell), multiple cymbals and gongs.

Drum-Kit History

The drum kit originated in the multiple drum sets played in theatre and musichall pits at the end of the nineteenth century. The drummer played the percussion part on a combination of bass drum, snare drum, cymbals and tom toms, and added in special effects on a range of other instruments, including woodblock, triangle, tambourine, castanets, slapstick and whistles.

The modern drum kit came into being with the invention of foot pedals for the bass drum and hi-hat in the jazz bands of the 1920s, in which drums, bass and rhythm guitar, banjo or piano formed the rhythm section. Previously, the bass drum and snare drum were placed side by side and played with sticks, or the bass drum was placed on the floor and kicked (which is why the bass drum is sometimes called a kick drum).

The original foot-pedal-operated cymbal, or low-boy, rested at floor level, which made playing on this cymbal with sticks awkward. The hi-hat, which places the cymbals at chest height, was developed by Gene Krupa (1909–73) – drummer in the Benny Goodman Orchestra, who played the famous drum solo in 'Sing Sing Sing' – and the Zildjian cymbal company in the late 1930s. The advantages of this new cymbal were quickly recognized by drummers and the hi-hat became a standard part of the kit.

Five Top Tracks

'When The Levee Breaks' Led Zeppelin
'Shuffle Master' Sam Lay
'I Wish You Would' The Yardbirds
'Brown Sugar' The Rolling Stones
'Stick Trick' Buddy Rich

Rhythm

The pulse played on bass drum and hi-hat with the feet provides the basis of most drum-kit rhythms. The drummer adds the snare-drum part with the left hand and the cymbal part with the right hand, playing either on the hi-hat or the ride cymbal. Improvisation is a key aspect of drum-kit playing, and the drummer may vary the rhythm by adding extra beats on the bass drum and snare drum.

The drummer may also vary a rhythm by altering the snare-drum and cymbal sounds. These include playing a click on the snare drum, by laying the head of the stick across the drum to hit the rim of the drum and the head at the same time, and using brushes or rattan sticks. The bell of the cymbal can be used to imitate

Keith Moon is a master of the extended drum solo.

a cowbell. In progressive rock, Latin and jazz styles, the drummer often plays more complex rhythms between the bass drum and snare drum.

Solos and Fills

Short drum fills and longer solos are added to vary the rhythm and mark out the musical structure. In rock, pop, blues and most jazz drumming, fills are played every fourth, eighth or sixteenth measure, and are timed to end on the first beat of the next phrase.

Longer solos can be built up by playing snare-drum rudiments around the kit, developing rhythms already played in the piece and free improvisation. Snare-drum rudiments are developed by splitting them between snare drum, bass drum and tom toms, by adding flams, drags and ruffs, and syncopated accented patterns.

Longer drum solos are found in many styles of music, and became a feature of swing and jazz modelled on the work of Gene Krupa, Buddy Rich (1917–87) and Art Blakey (1919–90), who made full use of the different sonorities available from the kit. Rock drummers in the 1960s and 1970s – including John Bonham (1948–80) of Led Zeppelin, Phil Collins (b. 1951) of Genesis and Keith Moon (1946–78) of the Who – developed extensive drum solos, like that in Led Zeppelin's 'Moby Dick', which John Bonham could extend to 30 minutes in live performance.

Harmonica

The birthplace of free reeds seems to have been eastern Asia. There, it is typical to place a small free reed, made of metal or bamboo, into a bamboo tube cut to the appropriate length so that its air column resonates at the reed's frequency, increasing the volume and allowing the player to allow it to sound, or to stop it, by opening or closing the airway.

The Spread of Free-Reed Instruments

There are few details, but it seems likely that it was from the *sheng* or similar that all western free-reed instruments have been developed. Organ-builders were early on the scene in the eighteenth century, but soon there were the first mouth-blown instruments such as the *aeolian* or *aeolina*, which was a simple set of free reeds mounted side by side. Like most western reeds, their vibrating tongues were bolted on to a plate rather than cut from it.

Harmonica

Soon the modern harmonica or mouth organ began to appear – essentially a row of reeds mounted side by side on a reed plate to make a diatonic or chromatic scale, with a slotted 'comb' to direct the breath to them. The scale is usually achieved by alternate blowing and sucking as one moves from channel to channel. This means that if one blows several at once, a chord is produced, with a different chord on the suck.

The chromatic harmonica, in its standard form has a hand-operated slider that opens and closes holes to direct the breath to one of two reed-banks tuned a half step apart. On tremolo harmonicas, pairs of reeds are slightly detuned to give a beating effect. Sophisticated playing techniques have developed, including bending notes (a style evolved by blues players) and manufacturers, early on in Germany and other parts of Western Europe, but now also back in the birthplace of the free reed, East Asia, are constantly creating new models to suit, and to add to the huge and ingenious range which exists, including the splendidly chugging bass harmonica.

Key Players

Slim Harpo
Howlin' Wolf
Junior Wells
John Lee 'Sonny Boy' Williamson
Sonny Boy Williamson II (Rice Miller)

Above: The harmonica is also known as a mouth organ. Right: Harmonica virtuoso Paul Lamb, who tours extensively with his band the Kingsnakes.

Piano

The most versatile of all keyboard instruments, the early pianoforte's development into the magnificent grand piano that we recognize today was made possible by a number of innovations and inventions that together brought the kind of power and projection that could happily compete with the sound levels of a full orchestra or jazz rhythm section.

A single cast-iron frame – perfected in the US – helped pianos to be able to withstand the increasing force brought to bear on them by performers and composers alike, as well as providing stability and the opportunity for more accurate tuning and better tension on the strings. The French manufacturer Erard provided the 'double escapement' action, allowing for fast repetition of the same note and providing the model on which the whole of modern piano technique was built. Laying the longer bass strings over the shorter high strings ('over-stringing') helped to redeploy the stress. Various prototypes using iron frames were explored, but eventually all of these elements came together in the 1859 patent by Steinway for an iron-framed, over strung, double-escapement grand piano.

The modern concert grand is a beautiful, impressive object and an engineering triumph: with over 10,000 parts, including those three pedals that still puzzle many a piano player, the left one mutes, the right sustains by letting all the strings resonate, and the one in the middle sustains only those notes originally held down.

Key Players

Albert Ammons
Leroy Carr
Champion Jack Dupree
Amos Milburn
Memphis Slim

The piano lends itself well to a wide variety of musical styles – the classical repertoire for the instrument is vast, but it is also prominent in other musical genres such as blues, jazz, rock'n'roll, folk and pop. The versatility offered by the keyboard enables the piano to work equally well as a solo, ensemble and percussive or rhythm section instrument.

Above: A concert piano consists of over 12,000 parts. Right: Classically trained pianist Charles Brown was a legendary performer of the blues.

Hammond Organ

The term electric, or electromechanical, organ is used to describe instruments that produce sounds using a dynamo-like system of moving parts – as opposed to electronic organs that employ solid-state electronics.

Laurens Hammond

In the same way that 'Hoover' is used instead of 'vacuum cleaner', the very name 'Hammond' has become synonymous with electric organs. The Hammond organ was developed by Laurens Hammond (1895–1973), a brilliant inventor who claimed to have no musical ability whatsoever.

Hammond graduated with an honours degree in mechanical engineering from Cornell University in 1916. Following a period of armed service in France during the First World War, he took up the position of chief engineer with the Gray Motor Company in Detroit. The invention of a silent, spring-driven clock gave Hammond enough capital to strike out on his own, and in 1928 he founded the Hammond Clock Company, which made a range of electric clocks, driven by another of his inventions – the synchronous electric motor.

However, as other clock companies went out of business during the Great Depression, Hammond's determination to remain solvent led him to develop other products, and he soon turned his attention to music. Though no musician himself, he recognized the importance of music and was keen to produce a system that could bring high-quality music-making to the domestic market.

Key Players

Al Kooper
Mark Naftalin
Alan Price
Jimmy Smith
Reuben Wilson

Development of the Electric Organ

In developing the electric organ, Hammond turned for inspiration to the underlying principles of Thaddeus Cahill's

Right: Influential musician Jimmy Smith was able to conjur some funky grooves from his Hammond organ.

ill-fated Telharmonium. Aided by his company treasurer (and church organist) William Lahey, Hammond used his engineering skill and experience to develop an electro-mechanical system of tone-wheel generators coupled with a keyboard. The Hammond tone-wheel organ was patented in 1934 and the Model A went into production in 1935, with Henry Ford and George Gershwin among the first customers.

The now-legendary B3 was first produced in October 1955 and quickly became a lasting favourite with musicians of all genres for its distinctive sound and versatility. The B3 is housed in a large wooden cabinet on four spindle legs, with separate power amplification and speaker system. The musician is presented with a pair of 61-note keyboards and a 25-note flat radial removable pedal board. The sound generated by the instrument is controlled by a series of rocker switches and drawbars. These drawbars lie at the heart of the Hammond sound, allowing the player to build up rich timbres by combining pure tones in differing combinations – in the same way that a church organist would use stops to combine pipes of different lengths.

PLAYING BLUES GUITAR

The blues has played a larger role in the history of popular music than any other genre. It is a direct ancestor to music styles as diverse as rock'n'roll, soul, funk and pop. Without the blues there would have been no Beatles, Jimi Hendrix, Led Zeppelin, James Brown, Stevie Wonder or Oasis, to name but a few!

The blues emerged out of the hardships endured by generations of African-American slaves during the late nineteenth and early twentieth centuries. By 1900, the genre had developed into a three-line stanza, with a vocal style derived from southern work songs. These 'call and response' songs were developed further by early blues guitar players, who would sing a line and then answer it on the guitar. By the 1920s, rural African-Americans had migrated to the big cities in search of work, bringing their music with them. Early street musicians such as Blind Lemon Jefferson (1893–1929), a guitar-playing blues singer, started to make recordings and these inspired the next generation of blues guitar players.

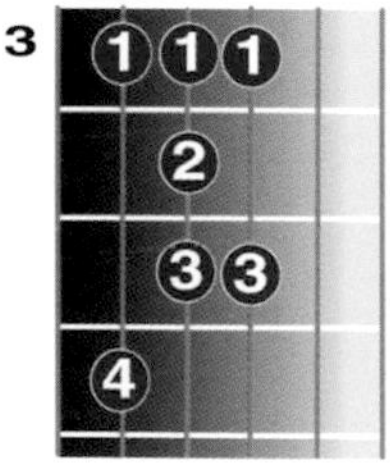

Blues scale.

Playing the Blues

Blues is based around the blues scale, which is a pentatonic minor scale with an added flat fifth note (the 'blue' note). Blues music is usually played in the keys of A, D, E and G as they are all easy keys to play on the guitar. The style has an odd harmonic structure, as the blues scale is usually played or sung over chords that are all dominant sevenths (e.g. A7, D7 and E7 in the key of A) or chords derived from them.

Blues Scale

The blues scale contains all the notes of the pentatonic minor scale, but with the addition of a ♭5 note. It is this note that gives the blues scale its distinctive blues flavour. All blues lead guitar playing uses the blues scale as its foundation. The interval spelling of the blues scale is 1 ♭3 4 ♭5 5 ♭7. C blues scale contains the notes C E♭ F G♭ G B♭.

Dynamic guitarist Son Seals performs at London's Hammersmith Odeon in 1977.

Acoustic Blues

Leadbelly, Son House, Big Bill Broonzy, Mississippi John Hurt, Blind Lemon Jefferson, Robert Johnson, Brownie McGhee, John Lee Hooker and Sam Lightnin' Hopkins are some of the best-known early blues players.

Although some of them, particularly in the later periods of their careers, used electric guitars, their style of playing remained barely unchanged from its acoustic roots, and all of these legendary bluesmen were finger-style players who could play a bass part and melody simultaneously.

In this style of playing the thumb plays the bass strings as an accompaniment to the melody, which is picked normally using just the index and middle fingers – the third and fourth fingers can be anchored on the guitar scratchplate to give the picking hand stability. The thumb has to play independently, regardless of what the fingers are doing. It is important that the thumb holds a steady beat and sets a regular 'groove'. Whilst you play the bass part with your thumb, the fingers can pick some blues licks or a melody.

Key Players

Big Bill Broonzy
Blind Lemon Jefferson
Lonnie Johnson
Robert Johnson
Charley Patton

To get an authentic blues sound, rest the side of the picking hand across the strings near the bridge. This will mute the bass notes and stop them overpowering the melody.

Much of the music in this style was mostly improvised, and designed to accompany a blues vocal line; therefore, to get the right feel it is important that your playing does not become too rigid – include variations for each verse you play.

Most traditional acoustic blues pieces are written in guitar-friendly keys, such as E and A, so that greatest advantage can be taken of the open bass strings; other keys occur mainly when a capo or an altered tuning is used.

Memphis Minnie, one of the finest female blues guitarists of all time.

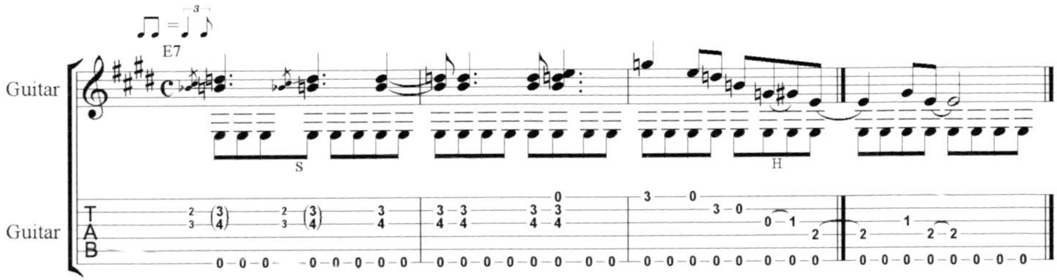

Example of acoustic blues finger-style playing: The low E string is played repeatedly with the thumb establishing a traditional blues rhythm in the bass. The opening chord is a D7 shape slid up to become E7; acoustic blues songs often feature slide-guitar playing and, even when they do not, the player often imitates a slide-playing style. Notice the contrast between the G and Gn notes (minor and major thirds) which creates a typical blues sound.

Electric Blues

Once blues players migrated from the country areas of the Mississippi Delta to the urban environments of cities like Chicago, they began increasingly to use electric guitar and perform with backing bands.

Guitarists like B.B. King, Buddy Guy, Muddy Waters, Freddie King and Albert King were the pioneers of electric blues playing. More recent blues players like Eric Clapton, Stevie Ray Vaughan and Robert Cray all drew their style from these players. Because electric blues players played within the context of a band, the emphasis shifted to lead and rhythm playing rather than finger-style playing. A wider range of keys was used – such as B♭, F and C – which suited the saxophone-and-trumpet horn sections that were often included in the band line-up.

The core of electric blues lead playing comes from the blues scale. This is enhanced by the use of a wide variety of string bends and vibrato – blues soloing does not sound authentic unless these techniques are employed.

Key Players

John Lee Hooker
Jimi Hendrix
B.B. King
Stevie Ray Vaughan
T-Bone Walker

Blues music has an unusual harmonic structure in that the chords used tend to be dominant sevenths (or their extensions) – which are extensions of major chords – whilst the lead playing is based on the blues scale – which is a variation of a minor scale. It is this harmonic 'clash' which gives blues soloing its unique tonality and character. However, many of the best blues players (most notably, B.B. King) go beyond the basic blues scale and include chord tones (often major third notes) in their lead playing. This gives their soloing a more lyrical and melodic sound than could be achieved using the blues scale alone.

Above: Blues guitarist Rory Gallagher – an exciting and energetic performer.

Example of electric blues solo: A 'lead-in' before the bar, and the use of string bends, makes this a typical Chicago-style solo. Notice how the major thirds of each chord are added to the basic blues-scale notes to create a more melodic sound. The basic dominant seventh chords have been extended to become dominant ninth chords in order to give a more mellow and sophisticated sound.

Playing Electric Blues

Electric blues stylists often embellish their phrases with expressive techniques such as string bending, sliding and vibrato. String bending should simply be thought of as another way of moving from one pitch to another on the fretboard.

To bend a string accurately, you must know your target note – this will usually be a note pitched a half step, a whole step or a step and a half above your unbent note. If your target note is a half step higher, for example, you can play the note behind the next fret up on the same string to hear what it should sound like. When you perform the bend, push the string over towards the bass strings until you hear your target note.

You can produce a blues slide effect when you play a note on a string and, while holding the string firmly down, slide along the fingerboard to another note. You can even slide across two or more strings at a time by barring your fretting finger across the strings and moving it along the neck in the same way. To obtain a vibrato effect, play a fretted note and move the string from side to side – across the fingerboard – with your fretting finger. This makes a sustained note sound more expressive or even aggressive.

Key Tracks

'Sunshine Of Your Love' Cream
'Born In Chicago' Paul Butterfield Blues Band
'Let's Work Together' Canned Heat
'Purple Haze' Jimi Hendrix
'All Right Now' Free

Above: A tremolo arm attached to the bridge of an electric guitar can be used to alter the pitch of the strings. Right: Whether you play in the style of Eddie Van Halen or B.B. King (pictured), being able to improvise is crucial to guitar playing.

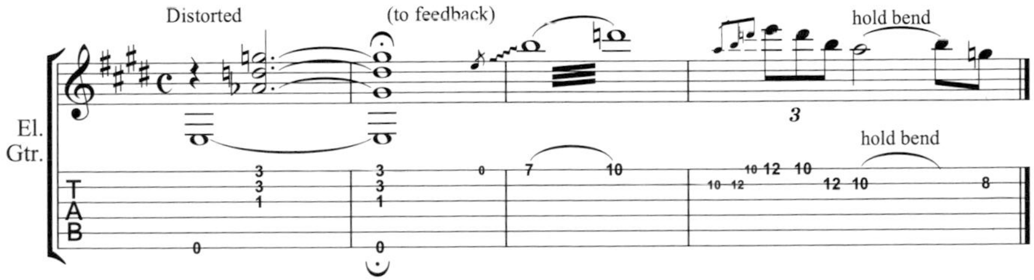

Blues Rock: Sliding the fingers from one note to another, instead of lifting the fingers off the strings, creates the blues sound, characteristic of blues rock. A freeform rhythm and performances embellished by long improvisations add to the sound.

Going Solo

There are many different approaches to soloing over a blues progression, but the simplest way to learn is to target the root notes of each chord in the progression. In the key of C, for example, the main blues chords are C7, F7 and G7. You can begin by playing the C pentatonic minor scale and targeting the notes C, F and G (which are all in the scale) over their respective chords. Try bending or sliding to these notes to make things sound more bluesy.

It is also a good idea to practise blues lead phrasing by using the 'call and response' approach favoured by early blues musicians; sing a phrase and then reply to it with a guitar line, and so on. This should help you to get an authentic blues feel, even if you're not a singer. It will enable you to put comfortable, natural rests between your phrases and notes so it all ends up sounding more musical and logical. You should also jam with other like-minded musicians, as this is not only fun but will also motivate you to become a better player.

Using a Bottleneck

Some blues players, including Elmore James and Duane Allman, have used a bottleneck made out of glass or metal to obtain a distinctive sliding effect between notes. Bottlenecks are inexpensive and fun to play with, but you'll need a little patience to master the technique properly. Special tunings such as D A D F# A D are often used for bottleneck pieces, as they enable the guitarist to play whole chords up the guitar neck with just one finger!

Key Tracks

'Dust My Broom' Elmore James
'I Believe' Elmore James
'Mean Old World' Duane Allman
'In My Time Of Dying' Led Zeppelin
'I Wanna Be Your Man' The Rolling Stones

Above: Elmore James took the Delta blues and brought it closer to rock'n'roll. Right: When using a bottleneck, the centre of the tube must rest over the centre of the fret, rather than just behind it.

Tens of thousands of blues songs are based around the most common chord-progression in the history of popular music: the 12-bar blues sequence.

|| C7 | C7 | C7 | C7 |

| F7 | F7 | C7 | C7 |

| G7 | F7 | C7 | G7 :||

Getting a Blues Sound

To get an authentic blues sound you'll need an appropriate guitar. Almost any acoustic instrument will do for acoustic blues, although resonators, guitars that use thin aluminium cones to mechanically amplify their sound, will give you a particularly 'bluesy' tone.

If you're after an authentic electric blues sound, you should pick an instrument similar to one played by your favourite blues artist. If you want to sound like B.B. King, for example, you should consider a Gibson ES-335, as this is the guitar he has favoured over the years, while a Fender Stratocaster will enable you to sound more like Robert Cray or Stevie Ray Vaughan, and a Telecaster would be essential for that biting Albert Collins sound.

Amplification is important too, and most blues artists favour valve amplifiers such as the Marshall Bluesbreaker combo or Fender's Twin and Deluxe models as they give a warm, fat sound with a big dynamic range.

Transistor amplifiers are cheaper but they sound more synthetic. If you're just playing guitar in your bedroom you should consider getting an amp modelling box such as a Line 6 POD, or a virtual amp software package such as IK Multimedia's AmpliTube or Native Instruments' Guitar Rig. Each of these comes armed with a surprisingly authentic set of blues presets, and you can use them without upsetting the neighbours.

Key Manufacturers

Fender
Gibson
Heritage
Jackson
G & L Guitars

Tone control settings are important as well; boosting an amplifier's bass and mid-range will give a fat B.B. King sound, while boosting the treble will help to emulate the 'icy' tones of Albert Collins. All in all, it is important to find a guitar tone that you feel comfortable with – if you sound great, you'll play well!

Keb' Mo's accessible, poppy blues style has ensured him several successful albums.

BIOGRAPHIES

Foreword: **Paul Jones**
Paul Jones was one of the young hopefuls who frequently 'sat in' with Alexis Korner's Blues Incorporated in 1962, before joining 1960s band the Mann-Hugg Blues, later known as Manfred Mann. After several top 10 hits, including two number ones, he went solo in 1966 and had a few more. Paul later embarked on a career as an actor, but by 1979, his deep-rooted love of the blues and R&B led to a return to music with the Blues Band. After 16 albums and a quarter-century of touring the world, Paul's inspired performances on harmonica and vocals continue to attract new generations of blues fans. He has been heard on TV and film soundtracks and on many albums by artists ranging from Percy Sledge and Tina Turner to Memphis Slim and Katie Melua. His songs have been recorded by an equally varied selection, from early Steppenwolf to Helen Shapiro and Ten Years After. His weekly blues show on BBC Radio 2 is a must-listen on Thursday evenings.

General Editor: **Julia Rolf**
Julia Rolf studied at University College, London and L'Università degli Studi, Pisa, and works in London as a music editor and writer. She was turned on to the blues at the tender age of eight via her dad's record collection, counting Elmore James and Robert Johnson among her early heroes. A self-confessed music geek, Julia has worked on a number of publications in this field, ranging in subject matter from opera and classical music to blues, jazz, rock and country.

Consultant Editor: **Philip Van Vleck**
Currently the pop music critic for the *Durham Herald-Sun* newspaper (Durham, NC), Philip Van Vleck also covers world music, blues, jazz and world jazz for *Billboard* magazine, and is a regular contributor to College Music Journal's *New Music Monthly* magazine, *Dirty Linen* magazine and *www.BMGmusic.com*. In addition to his music journalism, he holds a Ph.D. from Duke University and teaches in the history department at North Carolina State University in Raleigh.

Authors

Bob Allen (Influences: Country)
Bob Allen has spent the last quarter century as a country music journalist, historian and critic. He is former Nashville editor for, and has been a regular contributor to, the popular Nashville-based fan magazine, *Country Music Magazine*, since 1977. His writing on country music has appeared in *Esquire*, *Rolling Stone*, the *Washington Post*, the *Atlanta Journal*, and the *Baltimore Sun*. Allen is the author of *The Life And Times Of A Honky Tonk Legend*, the (unauthorized) biography of singer George Jones, and he has contributed to various historical and reference books on country music in recent years. He resides in Eldersburg, Maryland.

Rebecca Berkley (Instruments: Percussion)
Rebecca Berkley is a freelance writer and musician. She has taught percussion to students of all ages, as a private teacher and as a workshop leader, and has published percussion music. She also runs a community choir and directs music festivals with her husband.

Keith Briggs (Influences: Gospel)
Since 1983 Keith Briggs has been the reviews editor of the magazine *Blues And Rhythm: The Gospel Truth*. He has also contributed articles to this and other specialist publications as well as compiling and/or writing the notes for several hundred CDs.

Richard Buskin (Influences: 1950s and 1960s Pop; Rock)
A New York Times best-selling author, Richard Buskin has been a full-time freelance journalist specializing in the fields of popular music, film, television, and cultural affairs for the past twenty years. Having written for numerous music and film magazines around the world, he has also authored more than a dozen pop culture books. Among the most recent *are Inside Tracks: A First-Hand History of Popular Music from the World's Greatest Record Producers and Engineers* and *Sheryl Crow: No Fool to This Game*. A native of London, England, he lives in Chicago with his wife and daughter.

Andrew Cleaton (Instruments: Guitars, Hammond Organ)
Since gaining his masters degree in Music Technology from the University of York in 1990, Andrew Cleaton has enjoyed a varied career, spanning the fields of community music, higher education and the arts funding system. An accomplished composer and producer, Andrew is a founding co-director of Epiphany Music Ltd, offering creative music-technology solutions in production, education and consultancy.

Cliff Douse (Introduction; Styles of the Blues; Influences: Jazz; Playing Blues Guitar)
Cliff Douse has written hundreds of articles and columns during the past 10 years for many of the UK's foremost music and computer magazines including *Guitarist*, *Guitar Techniques*, *Total Guitar*, *Computer Music*, *Future Music*, *Rhythm* and *Mac Format*. He is also the author and co-author of several music books published by IMP, Music Sales, Music Maker and Thunder Bay. He is currently the editor of *Guitarist Icons* magazine (a quarterly special issue of *Guitarist* magazine) and is working on a number of new books and music software projects.

Ted Drozdowski (The Sixties; Contemporary Blues)
Ted Drozdowski is a freelance journalist and musician living in Boston, Massachusetts. He writes about popular culture, specializing in music. His writing has appeared internationally in a wide variety of publications

including *Tracks*, *Rolling Stone* and *Musician*. He is co-author of *The Best Music CD Art and Design* and appears on television and radio offering commentary on music. He was a research consultant for Martin Scorsese's PBS-TV series *The Blues* and has been awarded the Blues Foundation's Keeping the Blues Alive Award for Journalism. He leads the Mississippi-informed blues band Scissormen.

Colin Irwin (Influences: Folk)
London-based music journalist Colin Irwin has been writing about folk music for 25 years. He joined *Melody Maker* in the mid-1970s, eventually becoming assistant editor. He was editor of the weekly pop magazine *Number One* before turning to freelance writing and has presented several BBC series on folk music, both on radio and television. He is also a regular contributor to UK magazines *Mojo* and *fROOTS*, has written for *The Times*, the *Guardian* and the *Independent* and also wrote *The Name Of The Game*, a biography of ABBA.

Todd Jenkins (The Seventies)
Todd S. Jenkins is a contributor to *Down Beat*, *All About Jazz*, *Signal To Noise*, *The ZydE-Zine* and *Route 66* magazines. He is the author of *Free Jazz and Free Improvisation: An Encyclopedia* (Greenwood Press), *Eclipse: The Music of Charles Mingus* (Praeger), and a biography of pianist Jimmy Rowles. A resident of San Bernardino, California, Todd is a member of the American Jazz Symposium and the Jazz Journalists Association.

Howard Mandel (The Blues Story: Chapter Openers)
Howard Mandel is a writer and editor specializing in jazz, blues, new and unusual music. Born in Chicago, now living in New York City, he is a senior contributor for *Down Beat*, produces arts features for National Public Radio, teaches at New York University and is president of the Jazz Journalists Association. Mandel's *Future Jazz* (Oxford University Press, 1999) ranges from the AACM to John Zorn; he has written for *Musical America*, *The Wire* (UK), *Swing Journal* (Tokyo), *Bravo* (Rio de Janeiro), and many other periodicals.

Bill Milkowski (The Eighties)
Bill Milkowski is a regular contributor to *Jazz Times*, *Jazziz*, *Bass Player*, *Modern Drummer*, *Guitar Club* (Italy) and *Jazzthing* (Germany) magazines. He was named the Jazz Journalists Association's Writer of the Year for 2004. He is also the author of *JACO: The Extraordinary Life of Jaco Pastorius* (Backbeat Books), *Rockers, Jazzbos & Visionaries* (Billboard Books) and *Swing It! An Annotated History of Jive* (Billboard Books).

Garry Mulholland (Influences: Soul and R&B)
Garry is a music writer based in London, and has contributed features and interviews on pop, rock, dance and black music to *NME*, *Select*, the *Guardian*, *The Sunday Times*, the *Independent* and *Time Out*. His first book *This is Uncool: The 500 Greatest Singles Since Punk and Disco* was published by Cassell Illustrated in 2002.

Robin Newton (Instruments: Steel & Resonator Guitars; Banjo; Harmonica)
Robin Newton is active as a conductor, specializing in contemporary music. In 1997 he formed his own ensemble, e2k, with which he gives regular concerts in London. He has worked on several high-profile academic publications as writer and editor, chiefly for the *New Grove Dictionary of Music and Musicians* and the *Northern Arts* magazine *Artscene*.

Jim O'Neal (The Roots; The Teens)
Jim O'Neal is based in Kansas City and is founding editor of *Living Blues*, America's first blues magazine. He co-edited *The Voice of the Blues: Classic Interviews from Living Blues Magazine* (Routledge 2002), and he collects and sells soul, R&B, funk, jazz, country, folk, world/ethnic, gospel, soundtrack and rock'n'roll records as well as blues. His website, BluEsoterica.com, is a research forum for discussing new, obscure or overlooked details on blues.

Bob Porter (The Thirties; The Forties; The Fifties)
Bob Porter is a discographer, record producer and award-winning broadcaster and writer based in New Jersey. His syndicated blues program *Portraits in Blue* began its 24th year in autumn 2004. As well as serving on the board of directors of the Blues Foundation and being on the nominating committee for the Rock And Roll Hall of Fame, he has won two Grammies for his liner notes and produced more than 150 jazz and blues albums for artists such as Big Joe Turner and Illinois Jacquet. Porter has written for *Jazz Times Magazine*, *Down Beat*, *Jazz Journal* and *Discographical Forum*, amongst others. He contributed to the *Oxford Companion to Jazz*, and in 1992 was awarded the New Jersey Jazz Society's Outstanding Service Award.

Tony Skinner (Playing Blues Guitar)
Tony Skinner is the Director of the Registry of Guitar Tutors – the world's foremost organisation for guitar education. He is also the Principal Guitar Examiner for the London College of Music and has compiled examination syllabi in electric, bass and classical guitar playing and popular music theory. He has written and edited over 40 music-education books and is a regular contributor to *Total Guitar* magazine. Tony is widely respected as one of the UK's premier music educators.

David Whiteis (The Twenties)
David Whiteis, an internationally published critic and journalist with over 25 years of experience writing about blues, jazz, and other essential issues, currently writes on a regular basis for the *Chicago Reader*, *Down Beat*, *Living Blues*, *Juke Blues*, and others. He is the recipient of the Blues Foundation's 2001 Keeping the Blues Alive Award for Achievement in Journalism. His book, *I Mean It From The Heart: Stories and Portraits in Chicago Blues*, was published by University of Illinois Press in 2005.

PICTURE CREDITS

Dorling Kindersley Ltd: 514

Fender Musical Instruments Corporation: 490; 492

Foundry Arts
55; 97; 102; 117; 223; 233; 235; 249; 325; 335; 451; 459; 517

Hammond Suziki: 506

istock: 504

Todd S. Jenkins, 2003: 263

Lebrecht: 497

Live Photography: 515

London Features International: 19; 297; 373

Mark David Hill/hammond-organ.com: 507

C.F. Martin & Co., Inc., Nazareth, PA USA: 488

photodisc/Getty Images: 495; 496; 499; 502

Redferns Music Picture Library
31; 157; Glenn A. Baker Archives: 177; 341; 389; 411; 427; 467; BBC Photo Library: 365; Paul Bergen: 383; Chuck Boyd: 481; Henrietta Butler: 295; Delta Haze Corporation: 17; 21; 27; 35; 39; 41; 51; 67; 331; Ian Dickson: 276; 278; 501; Alan Dister: 281; 293; Amanda Edwards: 317; GAB Archives: 113; 119; 291; GEMS: 193; 225; 229; 251; 259; 387; 461; 469; Steve Gillett: 311; Harry Goodwin: 449; William Gottlieb: 121; William P. Gottlieb/Library of Congress: 489; Carry Hammond: 327; Tom Hanlet: 256–57; Paul Hoeffler: 369; Richie Howell: 479; Max Jones Files: 37; 43; 79; 115; 269; 401; 403; Ivan Keeman: 227; Robert Knight: 275; 282–83; 379; Elliott Landy: 134–35; Herman Leonard: 111; Andrew Lepley: 305; 319; Michel Linssen: 485; Steve Morley: 252–53; Keith Morris: 218; 219; 220; Leon Morris: 64–65; 309; 313; Michael Ochs Archives: 13; 29; 33; 47; 50; 52; 59; 63; 73; 75; 85; 89; 101; 105; 109; 127; 129; 131; 140; 142; 145; 147; 155; 174–75; 181; 183; 185; 187; 189; 191; 197; 199; 205; 215; 255; 267; 289; 343; 347; 349; 355; 359; 363; 371; 375; 377; 391; 393; 397; 407; 409; 417; 423; 429; 433; 435; 437; 441; 443; 445; 447; 453; 455; 463; 465; 471; 487; 491; 493; 505; Michael Ochs Archives/Venice CA: 138–39; Jan Persson: 137; 361; 381; Christina Radish: 367; David Redfern: 141; 231; 237; 307; 315; 405; 419; 431; 475; 477; Rick Richards: 457; Ebet Roberts: 273; 303; 345; 421; 473; 483; Philip Ryals: 519; Richard Upper: 512; Bob Willoughby: 415; Graham Wiltshire: 245; Charlyn Zlotnik: 271

Tony Russell: 425

Sylvia Pitcher Photo Library
15; 45; 56; 60; 93; 98–99; 107; 129; 133; 153; 167; 173; 178–79; 195; 207; 211; 212–13; 214; 216; 239; 241; 243; 247; 261; 285; 287; 329; 333; 351; 353; 357; 503; 509; 510; 516; B. Fisher: 149; 169; Tony Mottram: 385; B. Smith: 201; 277; 339; Weston Collection: 25; 69; 94; 123; 209; 265; 323; 395

Telarc & Heads Up: Tim Jackson: 301

Topham Picturepoint
23; 49; 71; 76; 81; 83; 90–91; 125; 151; 161; 163; 165; 321; 399; 439; Arena PAL: 299; Arena PAL/Christina Burton: 87; Mark Godfrey/The Image Works: 203

Universal/The Kobal Collection: 159

FURTHER READING

Abbott, L. & Seroff, D., *Out of Sight: The Rise of African American Popular Music, 1889–1895*, University of Missouri Press, 2003

Barlow, W., *Looking Up At Down*, Temple University Press, 1989

Berry, P., *Up From the Cradle of Jazz*, University of Georgia Press, 1986

Brooks, T., *Lost Sounds: Blacks and the Birth of the Recording Industry 1890–1919*, University of Illinois Press, 2004

Brunning, B., *Blues: The British Connection: The Stones, Clapton, Fleetwood Mac and the Story of Blues in Britain*, Helter Skelter, 2003

Charters, S.B., *The Country Blues*, Da Capo Press, Maryland, 1959

Chilton, J., *Let The Good Times Roll: The Story of Louis Jordan & His Music*, University of Michigan Press, 1997

Cohn, L. (ed.), *Nothing But the Blues: The Music and the Musicians*, Abbeville Press, 1993

Cohodas, N., *Spinning Blues Into Gold: The Chess Brothers and the Legendary Chess Records*, St. Martin's Press, 2000

Cook, B., *Listen to the Blues*, Charles Scribner's Sons, 1973

Dance, H., *Stormy Monday: The T-Bone Walker Story*, Louisiana State University Press, 1987

Davis, F., *The History of the Blues*, Hyperion, 1995

Dixon, R.M.W., Godrich, J. & Rye H. (eds), *Blues & Gospel Records, 1890–1943*, Clarendon Press, 1997

Dixon, W., with Snowden, D., *I Am The Blues: The Willie Dixon Story*, Da Capo Press, Maryland, 1989

Edwards, D., *The World Don't Owe Me Nothing*, Chicago Review Press, 1997

Ferris, W., *Blues From The Delta*, Anchor Press/Doubleday, New York, 1978

Friedman, M., *Buried Alive: the Biography of Janis Joplin*, Harmony, 1973

Gordon, R., *Can't Be Satisfied: The Life & Times of Muddy Waters*, Little, Brown and Company, 2002

Gurlanick, P., *Lost Highway*, Harper & Row, 1979

Henderson, D., *'Scuse Me While I Kiss the Sky: The Life of Jimi Hendrix*, Doubleday, 1978

Kooper, A., *Backstage Passes & Backstabbing Bastards*, Billboard, 1998

Lomax, A., *The Land Where the Blues Began*, Random House USA Inc., 1993

Lydon, M., *Ray Charles: Man and Music*, Riverhead Books, 1998

Murray, C.S., *Boogie Man: The Adventures of John Lee Hooker in the American Twentieth Century*, St. Martin's Press, 2000

Newman, R., *Blues Breaker: John Mayall And The Story of the Blues*, Sanctuary Publishing, London, 1995

Oakley, G., *The Devil's Music: A History of the Blues*, Da Capo Press, Maryland, 1997

Obrecht, J., *Rollin' and Tumblin': The Postwar Blues Guitarists*, Backbeat Books, 2000

Oliver, P., *Songsters & Saints: Vocal Traditions on Race Records*, Cambridge University Press, 1984

Oliver, P., *The Story of the Blues*, Pimlico, 1997

O'Neal, J., & van Singel, A. (eds), *The Voice of the Blues*, Routledge, 2002

Page, C.I., *Boogie Woogie Stomp: Albert Ammons & His Music*, Northeast Ohio Jazz Society, 1997

Patoski, J.N. & Crawford, B., *Stevie Ray Vaughan: Caught in the Crossfire*, Little, Brown and Company, 1993

Rosalsky, M., *Encyclopedia of Rhythm and Blues and Doo Wop Vocal Groups*, Scarecrow Press, Maryland, 2000

Rowe, M., *Chicago Blues*, Da Capo Press, 1982

Rowe, M., *Chicago Breakdown*, Drake Publishers, 1975

Santelli, R., *The Big Book of Blues: a Biographical Encyclopedia*, Penguin, 1994

Sawyer, C., *B.B. King: the Authorized Biography*, Quartet Publishing, 1982

Segrest, J. & Hoffman, M., *Moanin' at Midnight: The Life and Times of Howlin' Wolf*, Pantheon Books, 2004

Shaw, A., *Honkers and Shouters: The Golden Years of Rhythm and Blues*, Macmillan, London, 1978

Silvester, P.J., *A Left Hand Like God*, Da Capo Press, 1988

Southern, E., *The Music of Black Americans: A History*, Norton, New York, 1983

Tipaldi, A., *Children of the Blues: 49 Musicians Shaping a New Blues Tradition*, Backbeat Books, 2002

Titon, J.T., *Early Downhome Blues: A Musical and Cultural Analysis*, Atlantic Books, 1995

Ward, G., *The Rough Guide To The Blues*, Rough Guides, London, 2000

Wardlow, G.D., *Chasin' That Devil Music*, Miller Freeman Books, 1998

Waterman, D., *Between Midnight and Day: the Last Unpublished Blues Archive*, Thunder's Mouth Press, 2003

Wexler, J. & Ritz, D., *Rhythm and the Blues: a Life in American Music*, Alfred A. Knopf, 1993

Wilcox, D.E. & Guy, B., *Damn Right I've Got the Blues/Buddy Guy and the Blues Roots of Rock-and-Roll*, Woodford Press, 1993

Wolfe, C. & Lornell, K., *The Life and Legend of Leadbelly*, HarperCollins, 1992

Wolkin, J.M. & Keenom, B., *Michael Bloomfield: If You Love These Blues*, Miller Freeman Books, 2000

Wondrich, D., *Stomp and Swerve: American Music Gets Hot 1843–1924*, Chicago Review Press, 2003

Wyman, B. *Bill Wyman's Blues Odyssey: A Journey to Music's Heart and Soul*, Dorling Kindersley, London, 2001

INDEX

Page references in *italics* refer to illustrations, and those in **bold** to main articles on the subject. Page references which are concatenated with a dash take no account of intervening illustrations.